MARG

M000300444

The Little
AUSSIE
Fact
BOOK

Penguin Books

Penguin Books Australia Ltd
487 Maroondah Highway, PO Box 257
Ringwood, Victoria 3134, Australia
Penguin Books Ltd
Harmondsworth, Middlesex, England
Penguin Putnam Inc.
375 Hudson Street, New York, New York 10014, USA
Penguin Books Canada Limited
10 Alcorn Avenue, Toronto, Ontario, Canada M4V 3B2
Penguin Books (NZ) Ltd
Cnr Rosedale and Airborne Roads, Albany, Auckland, New Zealand
Penguin Books (South Africa) (Pty) Ltd
5 Watkins Street, Denver Ext 4, 2094, South Africa
Penguin Books India (P) Ltd
11, Community Centre, Panchsheel Park, New Delhi 110 017, India

First published by Pitman Publishing Pty Ltd, 1985; 4th edition 1988
Published by Penguin Books Australia Ltd 1993, 1995, 1998
This revised 8th edition published by Penguin Books Australia Ltd 2000

10 9 8 7 6 5 4 3 2 1

Cover design by Tony Palmer, Penguin Design Studio
Text design, maps, graphs and pagination by P.A.G.E. Pty Ltd
Printed and bound by South China Printing Co. Ltd, Hong Kong/China

National Library of Australia
Cataloguing-in-Publication data:

Nicholson, Margaret, 1931–.
   The little Aussie fact book.
   8th ed.
   ISBN 0 14 029241 1.
   1. Australia – Miscellanea. I. Title.
994

www.penguin.com.au

Breathes there the man, with soul so dead,
Who never to himself hath said,
'This is my own, my native land!'

Sir Walter Scott

This book is for my husband and our family,
and they all know the reasons why.

ACKNOWLEDGEMENTS

This book has evolved from numerous sources and I wish to sincerely thank the many people who helped me gather material.

I thank the staffs of the following organisations: Antarctic Division, Kingston, Tasmania; Australian Basketball Federation; Australian Ballet; Australian Bureau of Statistics; Australian Cotton Foundation; Australian Cycling Federation; Australian Information Service; Australian National Library; Australian Stock Exchange; Badminton Association Australia; Bloomin' Books, Caringbah; Children's Book Council of Australia; Department of Aboriginal Affairs; Department of Foreign Affairs; Department of Immigration; Department of the Prime Minister and Cabinet; Honours Secretariat; Image Library & Protocol of Sydney City Council; Image Library of the State Library of NSW; Maritime Services Board; Mitchell Library; Museum of NSW; National Confederation of Australian Sport; NSW Government Information Service; Opera Australia; Paralympic Federation of Australia; Parliament House Construction Authority, ACT; Parliament House Education Resources, ACT; Peat Marwick; Premier's Department of each state; Reserve Bank; Roads & Traffic Authority, NSW; Royal Botanic Gardens, Sydney; Sister Cities Association of Australia; Squash Australia; St Vincent's Hospital; State Protocol Departments; Tourist Commissions of each state; Water Resources Commission; Women's Hockey Australia.

I am indebted to the following people: Russell Best, flora and fauna; Peter Boyden, Antarctica; Ross Dundas, cricket; Pat Conlan, films; Jon Farkes, country music; Mark Hughes, rock music; Brooke Mann, musicals; Don Matthews, radio; Des Renford, swimming; Kate Reynolds, ballet; David Tarbottom, athletics; Claire Vince, opera ; John Williamson, foreword; Pat Yardley, art.

For permission to include copyright material I thank:

ABC Radio for photograph of Mike Carlton; ABC TV for Bananas in Pyjamas; Australian Antarctic Division, Tasmania for photograph by G. Ullman of Lambert Glacier and for photograph by D. Eastman of raising the Australian flag at Atlas Cove for the first Australian National Research Expedition, 1947; Australian Ballet for photographs of Steven Heathcote (*Spartacus*), Justine Summers, Damien Welch and Vicki Attard (*Divergence*); Barbara Leane & Associates for photograph of Sandy Gore; Basketball Australia for photograph of Shane Heal; Black Yak Management for photographs of The Whitlams; BMG Music for photographs of Screaming Jets, John Farnham, You Am I, Merril Bainbridge and Natalie Imbruglia; Brian Brownscombe for photograph of waratah; bruce pollack publicity for permission to reproduce photograph of Todd McKenney in *The Boy from Oz*; City of Sydney Archives and

Image Library for facsimile of Sydney's flag and coat of arms; City Rail for city/suburban rail network map; Clean Up Australia for photograph of Ian Kiernan; Mimmo Cozzolino for symbols reproduced from *Symbols of Australia*; Department of the Special Minister of State for Commonwealth flag and coat of arms; EMI Records for photographs of James Blundell and Slim Dusty; Fair Dinkum Road Company for photograph of John Williamson; Jon Farkes for photograph of Crosby Sisters; Government Printer, Sydney, for engraving *Arrival of the First Railway Train at Parramatta, from Sydney;* International Casting Service for photographs of Tony Martin and Ruth Cracknell; Ken Done Art and Design for photograph of Ken Done; Kraft Foods Ltd for Vegemite label; Massive Records for photograph of Dead Ringer Band; Mitchell Library for engraving *The Settlement at Sydney Cove 1788*; Murmur Records for photograph of silverchair; Mushroom Group for photograph of Yothu Yindi; NAISDA Inc., for photograph of Student Ensemble; National Gallery of Victoria for *The Rabbiters* by Russell Drysdale, *Shearing the Rams* and *The Sunny South* by Tom Roberts, and *Landing of Captain Cook at Botany Bay 1770* by E. Phillips Fox; National Library of Australia for engravings *Sturt's Party Threatened by Blacks . . .* by J. Macfarlane and *Attempted escape of prisoners from Darlinghurst Gaol* from *Illustrated Sydney News 1864*; National Library of Australia Rare Map Collection for permission to reproduce Thévenot's *Map of 1663 of Terra Australis Incognita*; Mark Nicholson for photograph of Hawkesbury River Bridge to Bridge water-skiing race; Northern Territory Tourist Bureau for photographs of Katherine Gorge; NSW Roads and Traffic Authority for photograph of Sydney Harbour Bridge and Metroads map; Opal Fields Pty Ltd, Sydney for photograph of opals; Opera Australia for photographs of the productions *Madame Butterfly* and *Cleopatra and Julius Caesar* and photographs of Cheryl Barker and Yvonne Kenny; Palace Films for still from *Redball*; Polygram Filmed Entertainments for still from *Paperback Hero*; Radio 2GB for photograph of Clive Robertson; Radio 2UE for photograph of John Laws; Radio 3AW Melbourne for photograph of Neil Mitchell; Radio 5AD Adelaide for photograph of Keith Martyn and Jeff Sunderland; Radio 6PR Perth for photograph of Howard Sattler; Reserve Bank of Australia and Australian Mint, Canberra for permission to reproduce facsimile currency; Roadshow for photograph of Savage Garden; Royal Botanic Gardens, Sydney for photograph by Jamie Plaza of Wollemi Pine; Shanahan Management for photographs of Barry Otto, Ben Mendelsohn, Miranda Otto, Toni Collette and Matt Day; Sony Music Australia for photographs of Troy Cassar-Daley, Tommy Emmanuel and Human Nature; State Library of NSW for transparency of

The Founding of Australia by Algernon Talmage; State Transit Authority for Sydney Ferries network map; *Sydney Morning Herald* for photograph by Andrew Meares of Fireworks at Stadium Australia; Sydney Port Authority for photograph of Darling Harbour and Bridge and Opera House scene; Sydney Theatre Company for photographs of Angie Milliken and Paul Goddard; TCN9 TV for photograph of Mike Munro; Tourism Commission of NSW for photograph of Sydney Opera House; Tourist Commission of ACT for photograph of Parliament House, Canberra; Victorian Tourist Commission for photograph of paddle steamer; WA Tourist Bureau for photographs of boab tree; Warner Music for photographs of James Morrison, Karin Schaupp and Regurgitator; Dennis Warren for photograph of boom-netting Great Barrier Reef; Women's Cycling for photograph of Rachael Linke.

Permission to reproduce the poem 'My Country' by Dorothea Mackellar was granted by the copyright holders, c/o Curtis Brown (Aust) Pty Ltd, Sydney. Permission to reproduce the poem 'Then and Now' by Oodgeroo of the tribe Noonuccal (formerly Kath Walker), Custodian of the land Minjerribah, was granted by the copyright holders, Jacaranda Wiley Ltd, Queensland. The Cross family, Armidale, NSW, kindly granted permission to reproduce the cartoon by the late Stan Cross.

Every effort has been made to trace ownership of copyright material used in this book; apologies are offered for any omission.

I have always considered myself fortunate to be an Australian. Just as most people need to experience a feeling of belonging, I feel I belong here. To understand this feeling it is necessary to know just what makes this country 'tick'. As well as recognising the forces shaping our lives today, we have to look back at events in our history and to people who have helped mould them, those who, at the time, probably did not even realise that they were part of the grand plan which has shaped our nation.

To me, Australia is a country always in a state of change, always incredibly diverse, always challenging yet accommodating and protective. Our lifestyle is equal to any in the world and even though at times it may not seem so, tolerance and acceptance is the rule rather than the exception.

My overriding hope when preparing this eighth edition was to encourage Australians to be more aware of their background and heritage. The book is by no means intended to provide exhaustive information on all aspects of Australia but rather it is designed to combine essential and practical information in a condensed form, which could be helpful to the average person wanting to know about our country.

I hope this little book gives you both pleasure and enjoyment and that it adds to your understanding of just what it is to be an Australian at the beginning of a new millennium, and why Australia, with all its excitement and colour, is one of the most beautiful and stimulating places on earth.

Margaret Nicholson 2000

It is understandable why this book sells so well. It is as down to earth in its approach as the Australian character – it is colourful and easy to understand.

Australians are at last realising how little we know about ourselves. This book is a brilliant way to start the wonderful path to rediscovering what it is to be Australian. Our Ambassadors would do well to study the contents thoroughly. Personally, I am learning all the 'Did You Know?' items first.

John Williamson

Prehistory

During the ice age, perhaps as early as 70 000 years ago, people and animals of the Northern Hemisphere began to drift southwards to escape the intense advancing cold, as well as to find new food supplies. As a result, more southerly groups were pushed even further south, causing a chain reaction of migration.

The ice had built up in the waters of the sea to form massive ice caps, lowering the level of water (estimated to be 70–90 metres lower than it is today). This uncovered bridges between land masses, nearly joining islands and making migration possible. People in crude craft were able to 'island hop', and perhaps it was possible for the first human inhabitants of Australia unknowingly to enter the great southern continent.

2 Possible paths of migration of the Australian Aborigines

Early human populations spread through migration.

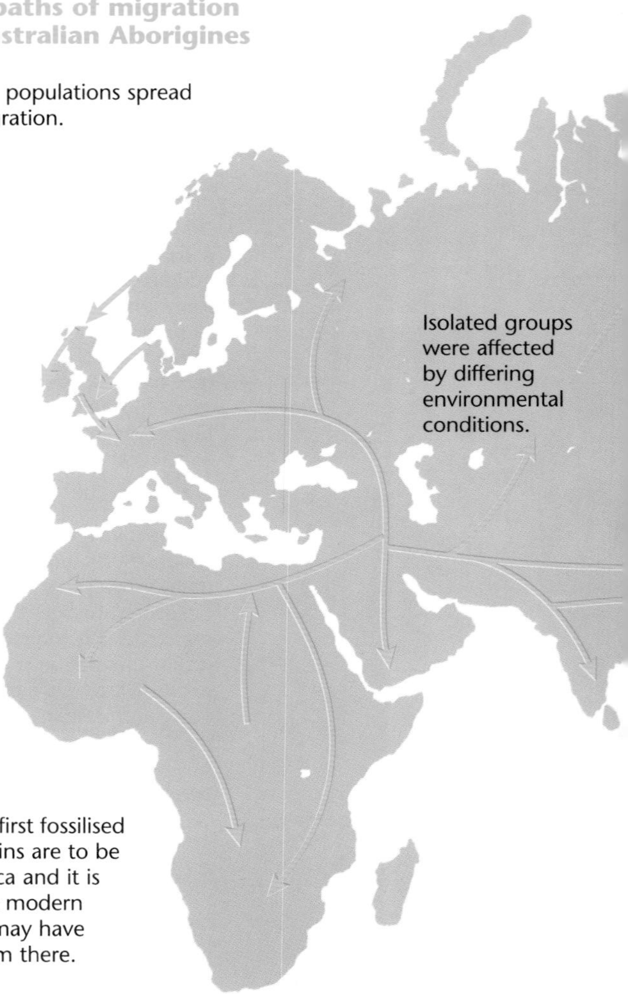

Isolated groups were affected by differing environmental conditions.

Some of the first fossilised human remains are to be found in Africa and it is believed that modern humankind may have emerged from there.

Possible paths of migration of modern humankind

Possible paths of migration of the Australian Aborigine

Rapid migration into America by hunters and gatherers is thought to have occurred about 15 000 years ago across the Bering Strait.

The intense cold of the Arctic produced mongoloid features – flat noses, small stature, virtually no facial hair – to prevent frostbite and heat loss.

In the tropics the dense forests, high temperatures and bright sunlight produced people of small stature with curly hair and dark skin.

Australian Aborigines are characterised by dark skin pigmentation, wavy hair and broad noses, all of which are adaptations to heat and intense sunlight.

It is believed that Tasmanian Aborigines may have originated in Polynesia.

Some Aboriginal tribal regions

Tiwi

Yoingu

Larrakia Mildjingi

Dalabon Gumatj

Kakadu

Ingaladdi

Wandjina

Lardil

Warramanga

Nyulnyul

Gurindji

Kalkadoon

Karadjeri

Walbiri

Pintubi

Wilgie Mia

Wenamba Arrernte

Pitjantjatjara Matuntara

Nakako

Dieri

Wongkonguru

Wirangu

Whadjuk

Archaeological sites found

- ● More than 30 000 years old

- ⫶ 15 000 – 30 000 years old

- ◉ 10 000 – 15 000 years old

Wik-mukan

Kongkandji

Kabikabi
Walawaka
Bigambul

Jagara
Galibal
Bandjalang
Kumbainggiri
Kamilaroi

Awabagai
Tharawal
Dharug
Worimi
Eora

Kameraigal

aurna

artangan
arijari
Wiradjiri
Mooroopna

Tjapruwong

Pennemukeer
anninher
Peeberrangner

Leetermairremener
Mouheneenner

Then and Now

*In my dreams I hear my tribe
Laughing as they hunt and swim,
But dreams are shattered by rushing
    car,
By grinding tram and hissing train,
And I see no more my tribe of old
As I walk alone in the teeming town.
I have seen corroboree
Where that factory belches smoke;
Here where they have memorial park
One time lubras dug for yams;
One time our dark children played
There where the railway yards are now,
And where I remember the didgeridoo
Calling to us to dance and play,
Offices now, neon lights now,
Bank and shop and advertisement now,
Traffic and trade of the busy town.
No more woomera, no more
    boomerang,
No more playabout, no more the old
    ways.
Children of nature we were then,
No clocks hurrying crowds to toil.
Now I am civilized and work in the
    white way.
Now I have dress, now I have shoes:
'Isn't she lucky to have a good job!'
Better when I had only a dillybag.
Better when I had nothing but
    happiness.*

Oodgeroo of the tribe Noonuccal
(formerly Kath Walker)

Aboriginal children.

Aboriginal culture

Australian Aborigines existed in almost total isolation for at least 60 000 years. They had no written history so only fragments of Dreamtime stories, cave paintings and etchings remain to record their remarkable past. Only in the last few decades has a systematic investigation revealed the rich and complex culture that they possessed.

It was, and still is, a culture based on strong spiritual ties which link them inexorably to the ancient land – a gift from the creator of the Dreamtime. It is believed the people are born of the spirit which inhabits the land, and on dying, return to the soil to be reborn. Each person is thought to be descended from either a plant or an animal and this becomes their 'totem', with its own taboos and rules of behaviour.

Before white settlement, most of the continent was occupied. Although their cultural and language patterns differed, the 600 or more scattered tribes existed in comparative harmony. They each occupied and hunted a recognised tract of land where sacred sites were protected, and boundaries, designated in the Dreamtime, were crossed only by invitation.

Tribal elders, who because of their wisdom were considered suitable for making decisions, upheld the laws. Every occasion demanded proper behaviour and breaches of law brought severe penalties.

Their economy was based on relentless daily activities of hunting and fishing by the men and gathering of seeds by the women. Drought and famine were interpreted to mean that the spirits were displeased and that 'man must make amends'. All made and repaired spears, boomerangs and digging sticks which were mainly made of wood. As well, Aborigines used ground-edge tools made of stone 10 000 years before their European counterparts.

Aboriginal society was a creative one and art, music, song and dance were integrated into both daily routine and spiritual ritual. The elders prescribed the form of ceremonial life, particularly the initiation, marriage and burial rites, in which the rest of the tribe, including songmen and artists, were totally involved. Also, corroborees and cave paintings reflected the powers of the Dreamtime. Symbolic designs were etched into most objects, from tools to the sacred Dreamtime stone, the *Tjurunga* (see 'Coat of Arms', p. 135).

Sorcery was not a daily occurrence although no one doubted its power. 'Pointing the bone', the most dreaded magic used, projected the power of evil hidden in the bone into the victim's body.

As the Aborigines confronted European settlers, the whole fabric of this fragile society was shaken. Early contact was usually made on the outskirts of towns where the materialistic values of the white people clashed with the cooperative sharing of the Aborigines. The myth that Australia was an uninhabited land when Captain James Cook discovered it gave the European settlers of the 18th and 19th centuries *carte blanche* to move into areas regardless of the consequences. The erosion of frontiers continued unheeded for over two centuries. Many Aborigines separated from their spiritual place and stable environment became dispossessed.

By 1850, concern was felt and segregation laws were passed to protect Aborigines from the poverty to which they were now exposed. Many were confined to missions and reserves run by white officials with extensive power and control. Some were used as a cheap source of labour by landowners who, although benevolent, still held great power. Others dwelt in a 'twilight zone' on the fringe of white society with little hope of recognition, where health, housing and education became endemic problems.

Changes in attitudes of both black and white people came after World War II. White society began to recognise its appalling lack of understanding and Aborigines became more aware of their national identity. In 1962 they were granted the right to vote in federal elections and were included in the census for the first time in 1967. National health services began to improve and housing and education services were made a priority. Land rights became an issue and by 1979 Aborigines were granted title to 144 former reserves. The High Court 'Mabo' judgement of 1992 ruled that Aborigines who could prove unbroken occupancy of land were able to lodge native title claims. In 1996 the controversial 'Wik' decision held that the grant of a pastoral lease did not necessarily extinguish native title and that in some circumstances the two could coexist. In 1998, the Federal Court of Australia ruled that native title could exist over coastal waters, and in the 'Yorta Yorta' native title claim the court ruled that, in some cases, 'the tide of history [had] washed away' entitlement.

Although much has been achieved in the last 50 years towards reconciliation and recognition of human rights of Aborigines, monumental problems still remain to be solved.

Aboriginal students perform a traditional dance in Wollongong, New South Wales.

European explorers and cartographers had long referred to a great land mass in the Southern Ocean as 'Terra Australis Incognita' (the unknown southern land). It was thought that to balance the large continental mass in the Northern Hemisphere a land mass must exist in the south.

Many explorers, spurred on by trade and constant reports by the Chinese and Malays who were frequent visitors to the area, sailed to the Southern Ocean, braving the vagaries of the weather and the uncharted seas to discover the Great South Land.

In 1606 Willem Jansz gave European navigators the first certain knowledge that Terra Australis existed. In the 17th century the western section was called New Holland, and in the 18th century the British established the penal colony of New South Wales on the east coast. It was not until the early 19th century, when it was established that these two sectors were part of the same land mass, that the navigator Matthew Flinders suggested the Great South Land be called Australia.

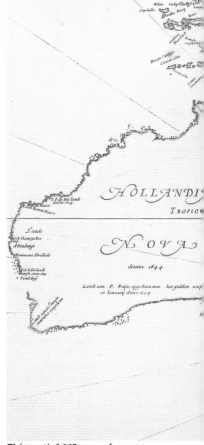

Thévenot's 1663 map of Terra Australis Incognita.

DID YOU KNOW?

In 1698, British adventurer and navigator William Dampier wrote in his journal: 'New Holland is a very large tract of land . . . I am certain that it joyns (sic) neither to Asia, Africa nor America'. (See his voyage of discovery on p. 10.)

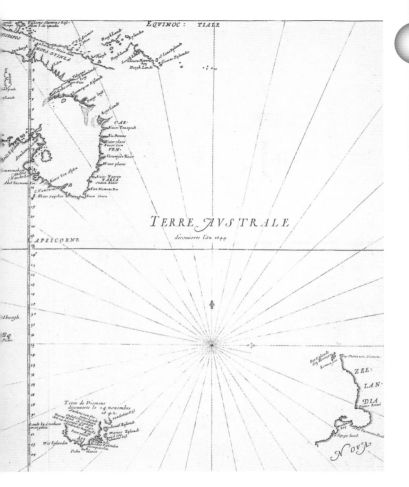

DID YOU KNOW?

The rugged Australian coastline has claimed
more than 500 ships. The earliest known is the
English ship *The Trial*, wrecked off the Western
Australian coast in 1662 with bullion estimated
to be worth $10 million in today's terms.

European voyages of discovery

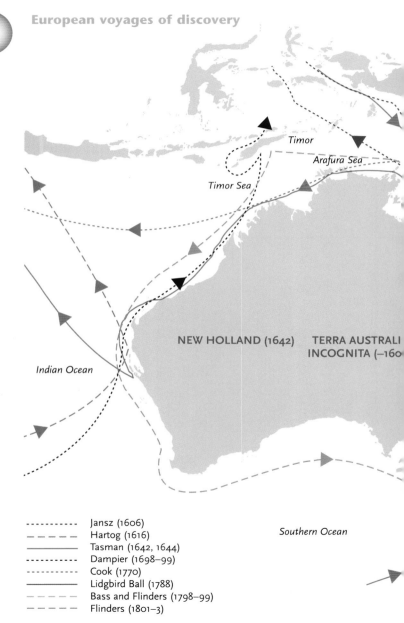

Timor

Arafura Sea

Timor Sea

NEW HOLLAND (1642)   TERRA AUSTRALI
INCOGNITA (–160

Indian Ocean

.... Jansz (1606)
— — — — Hartog (1616)
————— Tasman (1642, 1644)
-·-·-·-· Dampier (1698–99)
.... Cook (1770)
————— Lidgbird Ball (1788)
— — — — Bass and Flinders (1798–99)
— — — — Flinders (1801–3)

Southern Ocean

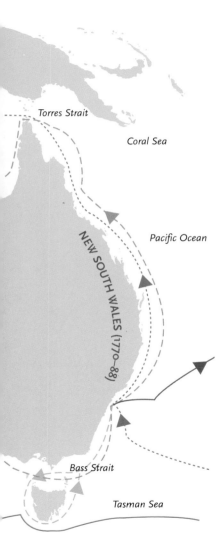

Torres Strait

Coral Sea

NEW SOUTH WALES (1770-88)

Pacific Ocean

Bass Strait

Tasman Sea

George Bass 1763–1808

A ship's surgeon; together with Matthew Flinders he circumnavigated Van Diemen's Land (Tasmania) in 1798, proving that it was an island.

Gregory Blaxland 1778–1853
William Charles Wentworth 1793–1872
William Lawson 1774–1850

These men were inland explorers. In 1813 they crossed the Blue Mountains west of Sydney and so opened up the fertile western plains to the colony.

Robert O'Hara Burke 1821–61
William Wills 1834–61

Burke, a policeman, and Wills, a surveyor, were the first Europeans to cross the continent from south to north. In 1860 they trekked from Melbourne to the Gulf of Carpentaria. On their return journey, because of exhaustion and lack of food, they slowly starved to death at Cooper Creek.

Wills memorial cairn at Cooper Creek, South Australia.

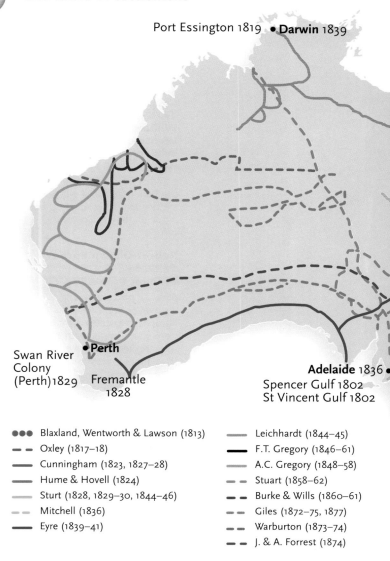

Port Essington 1819 ●**Darwin** 1839

●**Perth**

Swan River
Colony
(Perth)1829   Fremantle
                    1828

Adelaide 1836 ●
Spencer Gulf 1802
St Vincent Gulf 1802

●●● Blaxland, Wentworth & Lawson (1813)

– – Oxley (1817–18)

⎯⎯ Cunningham (1823, 1827–28)

⎯⎯ Hume & Hovell (1824)

⎯⎯ Sturt (1828, 1829–30, 1844–46)

– – Mitchell (1836)

⎯⎯ Eyre (1839–41)

⎯⎯ Leichhardt (1844–45)

⎯⎯ F.T. Gregory (1846–61)

⎯⎯ A.C. Gregory (1848–58)

– – Stuart (1858–62)

■ ■ Burke & Wills (1860–61)

– – Giles (1872–75, 1877)

– – Warburton (1873–74)

– – J. & A. Forrest (1874)

James Cook 1728–79

Cook landed in Botany Bay in 1770. At Possession Island, Torres Strait, he claimed the eastern coast of Australia in the name of King George III of Great Britain, and named it New South Wales.

William Dampier 1652–1715

A British privateer who visited the western coast of Australia in 1688 and again in 1699.

Edward John Eyre 1815–1901

An inland explorer, he crossed the continent from Streaky Bay, South Australia, to Albany, Western Australia, in 1839–41, a trek of almost 1600 kilometres.

Matthew Flinders 1774–1814

A British naval officer, he circumnavigated Australia in 1801–3, thus allowing the coastal mapping of Australia to be completed.

Dirk Hartog b. *c.*1570

A Dutch navigator who landed on an island off Western Australia in 1616, which was later named after him.

Hamilton Hume 1797–1873

He forged a route across the Great Dividing Range at Razorback (New South Wales) in 1814. Then in 1824, he and William Hovell conducted an expedition from Gunning (New South Wales) to Corio Bay (Victoria).

Port Bowen 1802

• Brisbane 1825

Port Macquarie 1818

○ Newcastle 1804
• Sydney

Port Jackson 1788

• Melbourne 1835

Port Phillip 1802

• Hobart 1804

Willem Jansz b. c.1550

A Dutch sea captain, he gave European navigators the first certain knowledge that Australia existed. In 1606 he landed on the west coast of Cape York Peninsula.

Ludwig Leichhardt 1813–48

He explored inland from Brisbane to Port Essington, Northern Territory in 1844, a 3200-kilometre trek. In 1848 he and an entire expedition disappeared without trace while trying to cross Australia from east to west.

Sir Douglas Mawson 1882–1958

Antarctic explorer and geologist who made many expeditions to the cold continent between 1907 and 1924. He was largely responsible for Australia gaining sovereignty over Antarctica between the 45° and 160° eastern meridians.

John McDouall Stuart 1815–66

He finally crossed the continent from south to north in 1862, after three attempted journeys into the interior.

Charles Sturt 1795–1869

An inland explorer who charted and named the Murray River in 1829.

Abel Tasman 1602–59

A Dutch navigator, he discovered Van Diemen's Land (Tasmania) and Statenland (New Zealand) in 1642.

Sir George Hubert Wilkins 1888–1958

He travelled beneath the arctic ice cap in 1931 in the US submarine *Nautilus* to within 1000 kilometres of the North Pole.

The intrepid explorers

'No country can possibly have a more interesting aspect . . . if a further trace into the interior is required . . . I respectfully beg leave to offer myself for the service. I see no end to travelling.' This was a request by explorer George William Evans in a letter to Governor Macquarie in 1815.

It has often been asked just why humans are gripped with the compulsive drive to explore. The Australian desert explorer Ernest Giles wrote: 'An explorer is an explorer from love and it is nature, not art that makes it so.'

The explorers were a diverse band. Some were highly educated government officials with scientific knowledge of surveying skills, others were fine bushmen with a natural talent for exploration, but the overriding love for the Australian landscape was common to all. It was said of Charles Sturt, the overland explorer, 'he quested because of his love for the interior of the continent and his ambition was to reach its very heart'.

Whatever their reasons, many explorers endured dreadful suffering in regions of impenetrable jungle or merciless

Sturt's party at the junction of the Murray and Darling Rivers, 1830.

desert. Colonel Peter Warburton, finding water at last after a particularly tortuous desert crossing, wrote in his journal, 'If we press on we risk losing our camels and dying of thirst. If we stand still we starve.'

Robert O'Hara Burke and William Wills were stranded with no food at Cooper Creek after their incredible trek from the Gulf of Carpentaria. Exhausted and starving, they gave up hope and waited for death. Burke's last diary entry read, 'weaker than ever . . . my legs and arms are nearly skin and bone'. The only survivor of his party was a man named King. He was found by Alfred Howitt's relief party who recorded, 'we found King sitting in a hut which the natives had made for him. He seemed exceedingly weak and we found it difficult to follow what he said'.

In retrospect, we can see that their judgement was sometimes questionable. For instance, in 1770 Captain Cook reported to the British Admiralty that Botany Bay was 'capacious, safe and commodious'. In 1788 Governor Phillip found it to be too exposed, and speedily moved the infant colony to Port Jackson, which he considered 'the finest in the world, where a thousand sail of the line might ride in the most perfect security'. When the Surveyor-General, John Oxley, described land in southern New South Wales as 'uninhabitable and useless for all purposes of civilized man', he would never have dreamed that the country between 34 and 35 degrees south and 147.34 degrees east would one day become the fertile Murrumbidgee Irrigation Area. Again, Francis Gregory, the leader of the first expedition into the mineral-rich Hamersley Range in Western Australia, commented in his journal, 'Of minerals I was unable to discover any, except iron'.

Many explorers took great pleasure in the beauty of the surrounding countryside. Sir Thomas Mitchell described the Nandewar Ranges of New South Wales as 'a beautiful variety of summits', while the Polish explorer, Sir Paul Strzelecki, described Mount Kosciuszko, our highest mountain, as 'a craggy scenic cone cresting the Australian Alps'. It was also with obvious

Landing of Captain Cook at Botany Bay, 1770 *by E. Phillips Fox.*

pleasure that Mitchell, exploring the south of the continent, wrote: 'It was not without some pride as a Briton, that I gave the name of the Grampians to these extreme summits of the southern hemisphere.'

The urgency to open up the interior was to enable the colony to expand beyond the confines of the coastal settlements. Although it took place in an atmosphere of excitement and challenge, it was mainly for the purpose of gain, a reason for which we may be dubiously proud.

However, there is good reason to value the courage of the intrepid explorers who, with passion and drive, journeyed into the unknown to open up new lands for the eager pioneer settlers.

Early European discovery and settlement

1642	Van Diemen's Land (Tasmania) discovered
1770	Botany Bay discovered
1774	Norfolk Island discovered
1788	Port Jackson (Sydney) settled; Lord Howe Island discovered
1802	Spencer Gulf and St Vincent Gulf discovered
1802	Port Phillip discovered
1804	Newcastle and Hobart settled
1818	Port Macquarie settled
1819	Port Essington discovered
1825	Brisbane settled
1828	Fremantle discovered
1829	Swan River Colony (Perth) settled
1835	Melbourne settled
1836	Adelaide settled
1839	Port Darwin discovered
1869	Darwin becomes a permanent settlement

DID YOU KNOW?

Between 1788 and 1856, 157 000 convicts were sent to Australia. This is only one-third of the total number sent to the United States.

Development of a nation

From 1788 to 1850 the government of the colony was in the tight control of New South Wales. Resentment ran high when laws passed by the New South Wales Legislative Assembly affected newer parts of the colony, hundreds of miles away. In 1850 the *Australian Colonies Government Act* was forced through parliament resulting in responsible government for each of the states. Each state now had its own governor.

1829

Western Australia

New South Wales

Van Diemen's Land

1650

Hollandia Nova

Van Diemen's Land

Mapping of coastline not completed until 1802

1851

New South Wales

Western Australia

South Australia

Victoria

Van Diemen's Land

1780

Terra Australis

New Holland

New South Wales

Van Diemen's Land

1859

Part of New South Wales

Queensland

Western Australia

South Australia

New South Wales

Victoria

Tasmania (1855)

1786–1824

unattached

New South Wales

Van Diemen's Land

1931

Northern Territory

Queensland

Western Australia

South Australia

New South Wales

Victoria

Australian Capital Territory

Tasmania

Hobart Town Gazette, 1843.

'Terra Australis Incognita' was inhabited by its Aboriginal people, who had their origins in remote antiquity.

1606 Willem Jansz lands on west coast of Cape York, Queensland

1616 Dirk Hartog lands on the island later named after him, off the west coast of Australia

1642 Abel Tasman discovers Van Diemen's Land (Tasmania) and Statenland (New Zealand)

1770 Captain James Cook lands at Botany Bay. He names the eastern coastline New South Wales for Britain

1788 Beginning of European settlement as a penal colony. Arrival of Governor Arthur Phillip and First Fleet at Botany Bay on 18 January and at Port Jackson on 26 January, when Phillip formally takes possession of the whole of the eastern part of the continent, including Tasmania

1793 First free settlers arrive

1796 Discovery of coal at mouth of Hunter River (Newcastle), New South Wales

1797 Introduction of merino sheep by John Macarthur

1798 George Bass and Matthew Flinders circumnavigate Van Diemen's Land (Tasmania) in the *Norfolk*

1802 Discovery of Port Phillip, Victoria, and of Port Bowen, Queensland by Lieutenant John Murray, and St Vincent Gulf and Spencer Gulf, South Australia, by Matthew Flinders

1804 Lieutenant David Collins establishes settlement at Hobart (Tasmania). First population headcounts, called 'musters', held in New South Wales and Tasmania; military personnel and Aborigines not counted

DID YOU KNOW?

Ten thousand years ago both the Europeans and the Australian Aborigines were hunters and gatherers. However, overpopulation in Europe forced agricultural development, whereas the Aborigines, with plenty of land, did not have to change their ways.

1807 First shipment of saleable wool to England

1808 The Rum Rebellion, deposition of Governor William Bligh

1813 Crossing of Blue Mountains by Gregory Blaxland, William Charles Wentworth and William Lawson

1814 Matthew Flinders suggests the name 'Australia' instead of New Holland

1817 The first bank, Bank of New South Wales (now Westpac), is established

1819 Lieutenant Phillip King discovers Port Essington (Northern Territory)

1822 Establishment of penal settlement at Macquarie Harbour, Van Diemen's Land (Tasmania)

1823 Brisbane River discovered by John Oxley and three convicts

1825 Separation of the administration of Van Diemen's Land from New South Wales. Establishment of settlement of Brisbane

1828 First official census taken: 36 000 convicts and free settlers, 2549 military personnel, Aborigines not counted

1829 Foundation of settlement at Swan River, Western Australia. Perth founded

1834 First settlement at Twofold Bay, New South Wales. Henty brothers form settlement at Portland (Victoria)

1835 Foundation of Melbourne, planned by Governor Sir Richard Bourke

1836 Settlement founded at Adelaide under Governor Sir John Hindmarsh

1838 Captain James Bremer establishes Port Essington (Northern Territory)

1839 Area around Darwin discovered by crew of the *Beagle*

1840 Abolition of convict transportation to New South Wales

1841 New Zealand proclaimed as a separate colony

1842 First elected council in New South Wales

1847 Melbourne proclaimed a city

1850 Sydney University founded. Representative government granted to Victoria, Van Diemen's Land (Tasmania) and South Australia

1851 Edward Hargraves discovers gold at Lewis Ponds, New South Wales. The Port Phillip District is created as a separate colony, named Victoria

1852 Abolition of convict transportation to Van Diemen's Land (Tasmania) and Norfolk Island

Attempted escape, Darlinghurst Gaol, 1855.

1854 Eureka Stockade riot at Ballarat, Victoria, sparked off by goldminers' objections to high mining licence fees

1855 Van Diemen's Land renamed Tasmania, commemorating its discoverer, Abel Tasman. Responsible government granted to New South Wales, Victoria and Tasmania

1856 Responsible government granted to South Australia

1857 Adult males granted the right to vote in Victoria

1858 Granting of the right to vote to adult males in New South Wales

1859 Queensland proclaimed a separate colony

1863 Northern Territory comes under the jurisdiction of South Australia. Discovery of gold at Kalgoorlie, Western Australia

1864 First sugar made from Queensland cane

1869 'Welcome Stranger' gold nugget found in Dunolly, Victoria. Darwin (Northern Territory) becomes permanent settlement

1872 Transcontinental telegraph completed. First cable message from Sydney to London

1876 Death of Truganini, last full-blooded Tasmanian Aborigine

1878 First telephone in Australia

1880 Ned Kelly, bushranger and rebel, captured

1883 Silver discovered at Broken Hill, New South Wales

1885 Australians go to war for the first time, as a New South Wales contingent is sent to Sudan, Africa. BHP mining company floated.

1889 Sir Henry Parkes' 'Tenterfield Address' on federation

1890 John Forrest becomes Western Australia's first premier

1899 First Australian contingent sent to Boer War in South Africa

1900 Federation: on 17 September Australia announces its intention to become independent from Great Britain

1901 On 1 January – the first day of the new century – the Commonwealth of Australia is proclaimed. First federal election. 1901 census: white population 3 773 801, Aborigines not counted

1902 Women granted the right to vote in federal elections

DID YOU KNOW?

The first ration list in 1788, per person per week, included 7 lbs (3.17 kg) of bread or flour, 7 lbs of beef or 4 lbs (1.81 kg) of pork, 3 lbs (1.36 kg) of peas, 6 oz (170 g) of butter, and 1/2 lb (225 g) of rice.

Desert sunset, Sturt National Park, New South Wales.

1908 Canberra chosen as the site for the national capital

1910 First Commonwealth bank notes issued

1911 Mawson leads expedition to the Antarctic. First Commonwealth census.

1913 First Commonwealth postage stamps issued

1914 World War I declared, 20 000 troops embark for overseas, devastating losses in battle of the Somme. German raider *Emden* sunk by HMAS *Sydney* in Indian Ocean

1915 BHP opens in Newcastle. ANZAC (Australian and New Zealand Army Corps) troops land at Gallipoli on 25 April and are evacuated on 19 December

1917 Completion of transcontinental railway

1918 First wireless message from London to Sydney. Armistice with Germany, 11 November. Australia House, London, opened by King George V

1919 Return of Australian troops from Europe. Ross and Keith Smith make the first flight from England to Australia

1920 Queensland and Northern Territory Aerial Services (QANTAS) formed by Hudson Fysh. White population 5 411 300

1922 Queensland is the first state to abolish the death penalty

1923 Sydney Harbour Bridge commenced

1926 Auction sales of wool begin

1927 Seat of government moves from Melbourne to Canberra

1928 Kingsford Smith flies from America to Australia in the *Southern Cross.* Flying Doctor Service begins. First traffic lights in Australia installed in Melbourne

1929 Beginning of Depression. Fall in exports. Commonwealth government mobilises gold reserves

1932 Sydney Harbour Bridge opened. Lang government in New South Wales dismissed

1933 BHP takes over steel works at Port Kembla, New South Wales

1935 Kingsford Smith lost without trace near the Bay of Bengal, flying from England to Australia. Ansett Airways set up by Reginald Ansett

1936 Hume reservoir completed

1938 Coca-Cola first made in Australia

1939 World War II declared. The last grain clipper race to England held

1940 20 000 Australian troops embark for service abroad. Introduction of food, petrol and clothing rationing

1941 Sinking of HMAS *Sydney* and HMAS *Canberra*. Australian troops besieged at Tobruk

1942 Darwin and Katherine bombed. Fall of Singapore. Battle of the Coral Sea. Japanese midget submarines in Sydney Harbour

1943 Industrial conscription introduced

1944 Pay-as-you-earn (PAYE) taxation begins. Japanese prisoners of war attempt mass breakout at Cowra, New South Wales; 234 killed

1945 World War II ends, demobilisation of 500 000 men and women begins

1946 United Nations grants trusteeship of New Guinea to Australia

Cooper Creek, South Australia.

1947 Commonwealth Arbitration Commission established. Arthur Calwell's immigration drive begins

1948 40-hour week introduced. General Motors-Holden produces first Holden car. Food and clothing rationing ends

1949 The right to vote granted to some Aborigines. Snowy Mountains Hydro Electric Scheme commenced. Robert Menzies (Liberal Party) becomes Prime Minister

1950 Petrol rationing ends. Australian troops join UN force in Korea

1951 ANZUS treaty signed by Australia, New Zealand and USA against aggression in Pacific

1952 Discovery of uranium at Rum Jungle, Northern

Territory. Nuclear experiments begin at Australian National University

1953 Atomic Energy Commission established. Television Bill passed. Atomic weapons tested by United Kingdom at Woomera, South Australia. South-East Asia Treaty Organisation (SEATO) founded

1954 Queen Elizabeth II makes first visit by a reigning monarch. Uranium discovered at Mary Kathleen, Queensland. Troops withdrawn from Korea. 'Petrov Affair': accusations of Communist espionage in Department of External Affairs

1955 Severe floods in eastern Australia cause havoc

1956 Olympic Games in Melbourne

1958 First nuclear reactor opened in Lucas Heights, Sydney

1960 Aborigines granted citizenship and therefore entitlement to Social Service benefits. Reserve Bank established

1961 Huge iron-ore deposits found at Pilbara, Western Australia

1962 Standard-gauge railway track opened between Brisbane, Sydney and Melbourne. Aborigines granted the vote. Australia grants approval to USA to build communication base at Exmouth, Western Australia, and space tracking station at Tidbinbilla, near Canberra

1964 HMAS *Voyager* sinks after collision with HMAS *Melbourne,* 82 lives lost. First flight of Blue Streak rocket launched at Woomera, South Australia

1965 Australian infantry battalion sent to Vietnam. Australia imposes economic sanctions against the Smith regime in Rhodesia

1966 Decimal currency introduced. Aborigines appeal to UN for human

Isolated Innamincka, South Australia.

rights recognition.
Sir Robert Menzies retires.
Harold Holt becomes
Prime Minister. Gough
Whitlam becomes leader
of the Labor Party. Metric
system of weights and
measures phased in

1967 Prime Minister Harold Holt
disappears at Portsea,
Victoria. Aborigines
included in census figures
for the first time.
Demonstration in
Melbourne against the
hanging of Ronald Ryan,
the last person to be
hanged in Australia

1968 First Australian heart
transplant performed.
John Gorton becomes
leader of the Liberal Party
and Prime Minister

1969 HMAS *Melbourne* collides
with USS *Frank E Evans*
with the loss of 74 lives.
Indian–Pacific railway
completed. Poseidon
company announces a
find of nickel; as a result,
share prices soar. Robert
Hawke is elected president

of the ACTU. Arbitration
Commission grants equal
pay to women for work of
equal value

1970 Vietnam Moratoriums:
large-scale demonstrations
against Australian and US
involvement in Vietnam
war. Mineral shares boom
ends. Tullamarine airport
opened in Melbourne

1971 Australia ends fighting role
in Vietnam. Lake Pedder in
Tasmania is flooded as
part of a hydro-electric
scheme

1972 Labor Party wins power
under the leadership of
Gough Whitlam.
Withdrawal of troops from
Vietnam. Formal ending of
White Australia Policy

1973 Eighteen-year-olds are
granted the right to vote
in federal elections. Queen
Elizabeth II to be known
as Queen of Australia

1974 Cyclone Tracy hits Darwin,
Northern Territory on
Christmas Day. Bankcard
introduced. Fully elected
assemblies set up in the

Broken Head, New South Wales.

Northern Territory and Australian Capital Territory

1975 Dismissal of Whitlam government by Governor-General Sir John Kerr. Return of Liberal–Country Party coalition to power under leadership of Malcolm Fraser. Papua New Guinea becomes independent. No-fault divorce introduced. The MV *Lake Illawarra* hits the Tasman Bridge, Hobart. Five Australian journalists killed in East Timor

1976 Flexitime approved for federal public servants

1977 Granville train disaster; 81 die

1978 Northern Territory becomes responsible for its own administration

1979 Aboriginal Land Trust gains title to 144 properties, all formerly Aboriginal reserves

1980 Campbell Inquiry into Australian financial system. Nugan Hand bank collapses. Baby Azaria Chamberlain allegedly taken by a dingo at Ayers Rock (Uluru)

1981 Severe drought affects large areas of Australia

1982 New South Wales introduces random breath testing. Franklin Dam controversy rages in Tasmania. Lindy Chamberlain found guilty of the murder of her daughter, Azaria. Devastating floods in Western Australia

1983 Robert (Bob) Hawke leads Labor Party into office after Prime Minister Malcolm Fraser is granted a double dissolution of parliament. Ash Wednesday bushfires devastate South Australia and Victoria. America's Cup victory by *Australia II*. Conservationists win battle against Franklin Dam project in Tasmania

1984 Prices and Income Policy Accord reached. Control of Ayers Rock (Uluru) given to local Aborigines. Milperra bikie massacre, seven people shot dead. World's first test-tube quads born in Melbourne

1985 McClelland Royal Commission into British nuclear testing in Australia. High Court Justice Lionel Murphy charged with allegedly having conspired to pervert the course of justice. Federal Treasury allows banking licences for 16 foreign banks

1986 Queen Elizabeth II signs a proclamation which finally severs some of Australia's historical, political and legal ties with United Kingdom, *Australia Act* comes into force. Lindy Chamberlain released on licence from jail. Russell Street police headquarters, Melbourne, bombed. Kevin Barlow and Brian Chambers convicted of drug trafficking and subsequently hanged in

Hamersley Gorge, Western Australia.

Malaysia. Fringe Benefits Tax introduced. High Court landmark ruling against Australasian Meat Workers' Union in dispute over wages and conditions in Mudginberri abattoirs in Western Australia

1987 Four men found guilty and one pleads guilty of murder in the Anita Cobby trial. The Milperra massacre trial – the longest-running in New South Wales legal history – ends with seven men being found guilty of murder, 21 guilty of manslaughter and 31 guilty of affray. Australian share market collapses. Seven people killed in Hoddle Street massacre, Melbourne. Vietnam veterans march in long-overdue 'Welcome Home' parade

1988 Australia celebrates bicentenary of white settlement. Queen opens new Parliament House. Charges against Lindy Chamberlain quashed

1989 Human Rights Commission estimates 50 000 children homeless. Queensland police and politicians flayed by Fitzgerald corruption report. 17 people killed in two ballooning disasters in the Northern Territory. 56 die in Australia's two worst coach crashes. Airline pilots' strike ends after 17 crippling weeks. Destructive earthquake in Newcastle, 12 dead. Environmentalists' victory over Wesley Vale pulp mill, Tasmania. Corporate failures emerge as result of 1987 share market collapse

1990 ANZAC contingent attends 75th anniversary of the landing at Anzac Cove, Gallipoli. Australian Navy represented in Gulf War. Worst recession for 40 years has widespread effects. HMAS *Voyager* survivor receives compensation after 26-year battle with government. Collapse of Bond Corporation and Pyramid Building Society. Australian hostages return from Baghdad. Fairfax Group placed into receivership

1991 Sydney hit by severe storms. Devastating Queensland floods. Banks affected by widespread losses. Tariff barriers and import quotas reduced. Sweeping reforms for Aborigines held in custody. Mining of uranium at Coronation Hill, Kakadu, banned. Heart transplant pioneer Dr Victor Chang murdered. Strathfield Shopping Plaza massacre in Sydney, nine dead. Paul Keating (Labor Party) becomes Prime Minister

1992 1c and 2c coins phased out. Unemployment 11.3%. Anglican Synod allows ordination of women priests. Sydney Harbour tunnel opens. Landmark Mabo High Court decision enables Aborigines with unbroken occupancy of land to claim title

1993 Highest unemployment ever. Unknown Soldier interred in the Hall of Memory, Canberra.

Ebor Falls, New South Wales.

Sydney wins year 2000 Olympic Games

1994 Four people die in New South Wales bushfires. National Crime Authority bombing in Adelaide. Bodies of seven murdered backpackers found in Belanglo forest, New South Wales. Nine dead in Seaview air crash. 12 die in Queensland bus crash. El Niño cycle brings devastating drought to eastern seaboard. Plastic $10 and $20 notes introduced. *Endeavour* replica leaves Fremantle, Western Australia

1995 Pay TV launched. Rugby Super League controversy rages. Balance of payments deficit historically high. Drought blankets eastern Australia. Plastic $50 note introduced. New South Wales Police Royal Commission into corruption has widespread ramifications. Salinity levels threaten Murray Basin

1996 Landslide victory to Liberals, John Howard becomes Prime Minister. Massacre at Port Arthur, Tasmania; 35 dead. Gun Summit bans certain automatic and semi-automatic weapons. Euthanasia legalised in Northern Territory. 18 soldiers die in Blackhawk helicopter crash in Queensland. Backpacker murderer Ivan Milat convicted. Martin Bryant given

35 life sentences for Port Arthur massacre. High Court Wik decision on pastoral leases

1997 Wood Royal Commission into police corruption ends after 370 days, sweeping changes recommended. Federal Senate overrides Northern Territory legislation on euthanasia. Federal government endorses major changes to financial sector after release of Wallis Report. BHP decides to quit steel-making in Newcastle by 1999.

The Pinnacle Desert, Nambung National Park, Western Australia.

Four Australians dead after bridge collapse at the Maccabiah Games in Israel. 18 killed in Thredbo landslide in New South Wales – Stuart Diver survives ordeal after 65 hours buried alive. Federal government imposes five-year freeze on tariffs on clothing, footwear and textiles. Gun buyback ends. Meltdown over Asian crisis. Devastating bushfires hit all states with tragic loss of life

1998 Asian crisis worsens, affecting economic markets. Severe floods hit many areas of northern Australia. Australia sends troops to Gulf combat zone. Constitutional Convention results in promise of public referendum on republic issue. Michael Hutchence, lead singer of INXS, dies tragically. Two American tourists disappear after being abandoned on Great Barrier Reef cruise. Four sailors perish in fire aboard HMAS *Westralia*. Landmark Federal Court ruling that native title can exist over coastal waters. Historical ruling in favour of native claims over large tracts of land in the Kimberley, Western Australia. Five volunteers die in Victorian bushfires. Federal Court rules that in some cases 'the tide of

Frangipani Bay, Cape York, Queensland.

history [had] washed away' entitlement, in native title claim. Prolonged dispute on waterfront reaches compromise settlement. Parcel bomber targets Taxation Office workers. Mining continues in Kakadu despite World Heritage listing. Sydney water contamination scare. Seven die in disastrous Sydney-to-Hobart yacht race

1999 Salt Lake City Olympic bid scandal erupts sending shock waves through the AOC. Unemployment hits 7.5%: lowest for decades. Exmouth, Western Australia devastated by Cyclone Vance: highest winds ever recorded on mainland Australia. Two CARE Australia volunteers in Kosovo, Yugoslavia, charged with spying. Hailstorm wreaks havoc in Sydney, bill exceeds $1bn. Australia takes in Kosovo refugees. GST to be introduced into Australian taxation system. Thirteen young Australians killed in freak Swiss flash flood. Four snowboarders disappear in Snowy Mountains. Federal Parliament passes historic declaration of 'deep and sincere regret' for past Aboriginal injustices. Australian troops lead Interfet peacekeeping force into East Timor. Historic overhaul of business tax system following the Ralph report. BHP Newcastle closes steel making after 84 years. Republic referendum results in a No vote

From the very first, when Governor Phillip was about to make the hazardous journey to New South Wales in 1787, the scenario was one of desperation and indifference. Although he sought better supplies and conditions for the convicts from the overcrowded British prisons, famine and pestilence blanketed the First Fleet like a venomous shroud. Depravity and thieving, horror and dread set the scene for its arrival at Botany Bay.

The struggling infant colony began with bitter disappointment. Lack of food, constant sickness and indolence seemed to set the pattern for the years to come. The country appeared to be a huge and empty land, hostile to British ideas and ways. The colony also had conflicting obligations.

Horse-drawn carriage, 1870s.

Sydney Cove (Port Jackson) 1788.

It had to contend with the commercial demands of the British government as well as the needs of the penal colony. There was nothing to suggest that the foundation of a prosperous nation could be laid from such a hopeless beginning.

Gradually, the tenacity of the colonists and their improved understanding of the land led to better times. Meanwhile, explorers blazed tracks into the interior and people began to spill out of the overcrowded towns and cities and into the country. Pioneers, squatters and free settlers followed in the tracks of the explorers and a spirit of self-reliance began to flourish in isolated communities. Compared to the confines of the English countryside there was space to breathe in this far-off colony in the antipodes, and the people liked it.

'The days of gold' from the 1850s to 1880s brought an uninterrupted boom to the colony, and tradespeople, clerks, shepherds and sailors all headed for the goldfields, gripped by 'gold fever'. Any kind of order in the towns or cities was disrupted, and although 'great excitement prevailed' and 'whole towns were in hysterics', Lieutenant-Governor La Trobe of Victoria contemptuously remarked 'The whole structure of society and the whole machinery of government is dislocated'.

Though trouble intermittently flared up on the goldfields due to various injustices and persecutions, the only major rebellion of the period, and of

Arrival of the first railway train at Parramatta, from Sydney.

the whole of Australian history, took place at the Eureka Stockade near Ballarat in December 1854.

Towards the latter part of the 19th century, railways and improved roads brought the country closer to the city and a new feeling of nationalism was born. Constitutionally, there was no such thing as an Australian citizen or an Australian nation, but people from both town and country wanted to be counted as one.

In his Tenterfield Oration of 1889, referring to the joining of all states in a federation, the revered statesman Sir Henry Parkes said, 'Surely what the Americans have done by war, the Australians could bring about by peace without breaking the ties that hold them to the mother country . . . We ought to set about creating this great national government for all Australia.'

The Commonwealth of Australia was proclaimed on the first day of the new century, 1 January 1901. Sir Edmund Barton, the first prime minister of Australia, remarked, 'For the first time in history we have a continent for a nation and a nation for a continent.'

A nation coming of age (1901–2000)

Although the young Commonwealth began the new century on a note of cautious optimism, it was obvious that it needed to be awakened to the demands of such a monumental experiment as Federation.

To establish a new identity was the main concern of most Australians, but the old loyalties and demands of Britain were strong. Australian 'soldiers of the Queen' marched to fight in the Boer War in South Africa, one which many saw as 'the most iniquitous war ever waged'.

Nevertheless, times were rapidly changing. The Commonwealth had blundered into a new century and progress came at a bewildering pace.

Kids afloat: Rhododendron Festival, Blackheath, New South Wales.

In 1905 the *Pure Foods Act* ensured quality and purity of food, substantially reducing infant mortality. Electricity had replaced gas lights; trams, trains and cars had superseded the horse, and the new inventions of the wireless, cash register and typewriter all led to an increased demand for skills. This was the machine age, and opportunity was everywhere, demanding that everyone become literate. The workers backed trade unions, and a five-and-a-half-day week and a £2 2s ($4.20) average weekly wage were introduced. Change was in the air worldwide, and Australia was making great strides in coming of age and keeping up with the rest of the world.

Yet loyalty to Britain persisted. When war broke out in 1914,

DID YOU KNOW?

The expected life span for Australians born in 1999 is estimated to be 76.95 years for males and 82.98 for females.

Australians again fought thousands of miles away from home. On 25 April 1915 the ANZACs began the bitter campaign against the Turks in Gallipoli, and a shocked nation learned of the long casualty list. All told, 416 809 men and women volunteered for the war, of which 59 258 were killed or reported missing in action.

Times were confusing for the returning 'diggers'. There were years of uncertain prosperity, followed by the Great Depression of 1929–32. This disaster affected all Australians: at one stage 30% of the workforce was unemployed, and those lucky enough to keep a job had restricted working hours or reduced wages.

Although suspicions of Japan's intentions in 1939 were mounting, it was again the trouble in Europe which plunged Australia into World War II. By 1945, 993 000 people had enlisted. As the casualty list grew, news from such places as the Middle East, Greece, North Africa and Tobruk was eagerly sought. On 8 December 1941 the Prime Minister, John Curtin, announced that Australia was at war with Japan. Singapore, Borneo, Java, New Guinea, the Kokoda Trail, the Coral Sea, Rabaul, the Owen Stanley Range and Changi prison became very well known in Australian households. In 1942 Darwin was bombed, with a loss of 238 lives. The war in Europe ended in May 1945, and under the threat of a widening of atomic warfare, after the bombing of Hiroshima and Nagasaki, the Japanese surrendered on 14 August 1945.

The postwar years brought growth and prosperity. With the signing of the ANZUS pact, Australia was at last making decisions without reference to Britain. In the 'cold war' atmosphere of the 1950s, Australian troops joined the British Commonwealth Brigade in Korea. Increased production and labour shortages brought full employment, and the rural and home-building industries flourished. A 40-hour week was introduced and the basic wage was £5 16s ($11.60) per week. A new immigration drive resulted in a more tolerant attitude towards Europeans and their cultures, and public awareness of the plight of Australian Aborigines grew. Education became more readily available, and there was more time for leisure and cultural pursuits.

During the 1960s there was affluence and prosperity with the mineral boom. Few people took notice of the war in Asia. However, the government argued that to retain US protection through the newly formed SEATO alliance, Australia must support the USA in Vietnam. Over 50 000 troops served in the war, with 400 deaths and 2000 injured. A moratorium clearly demonstrated that the majority of Australians were against our involvement, and

Beer Can Regatta, Darwin, Northern Territory.

after worldwide pressure, the USA ceased hostilities.

General dissatisfaction in the 1970s and 1980s saw political parties come and go, with a new wave of unrest sweeping the country. The White Australia Policy was dropped and Asian migration was encouraged. Australia was at last overcoming its feelings of isolation from Europe and finding a place in the Pacific region. Automation dramatically changed technology, and workers displaced by computers saw traditional jobs disappear, requiring them to retrain for new skills, or join the lists of the unemployed.

The race into the 1990s brought great change. Fiscal deregulation and the 1987 stockmarket crash and recession forced Australia to review its world position. Improvement of standards was essential to keep pace with the highly competitive nations of Asia. As well, multiculturalism through migration, a greater awareness of indigenous Australians and proposals for a republic began to change the Australian character.

The grand experiment begun in 1901 with Federation embraced a vision for the future of a cohesive nation. Now, even though enormous difficulties have been and still are to be overcome, and harsh realities have to be faced, there have been great triumphs and achievements. Notwithstanding the result of the 1999 Republic referendum, Australia is an independent nation, enabling it to enter the 21st century with confidence and dignity.

Geography

Location

Australia consists of two land masses: mainland Australia and Tasmania. It lies on and extends south from the Tropic of Capricorn in the Southern Hemisphere between latitudes 10°41' and 43°39'S and longitudes 113°9' and 153°39'E. It is bounded by the Pacific Ocean to the east, the Indian Ocean to the west, the Arafura Sea to the north, and the Southern Ocean to the south. The nearest neighbour is Papua New Guinea, 200 kilometres north. Timor is 640 kilometres to the north-west, New Zealand is 1920 kilometres east, and Antarctica is 2000 kilometres due south.

Area

The area of Australia is 7 682 300 square kilometres. Australia is about the size of the mainland states of the USA, excluding Alaska, and approximately 24 times the size of the British Isles.

Distances

Mainland east–west, 3983 kilometres; north–south, 3138 kilometres. Coastline, including Tasmania and off-shore islands, 36 735 kilometres.

Average monthly rainfall and temperatures around Australia

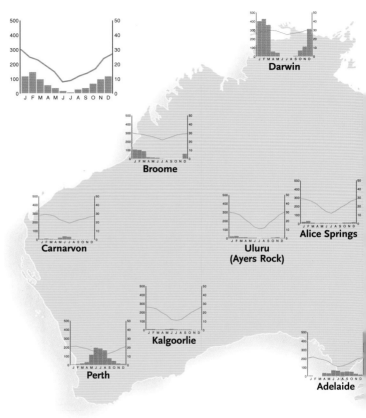

Darwin

Broome

Carnarvon

Uluru
(Ayers Rock)

Alice Springs

Kalgoorlie

Perth

Adelaide

■ Blocks show rainfall in millimetres

╲_ Curves show temperature in degrees Celsius

DID YOU KNOW?

The highest recorded temperature of 53.1°C
was at Cloncurry, Queensland, in January 1889.
The lowest recorded temperature of minus 23°C
was at Charlotte Pass, NSW on 28 June 1994.

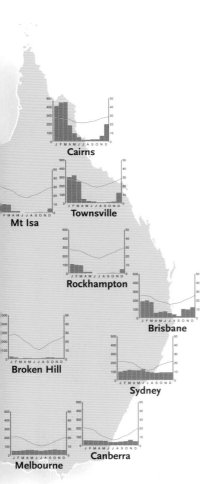

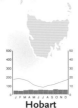

Climate

Australia is considered to be one of the driest continents on earth. However, because of its insular position and lack of natural features such as high mountain ranges, there are generally no great extremes of climate. Climate varies because of the size of the continent. The temperature ranges from 23°–26°C above the Tropic of Capricorn to 38°C in the arid plateaus and deserts of the interior. The southern areas are more temperate, although subject to wide variations such as high rainfall, great heat and irregular flooding and drought.

El Niño usually occurs in summer. Cold currents flow up the Peruvian coast from Antarctica and are warmed by equatorial currents circulating across the Pacific from Australia. Warmed winds blowing across the current's surface pick up moisture and deposit it on the Peruvian coast. The warm winds proceed across the central Pacific and in turn deposit rain on eastern Australia. Every three to eight years the equatorial current is exceedingly strong and noticeably warmer off the coast of Peru, resulting in strong winds bringing heavy rains and

DID YOU KNOW?

El Niño is Spanish for 'Christ child'. It was named by fishermen who noticed currents off Peru becoming unusually warm every three to eight years around Christmas time. La Niña is Spanish for 'girl child'.

floods. At this time, waters off Australia become noticeably cooler and winds weaken and are turned towards the Pacific, reducing rain-bearing clouds across eastern Australia, resulting in drought.

La Niña is the opposite phenomenon, which results in abnormally strong winds over the western Pacific blowing across unusually warm currents off the east coast of Australia, resulting in flooding rains.

Landform

Australia is one of the oldest continents, and because of the effects of 250 million years of erosion it has become the flattest land mass on earth. The shape of Australia was defined by the separation and rifting of the Australian continent from the super-continent Gondwanaland about 70 million years ago. It is considered to be the most stable land mass in the world, being free of any major mountain building events for the past 80 million years. Even so, Australia has a wide variety of landforms, mostly consisting of vast, ancient crustal blocks: the western plateau approximately 300 metres

The Three Sisters, Katoomba, New South Wales.

DID YOU KNOW?

The weather reports in Western Australia can take up to 15 minutes to deliver because of the number and diversity of climatic zones. They have ranged between 50.7°C at Eucla on 22 January 1906 and minus 6°C at Booylgoo Springs on 12 July 1969.

above sea level, the central eastern portion (a lowland which formed the bed of ancient seas), and the eastern highland running north and south along the eastern coastline. The lowest elevation is Lake Eyre (16 metres below sea level) and the highest peak is Mt Kosciuszko (2228 metres above sea level).

Time zones

There are three time zones within the Australian continent. The eastern states – Queensland, New South Wales, Victoria and Tasmania – are 30 minutes ahead of South Australia and the Northern Territory (including Broken Hill), and two hours ahead of Western Australia.

New South Wales, Victoria and Tasmania follow Eastern Summer Time but Queensland has decided not to adopt this practice. South Australia and the Northern Territory follow South Australia Summer time. These are subject to change, but the period usually falls between the months of November and February, and can extend for up to four weeks on either side. Tasmania has extended daylight saving to six months of the year, from early October to late March.

Time zones within Australia

Standard time zones

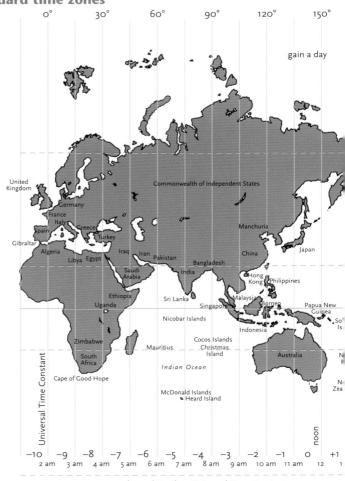

0°   30°   60°   90°   120°   150°

gain a day

United Kingdom

Commonwealth of Independent States

Germany
France
Italy
Spain   Greece
Gibraltar   Turkey
Algeria   Iraq   Iran   Pakistan
Libya   Egypt   Saudi Arabia   India
Ethiopia   Sri Lanka
Uganda

Manchuria

China   Japan

Bangladesh

Hong Kong   Philippines

Singapore   Malaysia   Borneo   Papua New Guinea

Nicobar Islands   Indonesia   So Is

Zimbabwe   Mauritius   Cocos Islands
South Africa   Christmas Island   Australia   N

Cape of Good Hope   *Indian Ocean*

McDonald Islands   N Zea
Heard Island

Universal Time Constant

noon

| −10 | −9 | −8 | −7 | −6 | −5 | −4 | −3 | −2 | −1 | 0 | +1 |
| 2 am | 3 am | 4 am | 5 am | 6 am | 7 am | 8 am | 9 am | 10 am | 11 am | 12 | 1 |

hours later than Universal Time Constant

DID YOU KNOW?

The world's largest cattle station, 30 028.3 square kilometres, is Strangeray Springs in South Australia. It is almost the same size as Belgium.

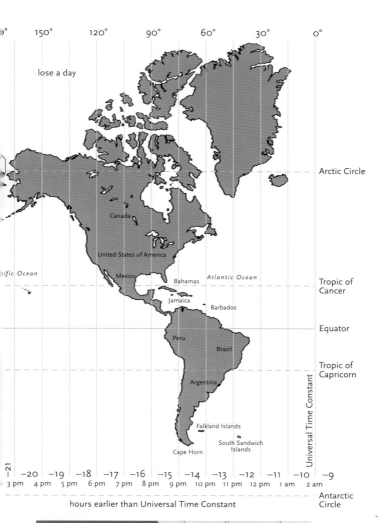

150° 120° 90° 60° 30° 0°

lose a day

Arctic Circle

Canada

United States of America

Pacific Ocean

Mexico

Bahamas *Atlantic Ocean* Tropic of Cancer

Jamaica

Barbados

Equator

Peru

Brazil

Tropic of Capricorn

Argentina

Universal Time Constant

Falkland Islands

South Sandwich Islands

Cape Horn

−21 −20 −19 −18 −17 −16 −15 −14 −13 −12 −11 −10 −9

3 pm 4 pm 5 pm 6 pm 7 pm 8 pm 9 pm 10 pm 11 pm 12 pm 1 am 2 am

Antarctic Circle

hours earlier than Universal Time Constant

DID YOU KNOW?

Due to extended hours of hot sunshine and searing winds, 89% of Australia's rainfall is lost through extreme rates of evaporation as compared to 60% in Europe and Africa and 48% in North America.

Great Britain

Gibraltar Malta Cyprus

Pakistan

India

Bangladesh

The Gambia

Nigeria

Sierra Leone Ghana

Lakshadweep

Kenya

Uganda

Sri Lanka Singapore

Malaysia Brunei Darassalam Papua New Guinea

Gilbert Islands

Nauru Kiribati

Seychelles Nicobar Islands

Zambia

Tanzania

Solomon Islands Tuvalu

Malawi

Mauritius

Cocos Islands Christmas Island

Indonesia

Western Samoa

Zimbabwe

Vanuatu Tonga Cook Islands

Australia

South Africa Swaziland Lesotho

Indian Ocean

Norfolk Island Lord Howe Island

New Zealand

Pacific Ocean

McDonald Islands Heard Island

Campbell Island

DID YOU KNOW?

Of all coloured peoples, the Australian Aborigines are ethnologically most akin to Caucasians.

Canada

Atlantic Ocean

Bermuda
Bahamas

Antigua and Barbuda
Jamaica   Dominica Barbados
St Vincent The Grenadines
Grenada
Trinidad and Tobago

Guyana

St Helena

Pitcairn

Falkland Islands
South Sandwich Islands
South Shetland Islands
South Orkney Islands

The Commonwealth of Nations is a worldwide association of nations and their dependent territories which recognises, or did recognise, the British monarch as its titular head.

The members share many customs and traditions because of their association with the former British Empire, of which they all formed a part. These include parliamentary systems of government, judicial systems and educational institutions which are similar to those of the United Kingdom. Although English is the official language, it is used widely in only eight member countries.

The main function of the Commonwealth is to encourage communication, exchange ideas, and develop mutual aid between its member nations.

DID YOU KNOW?

Australians can trace their ancestry to any one, or a mixture, of more than 60 nations.

44

Members of the Commonwealth of Nations and their dependencies

Member nations with dependencies	Status of dependency	Member nations with dependencies	Status of dependency
Australia		South Sandwich Islands	
Australian Antarctic	Territory	St Kitts-Nevis	Associated state
Christmas Is	Territory	Turks & Caicos Is	Associated state
Cocos Is	Territory	Grenada	
Coral Sea Is	Territory	Guyana	
Heard & McDonald Is	Territory	India	
Lord Howe Is	Territory	Jamaica	
Macquarie Is	Territory	Kenya	
Norfolk Is	Territory	Kiribati	
Bahamas		Lesotho	
Bangladesh		Malawi	
Barbados		Malaysia	
Belize		Maldives	
Botswana		Malta	
Brunei Darassalam		Mauritius	
Canada		Nauru	
Cyprus		New Zealand	
Dominica		Niue & Tokelau Is	Territory &
Gambia		Cook Is	associated
Ghana		Ross dependency	states
Gibraltar		Nigeria	
Great Britain		Pakistan	
Anguilla	Colony	Papua New Guinea	
Antigua	Associated state	St Lucia, St Vincent & the Grenadiers	Associated state
Barbuda		Seychelles	
Bermuda	Colony	Sierra Leone	
British Antarctic		Singapore	
British Indian Ocean Territory	Territory	Solomon Is	
British Virgin Is	Colony	South Africa	
Cayman Is	Colony	Sri Lanka	
Dominica	Associated state	Swaziland	
Falkland Is	Colony	Tanzania	
Gibraltar	Colony	Tonga	
Montserrat	Colony	Trinidad & Tobago	
Pitcairn	Colony	Tuvalu	
St Helena	Colony	Uganda	
St Christopher-Nevis		Vanuatu	
South Georgia		Western Samoa	
		Zambia	
		Zimbabwe	

Australia in proportion to Europe

DID YOU KNOW?

Because of the combustible nature of eucalyptus forests, Australia is considered to be one of the most explosive and fire-prone countries on earth. In 1995, the eastern seaboard bushfires cost the economy $153 million.

Australia in the western Pacific

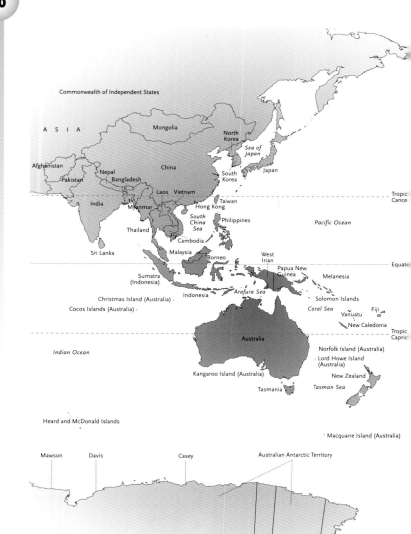

Commonwealth of Independent States

A S I A

Mongolia

North Korea

Sea of Japan

Afghanistan

Nepal
Pakistan   Bangladesh

China

South Korea

Japan

India   Myanmar

Laos Vietnam

Hong Kong

Taiwan

Tropic
Cance

Thailand

South China Sea

Philippines

Pacific Ocean

Cambodia

Sri Lanka   Malaysia   Borneo

West Irian

Papua New Guinea

Melanesia

Equato

Sumatra (Indonesia)

Indonesia

Arafura Sea

Solomon Islands

Christmas Island (Australia)

Cocos Islands (Australia)

Coral Sea

Vanuatu

Fiji

New Caledonia

Tropic
Capric

Australia

Norfolk Island (Australia)

Indian Ocean

Lord Howe Island (Australia)

Kangaroo Island (Australia)

New Zealand

Tasmania

Tasman Sea

Heard and McDonald Islands

Macquarie Island (Australia)

Mawson   Davis   Casey   Australian Antarctic Territory

Estimated world population for 2000 – 6 034.47 m

Country	Estimated population (million)	Surface area (km²)	Population density (per km²)
Australia	19.2	7 682 300	2
Belgium	10.2	30 513	334
Brazil	174.5	8 511 965	20
Canada	31.3	9 916 139	3
China	1257.5	9 569 961	131
France	59.1	551 500	107
Germany	82.1	357 010	230
India	1017.9	3 287 590	310
Indonesia	240.0	1 904 569	126
Italy	56.6	301 268	188
Japan	126.4	377 801	335
Malaysia	21.8	329 749	66
Netherlands	15.8	40 844	386
New Zealand	4.0	270 986	15
Norway	6.0	323 895	18
Pakistan	141.5	796 095	178
Philippines	81.0	300 000	270
Singapore	3.5	618	5663
South Africa	44.0	1 221 037	36
Sweden	8.9	440 945	20
Switzerland	7.2	41 293	174
UK	59.2	244 100	243
USA	275.3	9 372 614	29

Largest cities in western Pacific (millions)

Shanghai	13.5	Ho Chi Minh City	4.8
Beijing	12.3	Bandung	4.2
Tokyo	11.7	Sydney	3.9
Bangkok	10.5	Pusan	3.8
Seoul	10.3	Surabaya	3.8
Djakarta	10.0	Melbourne	3.3
Manila	9.5	Singapore	3.1
Hong Kong	6.3	Pyongyang	2.8
Osaka	6.3		

DID YOU KNOW?

Between the towns of Ooldia and Nurina in Western Australia is the world's longest straight stretch of railway, 478.4 kilometres long.

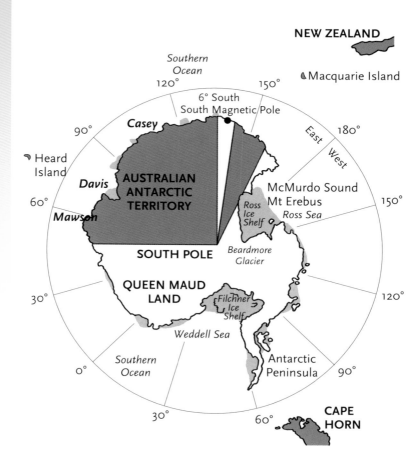

AUSTRALIA

Tasmania

NEW ZEALAND

Macquarie Island

Southern
Ocean
120°   150°

6° South
South Magnetic Pole

90°   East   180°
                                       West

Casey

Heard
Island

Davis   AUSTRALIAN
                 ANTARCTIC   McMurdo Sound
60°   TERRITORY   Mt Erebus   150°
                         Ross   Ross Sea
Mawson   Ice
                         Shelf

                 SOUTH POLE   Beardmore
                                    Glacier

                 QUEEN MAUD
                 LAND
30°   Filchner   120°
                          Ice
                          Shelf

                 Weddell Sea

      Southern   Antarctic
0°   Ocean   Peninsula   90°

           30°   60°   CAPE
                                    HORN

Location

Antarctica lies in the Southern Hemisphere below the latitude of 60°S and is 2000 kilometres due south from Melbourne. Mawson, Australia's first Antarctic station, is 5200 kilometres south-south-west of Perth.

Landform

Ice comprises more than 95% of the total surface and the other 5% is bare rock. The greatest rock exposures are in the Antarctic Peninsula and the Trans-Antarctic Mountains. Antarctica has enough ice to cover the whole of Australia with a mantle of snow nearly 2 kilometres thick.

Climate

Antarctica has one of the most hostile environments on earth. It experiences the coldest temperatures and the strongest winds and has the largest deserts. In coastal areas at 1000 metres, the mean annual temperature is minus 12°C, while in high parts, near 4000 metres, it falls to minus 60°C. The high plateau receives very little precipitation at all and is the world's largest and driest desert. A little

Raising the Australian flag at Atlas Cove, for the first Australian National Antarctic Research Expedition, 1947.

more snow falls in the lower areas and is equivalent to an annual rainfall of 5 centimetres – half as much as is experienced by places like Birdsville, Queensland. The quantity of ice present has been formed by the accumulation of snow over millions of years.

In winter it is so cold that the surrounding sea freezes to 200–300 kilometres off shore, and in summer the ice breaks to form pack ice. Under the influence of winds and tides the ice is distributed widely in the Southern Ocean, exerting a major influence on the world's weather patterns. During mid-winter Antarctica experiences 24 hours of darkness, and during mid-summer there are 24 hours of daylight.

DID YOU KNOW?

An international embargo on mineral exploration in the Antarctic will be enforced indefinitely.

An Antarctic traverse party en route between the Laresmann Hills and Mawson.

Population

There are no permanent inhabitants but world scientists are continually studying this vast continent; few stay longer than two years.

Australia maintains four scientific research stations, namely Casey, Davis and Mawson in the Australian Antarctic Territory and on Macquarie Island in the sub-Antarctic.

Flora and fauna

Because of Antarctica's intense cold and dryness, only simple algae, lichens and mosses, and a few tiny animals, such as mites, live there all year round. Many birds and animals breed on the fringes of the continent during summer, but move northward for the winter. These include penguins, albatross, snow petrels and various species of seals and whales. The ocean around the Antarctic has a distinct fish fauna of about 100 species, 75% of which are Antarctic 'cod' (not found in other seas) and hag-fishes, skates, squid and small eel-pouts.

DID YOU KNOW?

Sir Douglas Mawson led the Australasian Antarctic Expedition of 1911–14, which mapped 1500 kilometres of coast and up to 500 kilometres inland in places. He was the first Antarctic explorer to use morse code radio. It was his only link with the outside world when he and five companions were stranded during the long winter of blizzards in 1913 in Antarctica.

Population

The Australian population in 2000 is estimated to be 19.2 million. The national growth rate is 1.2 per cent. Because of the arid interior, the relatively recent settlement and the fertility of the coastlines, 88% are urban dwellers. Although Australia is considered to have one of the highest degrees of urban concentration in the world within the cities, the density of population is low by international standards, with an average of two persons per square kilometre. A striking feature of Australia's population is the large number of immigrants who have settled since World War II. At present, one in every four persons is either a first- or second-generation settler.

Population distribution

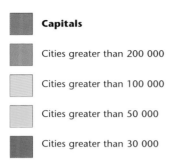

Capitals

Cities greater than 200 000

Cities greater than 100 000

Cities greater than 50 000

Cities greater than 30 000

Darwin 86 576

Boulder/Kalgoorlie
31 391

Perth
1 341 914

Bunbury 28 069

DID YOU KNOW?

The average number of persons per household has decreased from 3.31 in 1971 to 2.66 in 1998 due to a change in social attitudes leading to a reduction in the size of families. The average family has 1.77 children, well below population replacement, 22% of adults will never have children and 16% have only one child.

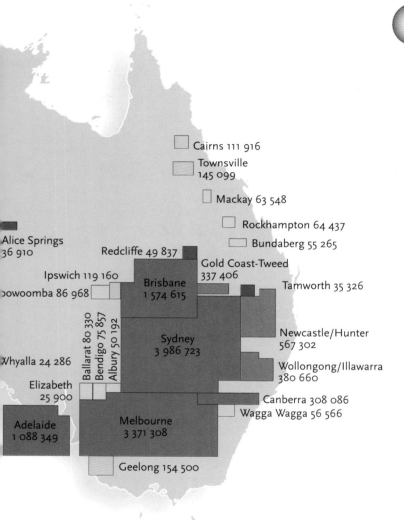

Cairns 111 916

Townsville
145 099

Mackay 63 548

Rockhampton 64 437

Bundaberg 55 265

Alice Springs
36 910

Redcliffe 49 837

Gold Coast-Tweed
337 406

Ipswich 119 160

Brisbane
1 574 615

Tamworth 35 326

Toowoomba 86 968

Ballarat 80 330
Bendigo 75 857
Albury 50 192

Sydney
3 986 723

Newcastle/Hunter
567 302

Whyalla 24 286

Wollongong/Illawarra
380 660

Elizabeth
25 900

Canberra 308 086

Wagga Wagga 56 566

Adelaide
1 088 349

Melbourne
3 371 308

Geelong 154 500

Burnie & Devonport 78 605

Launceston 98 352

Hobart 194 974

Population distribution

15% of the population is located in this area

25% of the population is located in this area

60% of the population is located in this area

TIMOR SEA

Darwin

Joseph Bonaparte Gulf

Kimberley Region

• Broome

INDIAN OCEAN

Great Sandy Desert

• Port Hedland

Gibson Desert

WESTERN AUSTRALIA

Great Victoria Desert

• Kalgoorlie

• Perth
• Fremantle

Great Australi Bight

• Albany

SOUTHERN OCEAN

DID YOU KNOW?

Marital figures for 1999 show 5.9 marriages per 1000 people. Median age for brides is 27.5 years and median age for bridegrooms is 29.7 years. 44% of men and 42% of women will never marry.

CORAL SEA

Arnhem Land

Gulf of Carpentaria

Cape York Peninsula

Cairns •

Great Barrier Reef

Townsville •

• Mount Isa

NORTHERN TERRITORY

PACIFIC OCEAN

Rockhampton •

• Alice Springs

QUEENSLAND

Simpson Desert

SOUTH AUSTRALIA

• Broken Hill

Brisbane

NEW SOUTH WALES

Spencer Gulf

• Mildura

Adelaide

• Newcastle

Sydney

Goulburn •

• Wollongong

• Albury

Canberra

VICTORIA

Ballarat

• Bendigo

Portland •

Geelong

Melbourne

Bass Strait

TASMAN SEA

• Launceston

TASMANIA

Hobart

Population changes since Federation

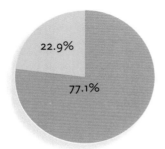

▲ % of people living in Australia, but born elsewhere

▲ % of native-born Australians

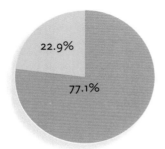

1900
total population 3 765 300

22.9%
77.1%

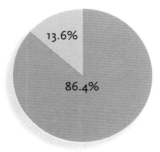

1930
total population 6 500 800

13.6%
86.4%

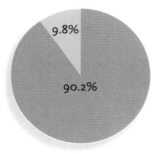

1947
total population 7 579 400

9.8%
90.2%

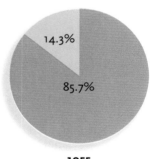

1955
total population 9 311 800

14.3%
85.7%

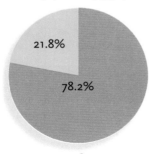

1981
total population 14 923 300

21.8%
78.2%

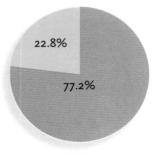

1993
total population 17 843 300

22.8%
77.2%

Birthplaces of overseas-born

1998–99
total population 19 100 000 (est.)

Main sources of immigration

UK and Ireland	6.28%
New Zealand	1.63%
Italy	1.33%
Vietnam	0.84%
Greece	0.71%
China	0.62%
Germany	0.62%
Former Yugoslavia	0.55%
Americas	0.55%
Philippines	0.52%
Netherlands	0.49%
Malaysia	0.43%
India	0.43%
South Africa	0.31%
Other European	3.77%
Other Asian	2.01%

United Kingdom
England, Wales, Scotland, Northern Ireland

Europe
Albania, Austria, Belgium, Bulgaria, Czech Republic, Denmark, Estonia, Finland, France, Germany, Greece, Hungary, Italy, Latvia, Lithuania, Malta, Netherlands, Norway, Poland, Portugal, Republic of Ireland, Romania, Slovak Republic, Spain, Sweden, Switzerland, Ukraine, Russia, former Yugoslavia

Middle East
Israel, Lebanon, Syria, Turkey, Egypt

Asia
China, Hong Kong, India, Indonesia, Japan, Malaysia, Myanmar, Pakistan, Philippines, Singapore, Sri Lanka, Vietnam

Africa
Mauritius, South Africa

Americas
Canada, South America, United States, West Indies Federation

Pacific Islands
Fiji, New Caledonia, New Zealand, Vanuatu

DID YOU KNOW?

Of the world's population, 44% now live in countries with births below population replacement.

Immigration to Australia ('000s)
Permanent and long-term residents

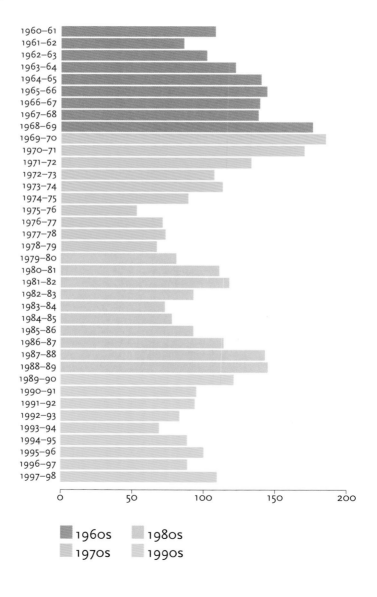

1960–61
1961–62
1962–63
1963–64
1964–65
1965–66
1966–67
1967–68
1968–69
1969–70
1970–71
1971–72
1972–73
1973–74
1974–75
1975–76
1976–77
1977–78
1978–79
1979–80
1980–81
1981–82
1982–83
1983–84
1984–85
1985–86
1986–87
1987–88
1988–89
1989–90
1990–91
1991–92
1992–93
1993–94
1994–95
1995–96
1996–97
1997–98

0   50   100   150   200

1960s   1980s
1970s   1990s

Australia's population and % growth rate 1998/99

Total population (est.)

	19 058 000	1.2
NSW	6 431 351	1.1
Vic	4 736 815	1.2
Qld	3 535 103	1.7
SA	1 504 730	0.5
WA	1 876 196	1.9
Tas	470 470	-0.3
NT	194 221	1.7
ACT	309 114	0.1

Spread of ages in Australia (%)

Age group

0–14	21.6
15–24	14.5
25–44	30.8
45–64	21.0
65+	12.1

Religions in Australia

Christian (%)

Roman Catholic	27.0
Anglican	22.0
Uniting Church	7.5
Presbyterian & Reformed	3.8
Orthodox	2.8
Baptist	1.7
Lutheran	1.4
Pentecostal	1.0
Jehovah's Witness	0.5
Church of Christ	0.4
Salvation Army	0.4
Other	2.4

Non-Christian (%)

Islamic	1.1
Buddhist	1.1
Jewish	0.4
Hindu	0.4
Other	0.4
No religion	16.6
Not stated	9.1

DID YOU KNOW?

Australia is the world's largest island and the smallest continent. It is also the largest continent occupied by one nation and the least populated.

The national flag.

The red ensign.

National floral emblem: golden wattle Acacia pycnantha.

For many years the Australian Blue Ensign was regarded as the official flag. This was a plain blue flag, with the Union Jack in the upper corner of the hoist, together with the seven-pointed Commonwealth star beneath. It also contained the five-starred Southern Cross. However, it had not been clearly established that any particular flag was the national flag.

In 1951 King George VI approved a recommendation by the government that the Australian Blue Ensign be proclaimed the national flag, and the Australian Red Ensign be the proper colour for merchant ships registered in Australia. The *Flags Act* was passed in 1953 by the Commonwealth parliament, making these the official flags of the Commonwealth.

The state flags are based on the plain Blue Ensign with the particular badge of each state added. The Northern Territory flag is based on colours found in desert regions, and the Territory's badge is added.

National animal emblem: kangaroo.

National gemstone: opal.

Coat of arms

The present coat of arms was granted in 1912 by King George V, following approval of substantial alterations by the Commonwealth government. It consists of a shield composed of six parts, each containing one of the state badges. These are surrounded by an ermine border, signifying the federation of the states into the Commonwealth. The shield is supported by two Australian animals, the kangaroo and the emu, standing on ornamental rests, behind which are small branches of wattle. The crest consists of the seven-pointed Commonwealth gold star, a symbol of national unity. At the base of the shield is a scroll on which is printed the word 'Australia'.

Anthems

The royal anthem, 'God Save the Queen', is used in the presence of Her Majesty the Queen or a member of the royal family.

The vice-regal salute, which consists of the first four and last four bars of the tune 'Advance Australia Fair', is used on all other occasions. For the words to Australia's national anthem, see p. 246.

Civilian honour awards

The Australian federal government bestows annual honour awards on people who have made outstanding contributions in their fields of endeavour. The awards are:

AC	Companion
AO	Officer
AM	Member
OAM	Medal of the Order

Colours

Green and gold are the national colours of Australia, and are used on all appropriate occasions, such as the Olympic Games.

DID YOU KNOW?

The oldest skeleton found in Australia was at Lake Mungo in south-west New South Wales. It is believed to be 38 000 years old and is the skeleton of an Aboriginal woman. It has traces of ceremonial ochre (a sign of culture), which is thought to be the oldest sign of ochre use ever discovered.

Public holidays and special days

January

1	New Year's Day
26	Australia Day

March

First Monday	Western Australia: Labour Day
	Tasmania: Eight-hour Day
Second Monday	Victoria: Labour Day
	Australian Capital Territory: Canberra Day

April

First full moon after equinox (may fall in March)	Easter holiday begins on Good Friday and continues until following Monday (in some states Easter Tuesday is also a public holiday)
25	Anzac Day

May

First Monday	Queensland: Labour Day
	Northern Territory: May Day

June

Second Monday	Queen's Birthday (except Western Australia)

August

First Monday	New South Wales: Bank Holiday

September

1	National Wattle Day (some states)
3	National Australia Flag Day

October

First Monday	New South Wales and Australian Capital Territory: Labour Day
6	Western Australia: Queen's Birthday
Second Monday	South Australia: Labour Day

November

First Tuesday	Melbourne, Victoria: Melbourne Cup Day
11	Remembrance Day

December

25	Christmas Day
26	Boxing Day (except South Australia)
28	South Australia: Proclamation Day

Australia's official name is the Commonwealth of Australia. Its form of government is a constitutional monarchy. The head of state is Queen Elizabeth II of the United Kingdom of Great Britain and Northern Ireland, who is also Queen of Australia. She is represented in Australia by the governor-general. The head of government is the prime minister, who is leader of the party or coalition of parties holding a majority in the federal parliament.

Australia is an independent self-governing member of the British Commonwealth of Nations, and a foundation member of the United Nations. It is in alliance with the United States of America and New Zealand in the ANZUS pact, and is a member of the South-East Asia Treaty Organisation (SEATO).

Australia is a federation of six states, with two internal federal territories – the Australian Capital Territory and the Northern Territory – and a number of external territories – Norfolk Island, the Cocos Islands, Christmas Island, Macquarie Island and Australian Antarctica between 45 degrees south and 160 degrees east – under its control.

Levels of government

Federal

Australia chose its executive form of government, consisting of a prime minister and cabinet, mainly from the British Westminster system. As well, some minor aspects of the United States congressional system were adopted.

The Australian federal parliament is generally responsible for matters of national importance. These include defence, external affairs, customs and excise, communications, foreign trade, social services, treasury and immigration. In addition it shares mutual responsibilities with the state legislatures. These include education, agriculture, energy services, health and law enforcement.

The Australian constitution, a document agreed to by the separate colonies in 1901 at Federation, limits the power of the federal government. To maintain strict control, the constitution can only be altered by a referendum.

There are two houses in the federal parliament, the House of Representatives (lower house) and the Senate (upper house).

The House of Representatives

This is often called the people's house as the 148 members are voted in directly by the people of Australia, with each member representing about 70 000 voters. The House consists of a government and opposition, it sits for 70–80 days each year, and it is limited to a three-year period. However, it may be dissolved sooner by the governor-general on the advice of the prime minister. Its main function is to debate and discuss bills, which are proposed new laws. The political party or coalition of parties holding majority support in the House have the right to form the executive government, with the leader of the party (or senior party) becoming prime minister. The official opposition consists of the major party or coalition of parties opposed to the government.

The number of members of the House of Representatives depends on the population of each state. In 1999 there were 148 members: 50 for New South Wales; 37 for Victoria; 27 for Queensland; 12 for South Australia; 14 for Western Australia; 5 for Tasmania; 2 for

DID YOU KNOW?

Australia is the only English-speaking country to have made voting compulsory in federal and state elections. This results in a voter turn-out of 95%.

the Australian Capital Territory and 1 for the Northern Territory.

The Senate

This is virtually a house of review, where the procedures are designed to allow debate on the merits or defects of any bill passed by the House of Representatives. The Senate can request amendments to, and can reject, any bill. In 1999 there were 76 senators, 12 from each state and 2 from each territory. Senators from states are elected for a six-year period and every three years half of the senators retire, but may stand for re-election. Senators from the territories are elected for three years.

The ministry

This consists of members of the government who are responsible for a particular area of policy. Most ministers are members of the House of Representatives; a few are from the Senate. They have specific departments of the public service to help them administer their portfolios. The prime minister is, by convention, always a member of the House of Representatives. Members who are not ministers or leading members of the opposition are called back-benchers.

The cabinet

This is an inner council and consists of the leading political figures (those with senior portfolios) of the government and the Senate, with the prime minister as chair. Junior ministers attend cabinet meetings only when matters affecting their departments are being discussed.

The executive council

This body has the task of advising the governor-general of major political decisions affecting the nation which have been made by meetings of the Cabinet.

The governor-general

This person is the Queen's representative in the Australian parliament, and is appointed by the Queen on the advice of the prime minister. All laws made by parliament finally depend on his/her assent.

Voting

Compulsory preferential voting is the most common system used in Australia. In voting for the House of Representatives, one candidate only from any one party is selected to represent each electorate. Every candidate must be voted for in order of preference. If no candidate receives an absolute majority, then there is a distribution of preference votes.

All Australians over the age of 18 are eligible to vote. Voting is compulsory for everyone except Aborigines. Aborigines may choose whether or not to register; if they register, they must vote.

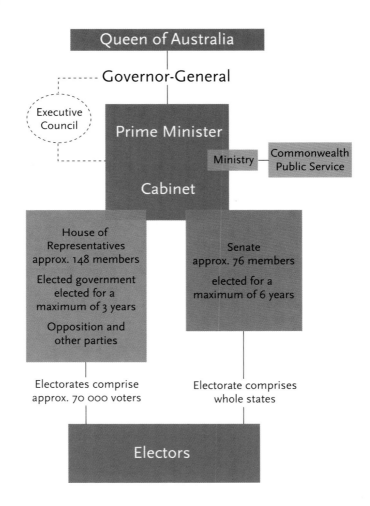

Queen of Australia

Governor-General

Executive Council

Prime Minister

Ministry

Commonwealth Public Service

Cabinet

House of Representatives approx. 148 members

Elected government elected for a maximum of 3 years

Opposition and other parties

Senate approx. 76 members

elected for a maximum of 6 years

Electorates comprise approx. 70 000 voters

Electorate comprises whole states

Electors

Distributing preference votes

All votes are sorted according to the voters' first choice and then counted. The candidate with the least number of votes is eliminated and his/her votes are distributed according to the voters' second choice. All votes are then re-counted and for the second time the candidate with the least number of votes is eliminated and his/her votes distributed according to the voters' next choice of candidate and so on. The first candidate who reaches 50% or more of the votes, wins.

Proportional representation is the other major electoral system in Australia. It is used in the Senate and in some state elections. Each senator represents a whole state; and as the electorate is so large, more than one candidate is elected for each state.

Procedures

A *double dissolution* of parliament is the dissolving of both the House of Representatives and the Senate due to a deadlock arising over the passing of a bill. This necessitates a general election of both houses.

The unusual procedure of a *joint sitting* of parliament occurs when a party wins a majority in the House of Representatives but not in the Senate, after a double dissolution. Both the House of Representatives and the Senate may sit jointly to work out a solution if a deadlock still exists.

Supply is the money granted by the passing of legislation before the end of the financial year in order to proceed until the next budget is passed.

Appropriation bills authorise the use of revenue collected by the government.

Separation of powers

At Federation in 1901, because of the necessity to protect the separate states from dominance by the proposed federal government, the Constitution provided for a *separation of powers*. Three bodies were to carry out these powers: the Legislative Power, consisting of the ministry, the House of Representatives and the Senate; the Executive Power, consisting of the governor-general, the ministry and government departments; and the Judicial Power, consisting of the High Court and other federal courts.

DID YOU KNOW?

The Australian Labor Party, the oldest surviving Labor Party in the world, celebrated its centenary in 1991. Its first meeting was held under a gum tree at Barcaldine, Queensland, in 1891.

State governments

Each state (except the Northern Territory and Australian Capital Territory) has an executive council consisting of the governor, the premier and selected ministers.

NORTHERN TERRITORY
Although still not a state, in 1978 became self-governing, with a fully elected Legislative Assembly

WESTERN AUSTRALIA
State governor
Cabinet consisting of premier and ministers
Legislative Assembly
Legislative Council

SOUTH AUSTRALIA
State governor
Cabinet consisting of premier and ministers
House of Assembly
Legislative Council

DID YOU KNOW?

The world's largest electorate (2 255 278 square kilometres) is Kalgoorlie, Western Australia.

State

State governments are also modelled on the British Westminster system, each having a premier as leader of the cabinet and ministry.

The state parliaments deal with domestic affairs such as housing, trade, education, industry and law enforcement within the states, as well as sharing mutual responsibilities with the federal parliament.

Local

The *Local Government Act* was passed in 1919. This gave power to areas as small as cities, municipalities and shires to provide a more satisfactory system of government within the local area with a mayor or president as leader. Australia has 900 bodies at local government level. They have varying responsibilities which may include urban planning, road construction, water, sewerage and drainage and local community activities.

QUEENSLAND
State governor
Cabinet consisting of
premier and ministers
Legislative Assembly

NEW SOUTH WALES
State governor
Cabinet consisting of
premier and ministers
Legislative Assembly
Legislative Council

AUSTRALIAN
CAPITAL TERRITORY
Legislative Assembly

VICTORIA
State governor
Cabinet consisting of
premier and ministers
Legislative Assembly
Legislative Council

TASMANIA
State governor
Cabinet consisting of
premier and ministers
House of Assembly
Legislative Council

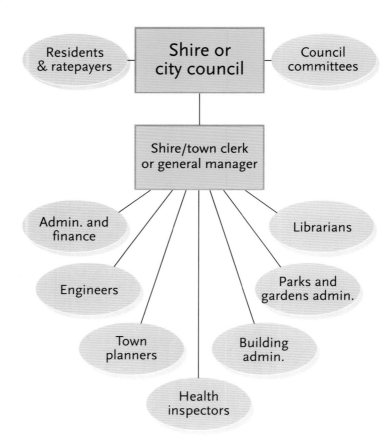

Voting is compulsory in some states

DID YOU KNOW?

In 1894, South Australia became the first colony
to extend political equality to women. In 1902
Australian women won the right to vote.

High Court of Australia
Federal Court
Family Court of Australia

appeals

Supreme Courts of the
six states and territories

appeals

District (County)
Courts of the six states
and territories

appeals

Local Courts
(previously called Courts of Petty Sessions)
of the six states and
territories

DID YOU KNOW?

There are approximately 175 local courts in each
state, which deal with 98% of all cases heard in
Australia.

PAYMENTS, PURCHASES, PRODUCTION

Australia has a prosperous western-style capitalist economy, which follows the system of free enterprise and orderly marketing of products. Rich in natural resources, Australia is a major exporter of agricultural products, minerals, metals and fossil fuels, so a downturn in the world's commodity needs can have a marked effect on the national economy. In 1991 the tariff barriers were eased by the Australian government forcing local manufacturing to become more competitive with imports.

Australia trades with two main blocs of countries. The most significant is the Asia-Pacific Economic Cooperation (APEC) group, which consists of nations such as Canada, USA, China, Japan, Indonesia, Singapore, New Zealand and Taiwan. The other bloc is the European Union (EU), with such countries as France, UK, Germany, Sweden, Switzerland and Italy.

Income and expenditure

The federal and state governments have separate areas of responsibility for raising and spending revenue. The financial year begins on 1 July.

Floating of the Australian dollar

In December 1983 the Government decided to allow the Australian dollar to *float*, that is, to establish its value in the foreign exchange market by the process of supply and demand. Prior to this the Reserve Bank set the value for the Australian dollar against the US dollar, on a daily basis.

Federal government income

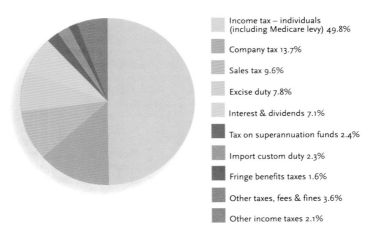

Income tax – individuals
(including Medicare levy) 49.8%

Company tax 13.7%

Sales tax 9.6%

Excise duty 7.8%

Interest & dividends 7.1%

Tax on superannuation funds 2.4%

Import custom duty 2.3%

Fringe benefits taxes 1.6%

Other taxes, fees & fines 3.6%

Other income taxes 2.1%

Federal government expenditure

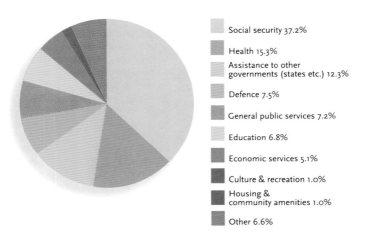

Social security 37.2%

Health 15.3%

Assistance to other
governments (states etc.) 12.3%

Defence 7.5%

General public services 7.2%

Education 6.8%

Economic services 5.1%

Culture & recreation 1.0%

Housing &
community amenities 1.0%

Other 6.6%

Basket of currencies – Trade Weighted Index

The *Trade Weighted Index* (TWI) is a measure of performance of the value of the Australian dollar against a 'basket' of such currencies as the US dollar, Japanese yen, English pound, German Deutschmark, New Zealand dollar etc. These are weighted in percentage terms to approximately the value of each country's trade with Australia.

State government income

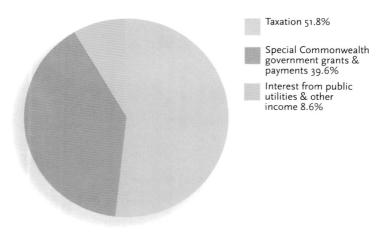

Taxation 51.8%

Special Commonwealth government grants & payments 39.6%

Interest from public utilities & other income 8.6%

DID YOU KNOW?

The first mass-produced all-Australian car came off the assembly line at Fishermens Bend, Victoria, in 1948. It was model 48-215, known as the FX Holden.

Expenditure

Federal versus State

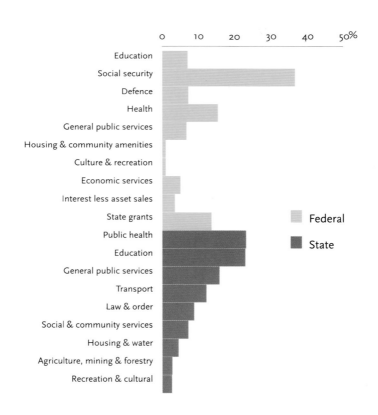

Destination and value of exports ($m)

Australia's main exports are coal, gold, iron ore, alumina, other minerals, petroleum products, meat, cereals, wool, cotton, transport equipment and manufactured goods.
Total $87.76 bn per year

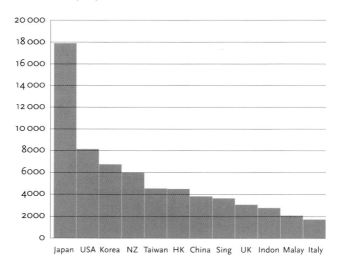

Balance of payments

Australia's balance of payments is not just the difference between exports and imports. It is made up of the following segments:

a) The inflow of money in payment for goods exported and the outflow of money in payment for goods imported. (This is called the Trade Account.)

b) The inflow of money for 'Services' and the outflow of money for 'Services'. (Services can include travellers' funds, freight and insurance costs, money gifts, royalty payments and payments for 'know-how' and the like – i.e. transactions of a mainly non-trade nature.)

c) The amount of dividends and interest on loans paid to foreigners less the amount of dividends and interest paid by foreigners. (This is called Net Income.)

Origin and value of imports ($m)

Australia imports mainly motor vehicles, petroleum oils, automatic data processing equipment, telecommunications equipment, medical and pharmaceutical products, organic chemicals, aircraft and associated equipment and clothing.
Total $90.68 bn per year

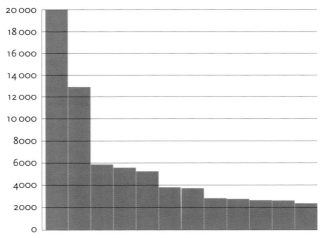

USA Japan UK China Ger Korea NZ Indon Taiwan Sing Italy Malay

For example, in 1997–98

a) Total export of goods	$87 766 m	
Total import of goods	$90 680 m	
Deficiency on Trade Account		–$2914 m
b) Inflow of money for Services	$25 550 m	
Outflow of money for Services	$26 314 m	
Deficiency on Services		–$764 m
c) Dividends/interest paid to foreigners (est.)	$28 021 m	
Dividends/interest paid by foreigners (est.)	$8 552 m	
Deficiency on Net Income		–$19 469 m
Total deficiency (adverse balance of payments)		$23 147 m

Adverse balance of payments is sometimes referred to as current account deficit.

Australian agriculture

1999

Total cattle population
26 800 000 (est.)

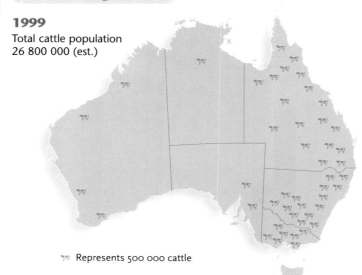

🐄 Represents 500 000 cattle

1999

Total sheep population
119 600 000 (est.)

Total wool production
1999 clip
694 500 tonnes (est.)

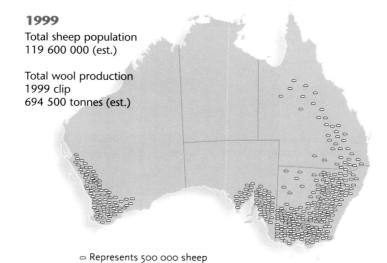

🐑 Represents 500 000 sheep

1999

Total wheat (est.)
9 243 000 hectares
16 566 000 tonnes

Total coarse grain (est.)
6 879 000 hectares
13 496 000 tonnes

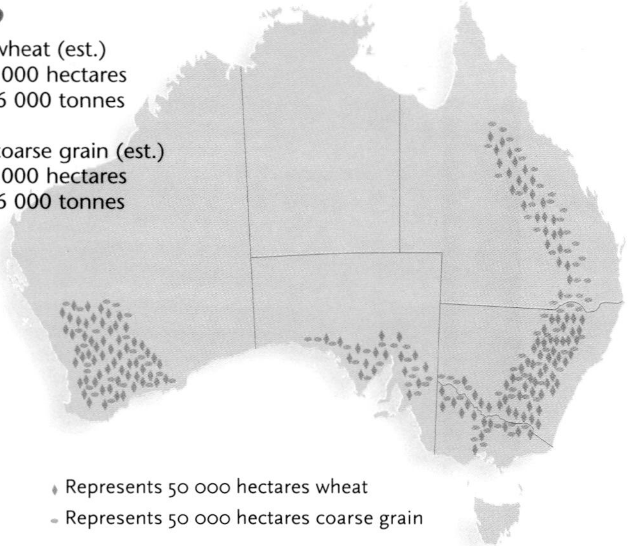

⸭ Represents 50 000 hectares wheat
◟ Represents 50 000 hectares coarse grain

1999

Total sugar cane (est.)
377 000 hectares (provisiorial)
35 889 000 tonnes (est.)

Total fruit and vines (est.)
195 000 hectares
2 376 000 tonnes

Total cotton (est.)
315 000 hectares
923 000 tonnes

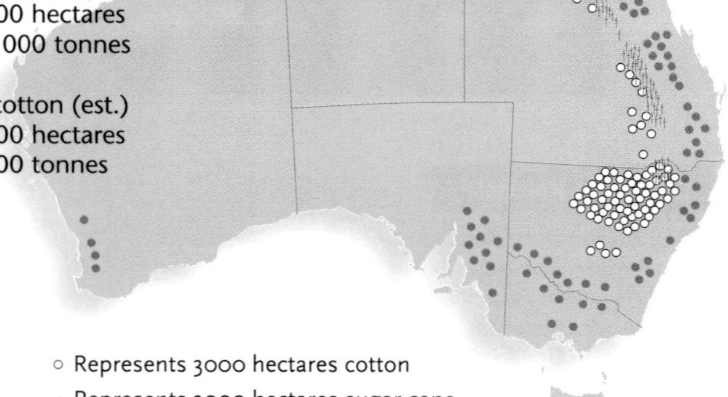

○ Represents 3000 hectares cotton
⸌ Represents 3000 hectares sugar cane
● Represents 3000 hectares fruit and vines

Mineral resources

Total value of mineral production $31.4 bn

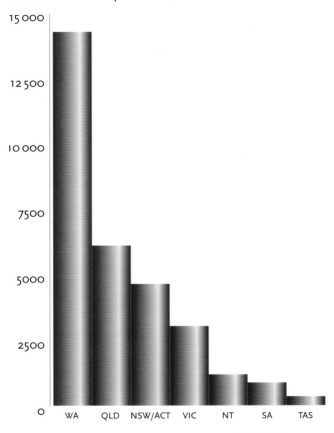

DID YOU KNOW?

The Argyle Diamond Mine, south of Kununurra in Western Australia, is the world's most modern and the main source of rare intense pink diamonds. Australia's three main opal fields are in Quilpie (Queensland), Lightning Ridge (New South Wales), and Coober Pedy (South Australia).

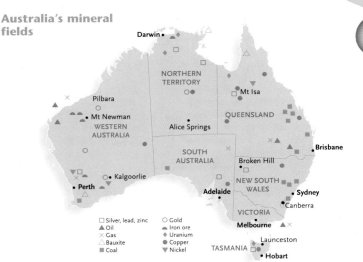

Australia's mineral fields

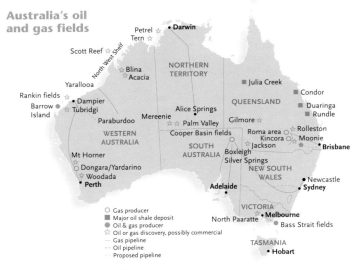

Australia's oil and gas fields

DID YOU KNOW?

Australia has 2500 kilometres of crude oil pipelines, 500 kilometres of petroleum product pipelines and 5600 kilometres of natural gas pipelines.

How the Australian dollar performs against the US dollar

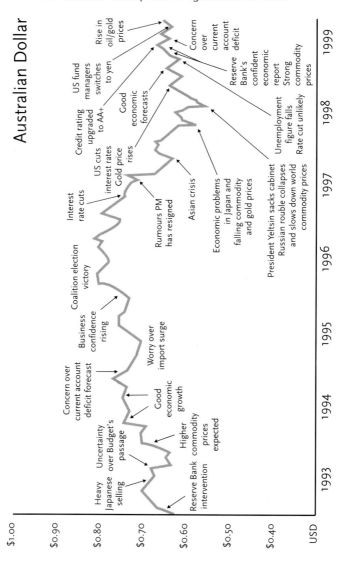

Australian Dollar

Heavy Japanese selling

Uncertainty over Budget's passage

Concern over current account deficit forecast

Reserve Bank intervention

Good economic growth

Higher commodity prices expected

Business confidence rising

Worry over import surge

Coalition election victory

Interest rate cuts

Rumours PM has resigned

Asian crisis

US cuts interest rates

Gold price rises

Credit rating upgraded to AA+

Good economic forecasts

US fund managers switches to yen

Rise in oil/gold prices

Economic problems in Japan and falling commodity and gold prices

President Yeltsin sacks cabinet Russian rouble collapses and slows down world commodity prices

Unemployment figure falls Rate cut unlikely

Reserve Bank's confident economic report Strong commodity prices

Concern over current account deficit

1993 1994 1995 1996 1997 1998 1999

$1.00
$0.90
$0.80
$0.70
$0.60
$0.50
$0.40
USD

Movements of shares on the Australian stock market

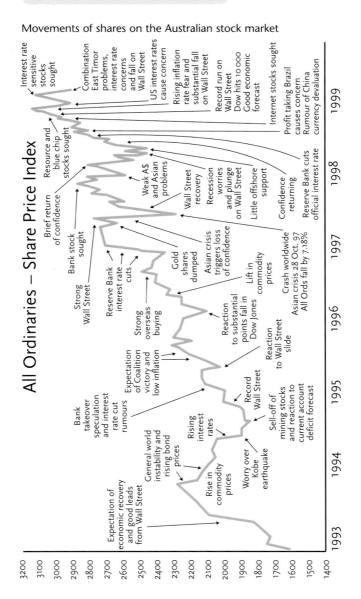

All Ordinaries – Share Price Index

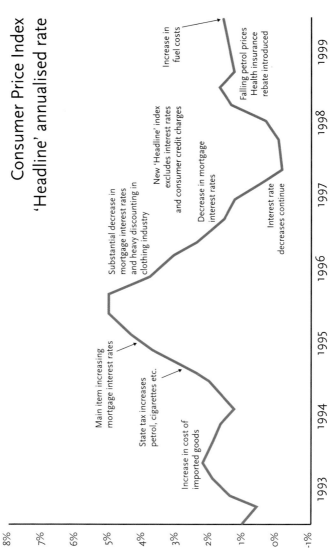

Consumer Price Index
'Headline' annualised rate

Measurement of rise and fall in cost of living

Increase in cost of imported goods

State tax increases petrol, cigarettes etc.

Main item increasing mortgage interest rates

Substantial decrease in mortgage interest rates and heavy discounting in clothing industry

New 'Headline' index excludes interest rates and consumer credit charges

Decrease in mortgage interest rates

Interest rate decreases continue

Falling petrol prices Health insurance rebate introduced

Increase in fuel costs

8%
7%
6%
5%
4%
3%
2%
1%
0%
-1%

1993 1994 1995 1996 1997 1998 1999

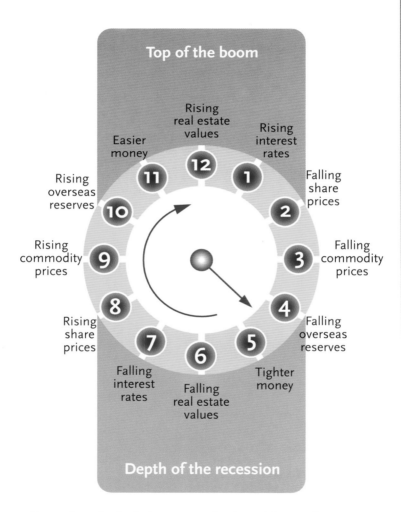

The stock market leads the economy by six to eight months.
The whole cycle can take anything up to eight years to complete.

Average weekly earnings of all employees ($) est.

800	
750	
700	
650	612.30
600	
550	548.10
500	
450	
400	
350	
300	307
250	247.60
200	
150	148
100	76
50	
0	6 11.60

1919   1948   1970   1975   1980   1982   1992   1998-99

DID YOU KNOW?

The highest-paid jobs for males are in the mining industry; for females, in the mining industry and community services (health, education etc.).

Until 1966 Australia followed the British system of currency, of pounds, shillings and pence. On 14 February 1966, decimal currency was introduced with the dollar ($A) being the unit of currency consisting of 100 cents (c). The currency has six coins and five notes in circulation as well as periodic commemorative notes and coins.

Coins

On all coins, the obverse side displays an image of Queen Elizabeth II, while the reverse side mostly depicts Australian native fauna.

The 5c coin has the echidna or spiny anteater, one of only two egg-laying mammals in the world.

The 10c coin shows a male lyrebird dancing, its magnificent tail spread and thrown forward over its head.

The 20c coin shows the only other egg-laying mammal, the platypus.

The 50c coin carries the coat of arms of the Commonwealth of Australia.

These coins are cupro-nickel.

The $1 coin portrays five kangaroos and has interrupted milling on the edge to assist the visually impaired.

The $2 coin has the bust of an Aborigine against the background of the Southern Cross.

These coins are made of aluminium-bronze.

Sometimes the 20c, 50c, and $1 coins are minted with a special design for commemorative

purposes and are circulated.

A $5 coin, a $10 coin (made of sterling silver) and a $200 coin (made of 22 carat gold) have been minted but are not generally circulated, although they are legal tender.

Notes

There are five notes ($5, $10, $20, $50, $100), each a different colour and increasing in size with value. All depict personalities and themes of Australian historical interest. They are all polymer (plastic) which allows the incorporation of sophisticated security features (most notably the clear window which can include printing and embossing). The plastic notes were first introduced in 1992 and Australia is the first country in the world to move all currency notes from paper to polymer.

The $5 note, predominantly mauve in colour, features a portrait of Queen Elizabeth II and gum leaves on the front, and Parliament House, Canberra, landscape plans and geometric shapes on the back. A gum flower can be seen in the clear window.

The $10 note, predominantly blue in colour, features a portrait of A.B. 'Banjo' Paterson, surrounded by microprinted excerpts from his famous poem 'The Man from Snowy River' on the front. On the back is a portrait of poet and champion of the oppressed Dame Mary Gilmore, surrounded by microprinted excerpts from her poem 'No Foe Shall Gather Our Harvest' with a bullock team in the background. The clear window has a windmill printed on it, along with embossed wave patterns.

The $20 note, predominantly orange in colour, features a portrait of Mary Reibey, who came to the colony as a convict and later became a respected businesswoman with interests in property and shipping. The reverse side commemorates the work of Reverend John Flynn, founder of the world-acclaimed Royal Flying Doctor Service. The clear window has a stylised compass printed on it, along with the embossing of the number '20'.

The $50 note, predominantly gold in colour, features a portrait of David Unaipon, an inventor and Australia's first published Aboriginal author, on the front, and Edith Cowan, a social worker and Australia's first female parliamentarian, on the back. The clear window has a stylised version of the Southern Cross printed on it, along with the embossing of the number '50'.

The $100 note, predominantly green in colour, features the internationally acclaimed opera singer Dame Nellie Melba. Her brilliant soprano voice was remarkable for its silvery timbre and even quality of range. On the back is a portrait of Sir John Monash, soldier, engineer and administrator, acknowledged for his outstanding leadership qualities in both military and civilian life. The clear window has a stylised image of a lyrebird printed on it along with the embossing of the number '100'.

PARTS

Australian Capital Territory

Two areas transferred to the Commonwealth of Australia by the state of New South Wales made up the Australian Capital Territory (ACT). In 1908 the larger area around Canberra was chosen for the federal capital site and in 1915 the smaller area of Jervis Bay, on the New South Wales coast, was transferred to the Commonwealth of Australia for development as a port. In 1993, after the formation of the Australian Capital Territory Legislative Assembly, the area around Canberra was deemed the Australian Capital Territory; Jervis Bay remains Commonwealth Territory.

Location

The Australian Capital Territory is in south-eastern New South Wales, west of the Great Dividing Range.

Area

The area around Canberra is 2400 square kilometres.

Landform

Rolling plains and grassland with gentle slopes becoming more mountainous towards the Namadgi National Park and Tidbinbilla Range.

Population

309 114, mostly residents of Canberra.

Climate

Mainly temperate; cold nights and cool to very cold days in winter, warm to hot days and cool nights in summer.

Administrative centre

Canberra is situated at the northern end of the Australian Capital Territory. It has an area of 805 square kilometres and a population of 308 086, of which 28 per cent are public servants. Average daily hours of sunshine: 7.2.

Main attractions

Parliament House, Lake Burley Griffin, National Gallery of Australia, High Court of Australia, Captain Cook Water Jet, Red Hill, Black Mountain, Telstra Tower, Australian War Memorial, foreign legations, Yarralumla (governor-general's residence), Vietnam war memorial.

Coat of arms

The coat of arms was granted in 1928 by King George V. It incorporates a shield depicting a triple-towered castle between the Sword of Justice and the Parliamentary Mace crossed, with a representation of the Imperial Crown. On one side stands a black swan, representing the Aboriginal people, and on the other a white swan, representing the European people in Australia. The motto is 'For the Queen, the Law and the People'.

Flag

The ACT flag features the Southern Cross and a modified version of the ACT coat of arms. It was proclaimed as the official flag in 1993.

Parliament House, Canberra.

Industries contributing to the Australian Capital Territory's gross state product

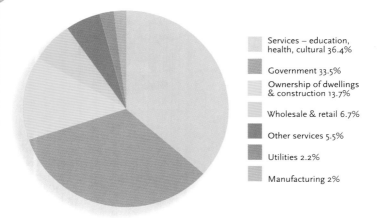

- Services – education, health, cultural 36.4%
- Government 33.5%
- Ownership of dwellings & construction 13.7%
- Wholesale & retail 6.7%
- Other services 5.5%
- Utilities 2.2%
- Manufacturing 2%

Major festivals and events

February	Royal Canberra Show
March	Canberra Festival
	National Folk Festival
May	Australian Science Festival
June	Canberra Festival of Drama
September	Floriade Festival
October	Rotary Embassy Open Day
	Days of Wine and Roses
	Oktoberfest

Sister city

Versailles (France)

DID YOU KNOW?

Parliament House, Canberra, covers 15% of a 32-hectare site, and is one of the largest buildings in the southern hemisphere. There are 4500 rooms and 250 000 square metres of floor area. The building is made of 300 000 cubic metres of concrete, enough to build 25 Sydney Opera Houses.

New South Wales

Population

6 431 351. The majority live in the three main cities – Sydney, Newcastle and Wollongong. Over half the people of the state live in Sydney.

Climate

Temperate and slightly humid in coastal areas, with the deserts of the interior experiencing cold nights and hot days. Irregular floods and droughts occur.

Location

New South Wales lies in the south-east of the continent and is bordered by the South Pacific Ocean, with Queensland to the north and Victoria to the south.

Area

It is the fourth-largest state in Australia, at 801 600 square kilometres (seven times larger than England).

Landform

Coastal slopes, plateaux and river flats are bounded by the Great Dividing Range, which runs north and south. West of the Dividing Range are rolling plains which deteriorate into semi-arid desert.

New South Wales animal emblem: platypus.

New South Wales floral emblem: waratah.

DID YOU KNOW?

Sydney Harbour Bridge has an arch span of 503 metres. The top arch is 134 metres above sea level. The overall length of the arch and its approaches is 1149 metres, with a deck width of 49 metres. The bridge weighs approximately 52 800 tonnes and the weight of the steel in the arch is 39 000 tonnes.

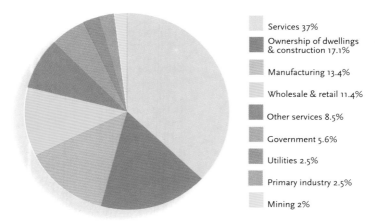

Services 37%

Ownership of dwellings & construction 17.1%

Manufacturing 13.4%

Wholesale & retail 11.4%

Other services 8.5%

Government 5.6%

Utilities 2.5%

Primary industry 2.5%

Mining 2%

State capital

Sydney was settled at Port Jackson, a sea inlet on the Pacific Ocean. The city has an area of 12 407 square kilometres (including Penrith and Hawkesbury) and a population of 3 986 723. Average daily hours of sunshine: 6.7.

Largest cities

Sydney	3 986 723
Newcastle/Hunter	567 302
Wollongong/Illawarra	380 660
Wagga Wagga	56 566
Albury/Wodonga	50 192
Tamworth	35 326
Broken Hill	21 297

Chief products

Agriculture:

Cotton, dairy products, fruit, honey, mutton, poultry, sugar, wheat, wool, timber, beef, sheep.

Fishing:

Many varieties of fish and shellfish.

Manufacturing:

Iron and steel, machinery, agricultural implements, chemicals, clothing, fertiliser, glassware, motor vehicles, paper, textiles.

Mining:

Coal, copper, gold, lead, mineral sands, silver, zinc.

Main attractions

Harbour Bridge, Opera House, Darling Harbour, Olympic Park at Homebush Bay, The Rocks area, Blue Mountains, Snowy Mountains, national parks, surfing beaches, fishing, wineries.

Coat of arms

The present coat of arms was approved in 1906 by King Edward VII. It consists of a shield with the red cross of St George. In the quarters are displayed sheaves of wheat and fleece from the sheep, representing the agricultural and pastoral industries of the state. The shield is supported by a lion and a kangaroo. The crest is a rising sun with rays, each tagged with the flame of fire. The scroll at the base bears the motto *Orta recens quam pura nites* ('Newly arisen, how brightly you shine').

Flag

The New South Wales flag is based on the Blue Ensign, with the state badge superimposed on the right-hand side. The badge consists of a golden lion on a red St George cross within a white circle. The badge was proclaimed in 1876.

Sydney Opera House.

Major festivals and events

January	Sydney Festival
	Tamworth Country Music Festival
February	Sydney Gay & Lesbian Mardi Gras
March	Orange Banjo Paterson Festival
	Royal Easter Show, Sydney
	Narrandera John O'Brien Bush Festival
April	Sydney Autumn Racing Carnival/Golden Slipper
	Tumut Festival of the Falling Leaf
June	National Rugby League State of Origin match
July	Lightning Ridge Opal & Gem Festival
August	Bledisloe Cup (Sydney)
September	Bowral Tulip Time Festival
	Sydney Spring Racing Carnival
October	Bathurst 1000 Car Races
	Grafton Jacaranda Festival
	Goulburn Lilac City Festival
	Forster Oyster Festival
	Newcastle Mattara Festival
November	Blackheath Rhododendron Festival
	Glen Innes Land of the Beardies Bush Festival
December	Sydney–Hobart Yacht Race (start)

Sister cities (selection)

Coffs Harbour	Hayama, Sasebo (Japan)
Cooma	Kamoto-cho (Japan), Taupo (New Zealand)
Lismore	Yamato-takada (Japan)
Manly	Avon, Bath (UK), Selma (USA), Taito-ku, Tokyo (Japan)
Newcastle	Arcadia (USA), Ube (Japan)
Orange	Kofu (Japan), Orange (USA), Timaru (New Zealand)
Sydney	Guangzhou (China), Hampshire, Portsmouth (UK), Nagoya (Japan), San Francisco (USA), Wellington (New Zealand)
Wollongong	Kimitsu (Japan), Lae (Papua New Guinea), Ohrid (former Yugoslavia)

DID YOU KNOW?

AMP Tower Centrepoint is the tallest building in the Southern Hemisphere, 324.8 metres above sea level.

Whichever way you enter Sydney, there is a feeling of anticipation. Whether it is by road from the north, crossing wide rivers and cutting through great sandstone canyons, or from the south through the forested plateaux of the Royal National Park, excitement builds. From the west, descending by road or rail from the Blue Mountains to the Cumberland Plain, great vistas of the city tantalise not only the tourist but also those who travel the rollercoaster ride down each day from the mountain towns and villages. Flying into Sydney at any time is breathtaking, but at night, after a long flight, it is pure magic. Entering the harbour by ship is something else again. Nowhere on earth is there such a waterway. When you round the craggy ramparts of the Heads, the harbour opens out to reveal great cliffs and valleys, coves and islands carved out aeons ago in the ice age and perched precariously on the harbour rim sits the expectant city, as if perpetually waiting for some other exciting event to occur.

● Sydney

Early Sydney

The harbour is and always has been the defining point of Sydney. It is where things happen. From the moment Captain Arthur Phillip decided to move the First Fleet from Botany Bay to Port Jackson, the die was cast. In the 1780s, Britain had lost the American colonies which had served as a dumping ground for British convicts. As a result, British prisons were teeming. Acting only on Captain Cook's 1770 report, Botany Bay was chosen as a place suitable to 'offload the problem'. Without further exploration or preparation, Captain Arthur Phillip RN was selected to lead the First Fleet and to establish a penal colony. One thousand and thirty people, consisting of 750 convicts and three companies of marines, were hastily despatched in two warships, *Sirius* and *Supply*, and nine chartered merchantmen. After almost nine agonising months at sea, Phillip found the exposed anchorage of Botany Bay to be unsuitable. Port Jackson, which had been named by Cook but bypassed at the time, looked a promising alternative. Phillip wrote in his journal that it proved to be 'the finest (harbour) in the world, where a thousand sail of the line might ride in the most perfect security'. On 26 January 1788 the First Fleet sailed into Port Jackson, where Phillip disembarked the emaciated company at Sydney Cove and proclaimed the foundation of

the colony for King George III of England.

For the Aboriginal harbour dwellers – the Eora people and their neighbours the Tharawal and the Dharug – the arrival of the First Fleet was cataclysmic. They dwelt in an environment unaware of the existence of the outside world. They knew no natural enemy, food was in abundance, the climate was congenial and they had time for leisure. Their history and traditions were etched into sandstone rock (paintings can still be found in caves and on surrounding plateaux). This meeting with Europeans foreshadowed the disintegration of their society.

A long and bitter struggle for survival was fought by the floundering colony on the site where the central business district of Sydney now stands. With remarkable courage and determination, Phillip faced enormous problems. Lack of military discipline, unruly convicts, an unskilled workforce and a shortage of proper medical and food supplies all but annihilated the settlement. Although Phillip did much to befriend them, within three years of the arrival of the First Fleet the Aboriginal population had been decimated by two-thirds, leaving the survivors physically and emotionally weak and reliant on the new settlement.

In the next two decades, slowly and against all odds, Sydney began to step forward. From the rudimentary higgledy-piggledy of makeshift shelters

Landing at Sydney Cove from **The Founding of Australia** *by Algernon Talmadge.*

huddled near the harbour, a rough and ready society began to emerge. Always burdened by its history of criminal activity and with ignorance and misery lurking around every corner, convicts, emancipists and free settlers alike began to settle in the unholy atmosphere. Away from the dictates of Europe, to some this was freedom never before known, but for those who had exchanged one cruelty for another things were no different. Regardless, the town began to mushroom. Most built their own huts and cultivated whatever land suited them. Roads were little more than strips of cleared land and town planning was at the whim of the governor of the time. Unfortunately, the Colonial Office in far-off England withdrew men of vision like Governor Macquarie and replaced them with less inspired individuals who had no plan for the future. A chaotic subdivisional history ensued, with buildings and street alignments drawn up more for profitability than good drainage and orderly development. This lack of concern and the formidable demands of merchants and those privileged enough to hold private property dictated where and to whom the land was allocated. Unimaginable slums developed. By 1840, with more free settlers than convicts, the population began to shift outwards. The Blue Mountains had been breached in 1813 and land to the west was beginning to be settled.

As the country dragged itself out of the 1840s depression, wealth from wheat, wool and gold brought for some a new spirit of exuberance and independence. Now a city, Sydney was showing signs of prosperity. It seemed to be open to all who would come, and despite the realities, people stayed. Rail, tram and ferry services began opening up new areas. There was a pervasive feeling of optimism and confidence, an indifference to law and order and a strong belief in a 'fair go' for all. With endless opportunities, the town came to life. Always slightly seedy and disorderly, it was this hotch-potch of humanity at the other side of the earth that attracted people. Sydney had long outstripped its designated boundaries, and now it sidestepped world opinion that it was 'an antipodean backwater lacking true direction' and continued on unimpeded.

Federation to the postwar boom

At the turn of the century, the seven Australian states formed a Federation. This seemed to be a chance for a new beginning, but the self-seeking merchants, corrupt councils

Sydney Harbour Bridge.

and depressed economy of Sydney gave no quarter. The 'unplanned ugliness' of Sydney resulted in an accumulation of filth, vermin and eventual plague which at long last galvanised the city fathers into action. They finally called a halt to the unrestrained greed and in the aftermath of the plague, major reforms were imposed. Health regulations were introduced, building and road codes were enforced and water, sewerage and drainage were vastly improved. The harbour, which had long been the cesspool for drainage from the city, began to be managed by the Sydney Harbour Trust. Although it took years, the slums were cleared and their forlorn occupants rehoused. At last Sydney was cleaning itself up and becoming a city worth living in.

The next 50 years were turbulent. With two world wars and the Great Depression, life seesawed between good times and bad. In the 1920s the harbour bridge was commenced. One million Sydneysiders, disregarding the adversity of the times, embraced the opening in 1932 with gusto and partied unabated for two weeks. The bridge enabled the North Shore to flourish and opened up new areas further on towards leafy Hornsby.

Rampant urban development continued in the 1950s. The postwar boom created a feverish desire for most Australians to own their own home as well as their own car.

The modern city of Sydney.

Dormitory suburbs sprawled west to the buttress of the mountains and north to the Pittwater peninsula. In the south, the orchards and dairy farms of Camden and Campbelltown were overtaken by huge estates, which housed many families of the postwar baby boom. At the same time the desirable harbour dress circle, the domain of millionaires, was bought and sold in a constant jostle for a stake in a view beyond the dreams of most. Ironically, these properties had had to be periodically vacated in the early days because of the stench from the harbour, and in World War II, the appearance of enemy submarines, which had broken through the wartime safety net, caused further concern and departures. But now these top spots were at a premium.

Development in the 1960s was brisk and ruthless, resulting in an overabundance of office towers appearing on every corner of the CBD. Although public opposition was strong and vocal, some heritage buildings were sacrificed in the need to satisfy the rush of developers. This changed the character of the city forever.

The proceeds from 496 lotteries enabled one of the man-made wonders of the world to be built on the harbour. In 1973 the curtain rose on the Sydney Opera House, and since then this Australian icon has played host to thousands of guests from far and wide. Its galleon presence on Bennelong Point makes it a fitting partner to the arched bridge behind, creating a vista which is recognised worldwide and a spectacle that is hard to beat.

Sydney today

The 1980s and 90s brought incredible change. The fluctuating fortunes of big business and entrepreneurs saw the city crown itself with high-tech towers of steel and glass. Overdue freeways cut great swathes through bushland and suburbs alike and some rough areas of the city, previously considered too dangerous to enter, were transformed into canyons of elegant high-rise apartments and tourist haunts. The spotlight, of course, is still on the spectacular harbour. It is where the city celebrates and no excuse is needed for Sydneysiders to flock there in their thousands. It is also the commerical gateway to Australia and the main working port for overseas trade. Commerce and industry always vied with real estate, and when some warehouses and container terminals relocated to Botany Bay there was a rush to rebuild on their deserted sites. Although it has lost some of its workaday busyness, the harbour is now ringed with heady, high-rise tourism ventures and fast-money commerce. Always fickle, Sydney now embraces the variety offered by multi-culturalism and accepts wholeheartedly the colour and excesses of a society willing to try anything at any price. The bedraggled past seems to be another world and there is no looking back.

Today, despite its shortcomings, Sydney is a rich and dynamic place. The possibilities in such a vibrant atmosphere are endless. The city's natural beauty overrides everything, the climate is superb

CBD and environs

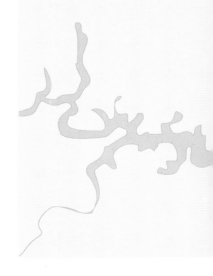

PARRAMATTA

HOMEBUSH
BAY
Olympic
Park •

BURWOO

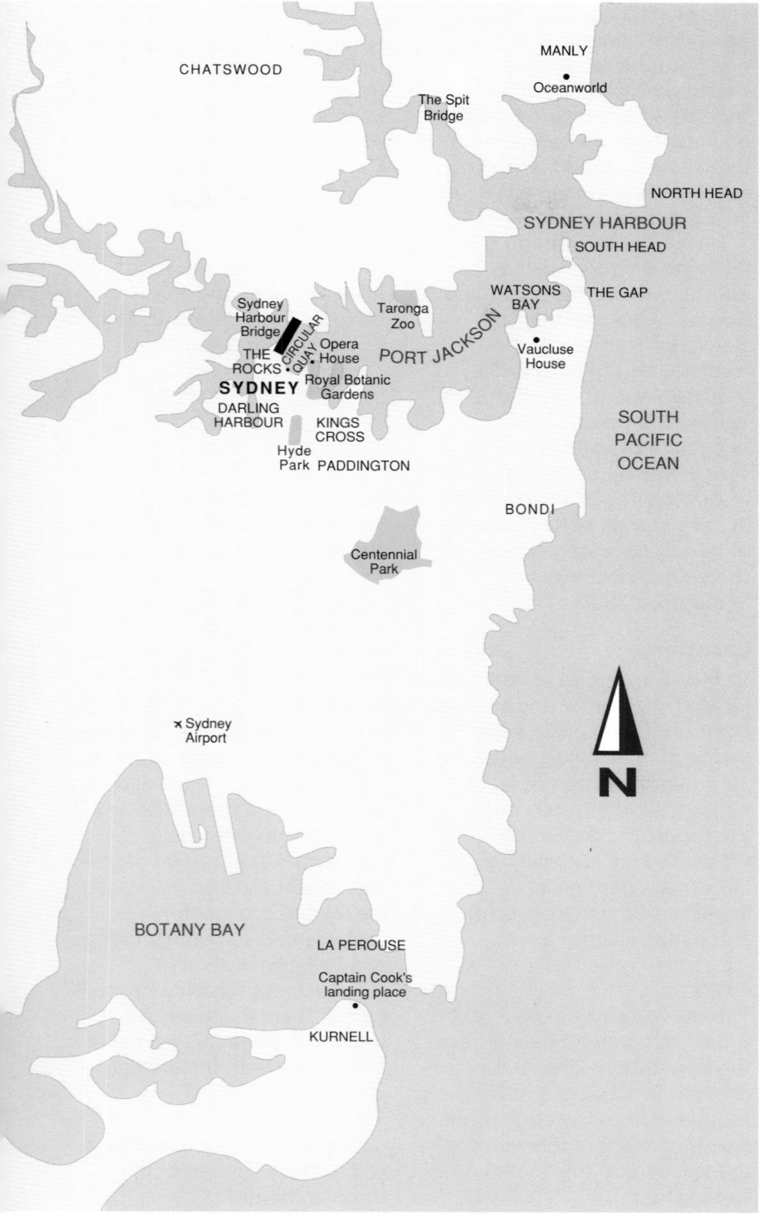

CHATSWOOD

MANLY
● Oceanworld

The Spit
Bridge

NORTH HEAD

SYDNEY HARBOUR

SOUTH HEAD

WATSONS
BAY   THE GAP

Sydney
Harbour
Bridge

Taronga
Zoo

PORT JACKSON

Vaucluse
House

CIRCULAR QUAY

Opera
House

THE
ROCKS

Royal Botanic
Gardens

SYDNEY

DARLING
HARBOUR

KINGS
CROSS

SOUTH
PACIFIC
OCEAN

Hyde
Park PADDINGTON

BONDI

Centennial
Park

✕ Sydney
Airport

N

BOTANY BAY

LA PEROUSE

Captain Cook's
landing place
●

KURNELL

and the views are spectacular. Beaches are only a short bus ride from the centre and theatres, restaurants, pubs, galleries and museums are in abundance. It doesn't seem to matter what you do when you get there; the excitement is just in being there.

Flushed with winning the Olympic bid, Sydney has had another excuse for a building boom. Like a spectacular stage set, Homebush Bay – formerly an ugly, disused industrial site on the banks of Parramatta River – has become a mega sporting venue worthy of the honour of hosting the 2000 Olympics. Sydney stands poised in all its glory to celebrate and enjoy the world's focus in September 2000.

Location

Sydney was settled at Port Jackson, a sea inlet on the east coast of Australia flanked by the Tasman Sea, part of the South Pacific Ocean. It is the largest city in Australia and the capital of New South Wales. Sydney is a leading industrial, commercial, financial and transport centre and a major port.

Area

The city has an area of 12 407 square kilometres, ranging from the Hawkesbury River in the north to Port Hacking in the south and from the ridge of the Blue Mountains in the west to the seaboard of the South Pacific Ocean.

Population

3 986 723, mostly descended from British stock and more recently from Asia and southern Europe. Twenty per cent of Australia's total population and 62% of the New South Wales population live in Sydney.

Landform

A vast, undulating tract of lowland extending from Windsor in the north to Penrith in the west and to Camden in the south is flanked by sandstone plateaux: the Hornsby, Woronora and Blue Mountains plateaux. The whole area is dissected by considerable stream erosion, which over time has exposed sheer cliffs and remnant ridges. The coastline alternates between sandstone headlands and numerous crescent beaches.

Climate

Sydney experiences a temperate climate with no great extremes. December, January and February are the hottest months, when temperatures can reach 38 degrees Celsius (100 degrees Fahrenheit) and beyond. Winters are mild to cool, with July temperatures sometimes falling to 12 degrees Celsius (53.5 degrees Fahrenheit) and below. There is virtually no snow, but occasional sleet and frosts occur with the average annual rainfall being 1200 millimetres. Heavy downpours and thunderstorms with hail are features of the summer months.

Coat of arms

From the time Sydney became a city in 1842, the coat of arms has never had a static image. Changes seem to follow the tide of history and the present image was adopted in 1994. It consists of a shield flanked by a coiled rope and the Rainbow Serpent. These acknowledge the history of European settlement in Sydney as well as its original Aboriginal inhabitants, the Eora people. The whole is topped by a six-point star. Within the shield there are simplified versions of three coats of arms. The first is of Viscount Sydney, after whom the city was named, then Captain Cook's, representing the British contribution, and lastly that of Thomas Hughes, the first Lord Mayor of Sydney (1908). The bottom half of the shield incorporates a crown and an anchor, both of which are working symbols of a seaboard city.

The flag

The city flag has flown from the Sydney Town Hall since 1908. The top third consists of three designs similar to those in the coat of arms. The bottom half depicts a sailing ship, with subdivision of the field into blue and gold, indicative of a shipping port in the Golden South.

The floral emblem

Banksia ericifolia was first documented by Sir Joseph Banks when Captain Cook came to Botany Bay in 1770. The species is indigenous to the foreshores of the harbour and heathlands and still survives in abundance to serve as a symbol of Australia's oldest city.

Sydney floral emblem: banksia.

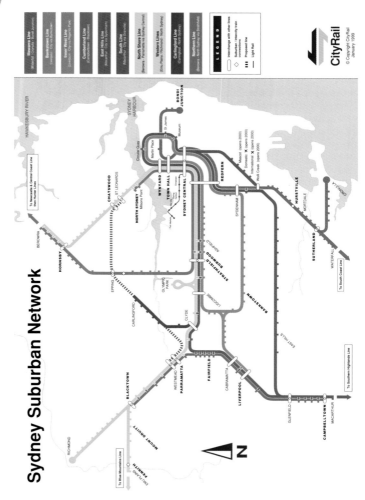

Sydney Suburban Network
Illawarra Line (Waterfall / Cronulla - Bondi Junction)
Bankstown Line (Liverpool - City via Bankstown)
Inner West Line (Liverpool - City via Regents Park)
Cumberland Line (Campbelltown - Blacktown)
East Hills Line (Macarthur - City via Sydenham)
South Line (Macarthur - City via Granville)
North Shore Line (Berowra - Parramatta via Sydney Central)
Western Lines (Emu Plains / Richmond - North Sydney)
Carlingford Line (Carlingford - North Sydney)
Northern Line (Berowra - North Sydney via Strathfield)
LEGEND
Interchange with other lines
Suburban / Intercity train connections
Proposed line
Light Rail
CityRail
© Copyright CityRail January 1999
HAWKESBURY RIVER
SYDNEY HARBOUR
To Newcastle & Central Coast Line then Hunter Lines
BEROWRA
HORNSBY
CHATSWOOD
ST LEONARDS
NORTH SYDNEY
Milsons Point
WYNYARD
TOWN HALL
SYDNEY CENTRAL
Circular Quay
Martin Place
St James
Museum
BONDI JUNCTION
REDFERN
Mascot (opens 2000)
Domestic (opens 2000)
International (opens 2000)
Wolli Creek (opens 2000)
SYDENHAM
HURSTVILLE
MORTDALE
CRONULLA
SUTHERLAND
WATERFALL
To South Coast Line
EPPING
OLYMPIC PARK
ASHFIELD
BURWOOD
STRATHFIELD
LIDCOMBE
BANKSTOWN
CARLINGFORD
CLYDE
EAST HILLS
To Southern Highlands Line
BLACKTOWN
WESTMEAD
PARRAMATTA
FAIRFIELD
CABRAMATTA
LIVERPOOL
GLENFIELD
CAMPBELLTOWN
MACARTHUR
RICHMOND
MOUNT DRUITT
PENRITH
EMU PLAINS
To Blue Mountains Line
N

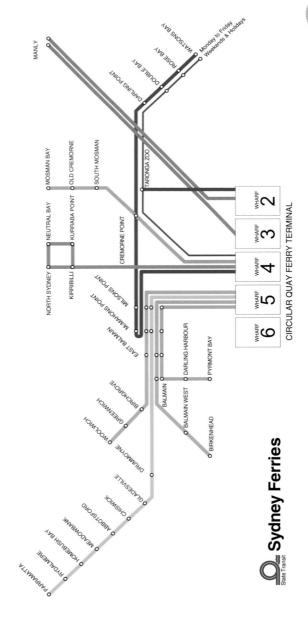

Sydney Ferries
State Transit

Distances

Sydney to:	
Canberra via Metroad M5, South Western Motorway, Hume Highway (National Route 31), then Federal Highway	290 km
Melbourne via Metroad M1 (south), Princes Highway (National Route 1)	1043 km
Melbourne via Metroad M5, South Western Motorway, Hume Highway (National Route 31)	868 km
Brisbane via Metroad M1 (north), Sydney–Newcastle Freeway (National Route 1 north), Pacific Highway	975 km
Brisbane via Metroad M1 (north), Sydney–Newcastle Freeway (National Route 1 north), New England Highway	1017 km
Adelaide via Metroad M4, National Routes 32, 24 and 20 (Great Western, Mid Western and Sturt Highways)	1419 km
Adelaide via Metroad M5, National Routes 31 and 20 (Hume and Sturt Highways)	1427 km
Perth via Adelaide	4144 km
Darwin via Bourke and Mt Isa (Queensland)	3991 km
Newcastle via Metroad M1 (north), Sydney–Newcastle Freeway (National Route 1 north)	170 km
Wollongong via Metroad M1 (south), Princes Highway (National Route 1 south)	80 km

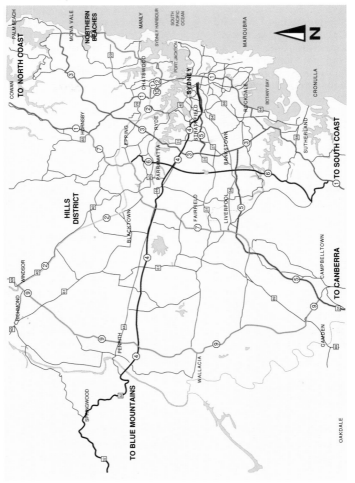

Tolls are payable on some Metroads and Motorways.
The Sydney–Newcastle Freeway is sometimes referred to as the F3.

Major attractions

Sydney Harbour and the Bridge, Circular Quay and the Opera House, The Rocks, Darling Harbour (including National Maritime Museum, Powerhouse Museum, Sydney Aquarium and Sydney Fish Market), Taronga Zoo, colonial buildings in Macquarie Street, State Library, Parliament House, Hyde Park Barracks, Hyde Park, Martin Place, Strand Arcade, AMP Tower Centrepoint, Queen Victoria Building, Town Hall, Museum of Sydney, Art Gallery of New South Wales, The Domain, Mrs Macquarie's Chair, Royal Botanic Gardens, Kings Cross, Woolloomooloo, Paddington, Centennial Park, Vaucluse House, Watsons Bay, South Head and The Gap, Homebush Bay Olympic site, Manly and Oceanworld, North Head, beaches extending from Palm Beach in the north to Cronulla in the south.

Day trips from Sydney

Ku-ring-gai Chase National Park

Located 40 kilometres north of the city, this park encompasses rugged sandstone country, crisscrossed by extensive systems of waterways. The high plateau area overlooks inlets of the Hawkesbury River as it merges into Broken Bay. The park is renowned for its vast array of wildflowers and numerous Aboriginal rock paintings. Main destination points are Bobbin Head, Coal and Candle Creek, Akuna Bay and Commodore Heights.

Royal National Park

Created in 1879, this was the first national park in the world. It is a high sandstone plateau and forested area, dissected by steep valleys. There are coastal cliffs with sheltered coves and beaches. The park is located about 40 kilometres south of the city along the Princes Highway and is a favourite picnic spot.

City of Parramatta

The Parramatta area can be reached from the city by road via the Great Western Highway or in an hour by ferry from Circular Quay. Confined within the boundaries of the metropolitan area, this modern city has major historical buildings which bear testament to the time when Parramatta was the political, social and agricultural centre of the colony.

Windsor, Richmond and Upper Hawkesbury

Situated on the rich and fertile flood plains of the Hawkesbury River about 70 kilometres from the city, these were the market gardens of the early colony. Early 19th-century buildings are still in existence and the magnificent river and stands of untouched bushland make this area well worth a visit.

Katoomba and the Blue Mountains

West of the city the Great Western Highway winds up the escarpment of the Blue Mountains plateau and reaches Katoomba, 105 kilometres from Sydney. The area is renowned as one of Australia's greatest tourist attractions. Echo Point, the famous Three Sisters and the Giant Stairway are all part of the great sandstone cliffs and precipices rising from the deep, wooded Jamison Valley. Bushwalking, rock climbing, abseiling, riding the Scenic Railway and Skyway and admiring the magnificent views are just a few of the wonderful attractions of this unique area.

Jenolan Caves and Hartley

Twenty kilometres further north-west from Katoomba the highway reaches the historic convict-built settlement of Hartley, which is well worth a visit. Shortly after the village, you can turn left and travel 8 kilometres to the fantastic natural wonder of Jenolan Caves, where seven caves are open for inspection. These limestone caves are the best known in the state and are famous for their abundance of stalagmites and stalactites. Jenolan Caves House is the epitome of early 1900s guesthouse grandeur.

Hunter Valley and vineyards

Only two hours drive to the north of Sydney is Australia's oldest commercial wine-producing area. Some of the

Tulip time at Bowral, southern highlands.

best wines in the world come from this thriving region and the proliferation of vineyards over the last twenty years has seen a burgeoning tourist industry develop, making the area one of the most popular day trips out of Sydney.

Newcastle

A major industrial city and important port located on the Hunter River estuary, Newcastle has a lot to offer the discerning tourist. The beaches are extensive, fishing is plentiful and the scenic hinterland is only twenty minutes from the CBD. Most of the city is built on ridges and hills, giving wonderful views of the coastline and distant mountains. Lake Macquarie, the largest coastal saltwater lake in the Southern Hemisphere, is 25 kilometres south of Newcastle and a natural playground for boating, water-skiing, swimming and fishing.

Pearl Beach, on the Central Coast of New South Wales.

Central Coast

Along the coast north of the Hawkesbury River, between Sydney and Newcastle, are numerous towns and villages forming a ribbon development from Broken Bay to Budgewoi. The area has great sweeps of unspoilt beaches fringed at times by stands of low coastal forest. The low-lying coastal flats are broken by a series of lagoons and lakes providing wonderful waterways and wetlands, all of which can be accessed by a comprehensive road system.

Palm Beach

To get to this wonderful area 48 kilometres from the city, you can ride the ferry to Manly and travel north along Pittwater Road. Alternatively, you can go by road via The Spit Bridge through to Barrenjoey Road, past the beaches of Curl Curl, Dee Why and Collaroy. Apart from the lovely beach, there is surfing and boating on Pittwater and the climb to Barrenjoey Lighthouse is well worth the effort.

Wollongong

Wollongong is a busy service, industrial and tourist city built in the shadow of the Illawarra escarpment, 80 kilometres south of Sydney. It can be reached by rail or road via the Princes Highway. Sublime Point, at the top of Bulli Pass, is one of the most spectacular views in Australia. An historic lighthouse overlooks Belmore Basin and is open for public inspection.

Southern Highlands

Ranging from undulating woodland to rugged cliffs and ravines, the Illawarra escarpment and Morton National Park are picturesque and a treat for tourists. The quaint villages, ordered landscapes and cool fresh climate provide a mecca for travellers wishing to escape the busy city.

Victoria

State capital

Melbourne is situated on the Yarra River, on Port Phillip Bay. It has an area of 6109 square kilometres and a population of 3 371 308 (about seven-tenths of the state's population). Melbourne's motto is *Vires acquirit eundo* ('We gather strength as we grow'). Average daily hours of sunshine: 5.7.

Largest cities

Melbourne	3 371 308
Geelong & environs	154 150
Ballarat	80 330
Bendigo	75 857
Shepparton	41 910

Location

Victoria lies in the south-eastern corner of the continent.

Area

It is the smallest state on the mainland, and is 227 600 square kilometres in area.

Landform

Mountainous areas in the north-east and semi-desert areas in the north-west. Most land is well suited to farming, and as a result Victoria is often referred to as 'The Garden State'.

Population

4 736 815. Victoria is the most densely populated and the most urbanised of all the states.

Climate

Generally temperate, although the climate is subject to wide variation. High rainfall, extremes of summer heat and irregular floods and droughts occur.

Victorian animal emblem: Leadbeater's possum.

Victorian floral emblem: pink heath.

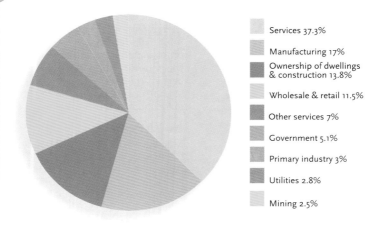

Services 37.3%

Manufacturing 17%

Ownership of dwellings & construction 13.8%

Wholesale & retail 11.5%

Other services 7%

Government 5.1%

Primary industry 3%

Utilities 2.8%

Mining 2.5%

Chief products

Agriculture:

Cattle, forest products, fruit, hay and straw, milk and dairy products, poultry and eggs, sheep, vegetables, wheat, wool.

Manufacturing:

Building materials, chemical products, clothing, farm machinery, footwear, light engineering, motor vehicles, textiles, meat, dairy products.

Mining:

Brown coal, natural gas, oil.

Main attractions

Melbourne Cup (began 1861), Australian Rules football, National Tennis Centre, Phillip Island (penguins), Formula One Grand Prix, wineries, prospecting, riverboat cruising, surfing, snowfields, national parks, sailing, fishing.

DID YOU KNOW?

The secret ballot box, the most prized symbol of democracy, was pioneered in Victoria in 1856.

Coat of arms

The present coat of arms was granted by Queen Elizabeth II in 1972. It incorporates a shield with five stars representing the constellation of the Southern Cross. On either side stands a female figure, one representing peace and the other prosperity. The figure of peace is holding an olive branch and the figure of prosperity is holding a cornucopia, or horn of plenty.

The crest consists of a kangaroo bearing in its paws an Imperial Crown. Below the shield is the motto 'Peace and prosperity'.

Flag

Victoria was the first state to have its own flag. The flag is made up of the Blue Ensign with the badge of the state. This consists of the five white stars of the Southern Cross in the fly, above which is a crown. The flag was used as early as 1870.

Paddle-steamer on the Murray River.

Major festivals and events

January	Australian Open tennis, Melbourne
	Cobram Peaches and Cream Festival (biennial)
March	Australian Formula One Grand Prix, Melbourne
	Ballarat Begonia Festival
	Beechworth Golden Horseshoes Festival
	Bendigo Easter Fair
	Melbourne Moomba Festival
	Melbourne Food & Wine Festival
	Port Fairy Folk Festival
	Stawell Gift (Easter Monday)
April	Castlemaine State Festival (biennial)
	Melbourne International Comedy Festival
	Bright Autumn Festival
June	Echuca Steam, Horse and Vintage Car Rally
August	Melbourne Writers' Festival
September	Australian Football League Grand Final
	Halls Gap Wildflower Exhibition
	Royal Melbourne Show
	Tesselaar's Tulip Festival, Silvan
October	Australian 500cc Motorcycle Grand Prix, Phillip Island
	Euroa Wool Week
	Melbourne Festival of the Arts
October/	
November	Spring Racing Carnival
November	Benalla Rose Festival
	Mansfield Mountain Country Festival
	Melbourne Cup

Sister cities (selection)

Altona	Anjo (Japan)
Bendigo	Los Altos (USA)
Box Hill	Matsudo (Japan)
Frankston	Suson (Japan)
Melbourne	Boston (USA), Florence (Italy), Osaka (Japan), Thessalonika (Greece), Tianjin (China)
Portland	Uchiura-cho (Japan)
Shepparton	Esashi (Japan), Florina (Greece), Resen (former Yugoslavia)
Swan Hill	Grand Junction (USA), Yamagata (Japan)
Warrnambool	Miura (Japan), Palmerston (New Zealand)
Yarrawonga	Katsuyama-mura (Japan)

Queensland

State capital

Brisbane is situated on the Brisbane River, on the east coast. It has an area of 3080 square kilometres and a population of 1 574 615. Average daily hours of sunshine: 7.5.

Largest Cities

Brisbane	1 574 615
Gold Coast/Tweed	380 270
Townsville & environs	145 099
Cairns	111 916
Rockhampton	64 437
Mackay	63 548
Mount Isa	22 061

Location

Queensland lies in the north-east of the continent, bordered by the Pacific Ocean to the east and Torres Strait to the north.

Area

Second-largest state in Australia; 1 727 200 square kilometres.

Landform

The north coast is sheltered by islands and the Great Barrier Reef system. Behind the coastal slopes of the Great Dividing Range and river flats are rolling plains. Then the land becomes semi-arid desert.

Population

3 535 103, mostly in four coastal areas.

Climate

The climate is mainly tropical, with two main seasons – wet and dry. Queensland is known as 'The Sunshine State' because of pleasantly warm winters and long hours of sunshine.

Queensland animal emblem: koala.

Queensland floral emblem: Cooktown orchid.

Industries contributing to Queensland's gross state product

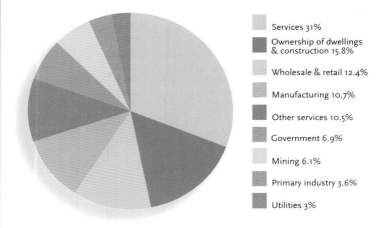

- Services 31%
- Ownership of dwellings & construction 15.8%
- Wholesale & retail 12.4%
- Manufacturing 10.7%
- Other services 10.5%
- Government 6.9%
- Mining 6.1%
- Primary industry 3.6%
- Utilities 3%

Chief products

Agriculture:

Barley, cattle, cotton, fruit, maize, peanuts, pigs, sheep, sugar, tobacco, wheat, wool, fishing, prawning.

Manufacturing:

Basic metal products, brick making, dairy products, electricity generation, meat products, ready-mixed concrete, timber and log processing.

Mining:

Bauxite, coal, copper, gold, lead, mineral sands, nickel, salt, tin, uranium, zinc.

Main attractions

The Great Barrier Reef (a complex organic system and one of the greatest biological wonders of the world), Gold Coast, Sunshine Coast, Cape York Peninsula, Indianapolis car race, surfing beaches, fishing, palm-fringed coastline, tropical islands, prospecting, national parks, tropical rainforests.

DID YOU KNOW?

The World Natural Heritage-listed Great Barrier Reef is the longest coral reef in the world, extending over 2012.5 kilometres. It is the world's largest marine park.

Coat of arms

The present coat of arms was granted by Queen Elizabeth II in 1977. Within the shield are a bull's head and a ram's head in profile, representing the pastoral industry. There is also a mound of quartz emerging from a golden pyramid, in front of which is a spade and pick, representing the mining industry. In the other quarter is a sheaf of wheat, representing the agricultural industry. The shield is supported by a red deer and a brolga. The crest comprises the Maltese Cross superimposed by the Imperial Crown. These are held between two stalks of sugar cane. At the base is the motto *Audax at fidelis* ('Bold, aye, but faithful too').

Flag

The flag of Queensland is based on the Blue Ensign, with the state badge superimposed on the right-hand side. It has a blue Maltese Cross with the Imperial Crown in the centre. The badge was proclaimed in 1876.

DID YOU KNOW?

Tully in Queensland is the wettest town in Australia, with an average annual rainfall of 355.6 centimetres.

Major festivals and events

April	Mt Isa Country Music festival
	Winton Waltzing Matilda Festival
May/June	Queensland Winter Racing Carnival
July	Rainbow Beach Fishing Classic
	Townsville Australian Festival of Chamber Music
August	Royal Brisbane Show ('The Ekka')
September	Mackay Sugartime Festival
	Maryborough Heritage City Festival
	Toowoomba Carnival of Flowers
	Yeppoon Pineapple Festival
October	Bundaberg Arts Festival
	Cairns Reef Festival
	Gympie Gold Rush Festival
	Ipswich Jacaranda Festival
	Rockhampton Arts in the Park
November	Brisbane Livid Festival
December	Woodford Folk Festival

Sister cities (selection)

Brisbane	Brisbane, California (USA), Kobe (Japan), Nice (France)
Cairns	Hiwasa-cho (Japan), Lae (Papua New Guinea), Scottsdale (USA), Sidney (Canada)
Rockhampton	Ibusuki (Japan)

Boom netting, Great Barrier Reef, Queensland.

South Australia

State capital

Adelaide, situated on the Torrens River in St Vincent Gulf, is sheltered by the Mount Lofty Range. The population is 1 088 349, and its area is 1870 square kilometres. Average daily hours of sunshine: 6.9.

Largest cities and towns

Adelaide	1 088 349
Elizabeth	25 900
Whyalla	24 286
Mt Gambier	23 055
Port Pirie & environs	18 412
Port Augusta	13 995

Location

South Australia occupies a central position on the southern coastline. Seaward is the Great Australian Bight.

Area

It is the third-largest state, and covers one-eighth of the total area of Australia. It is 984 000 square kilometres in area, with a coastline of 3700 kilometres.

Landform

Undulating hills, grasslands and valleys. Semi-arid to arid deserts to the north.

Population

Sparsely populated, with 1 504 730 people, mainly concentrated in the south-east corner of the state.

Climate

Mostly a Mediterranean climate, warm to hot in summer, and cool in winter. It is the driest state, with four-fifths of its total area receiving less than 254 millimetres of rainfall a year.

South Australian animal emblem: hairy-nosed wombat.

South Australian floral emblem: Sturt's desert pea.

Industries contributing to South Australia's gross state product

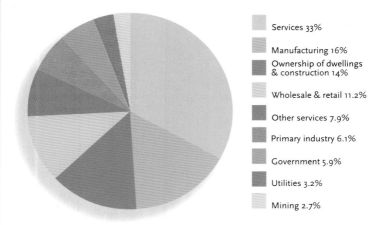

Services 33%

Manufacturing 16%

Ownership of dwellings & construction 14%

Wholesale & retail 11.2%

Other services 7.9%

Primary industry 6.1%

Government 5.9%

Utilities 3.2%

Mining 2.7%

Chief products

Agriculture:
Wheat, wine, almonds and dried fruits, barley, beef, vegetables, fruit, wool.

Manufacturing:
Carriages and wagons, chemicals, cotton, electrical goods, iron and steel, machinery, motor vehicles, pipes.

Mining:
Barytes, coal, copper, dolomite, gypsum, iron ore, natural gas, opals, salt, talc.

Main attractions
Vineyards in Barossa and Clare Valleys, Flinders Ranges, opal fields, Blue Lake (Mt Gambier), Yorke and Eyre Peninsulas, Kangaroo Island, Moonta and Burra Burra copper mine sites, Victor Harbor, Nullarbor Plain, Great Australian Bight Marine Park, whale watching.

DID YOU KNOW?

The Murray River flows with its own current through Lake Alexandrina, South Australia, on its course to its mouth at the Southern Ocean.

Coat of arms

The present coat of arms was conferred by Queen Elizabeth II in 1984. It incorporates a shield with a piping shrike displayed standing on the branch of a gum tree. The shield rests on a grassy mound from which two vines grow, entwining the stakes of the shield; on either side, stalks of wheat and barley appear and lying on the mound are two cog wheels and a miner's pick. All these represent aspects of industry in South Australia. Above the shield is a crest of four sprigs of Sturt's desert pea and at the base is a scroll with the words 'South Australia'.

Flag

The flag of South Australia is based on the Blue Ensign and has the badge of the state superimposed on the right-hand side. It consists of a piping shrike with wings outstretched on a yellow background. This was adopted in 1904.

DID YOU KNOW?

The Great Artesian Basin is the largest in the world, with an area of 1 716 200 square kilometres. It stretches from south-west Queensland and north-west New South Wales into the Northern Territory and South Australia. Artesian water occurs over 60% of the continent.

Major festivals and events

January	Adelaide Schützenfest
February	Adelaide Festival of the Arts & Adelaide Fringe Festival (even-numbered years)
	Womadelaide (odd-numbered years)
	Mt Gambier Country Music Festival
	Tanunda Oompah Fest
March	Kapunda Celtic Music Festival
	Tanunda Essenfest
Easter	Barossa Valley Vintage Festival (odd-numbered years)
April	Australian Festival for Young People, Adelaide (odd-numbered years)
May	Adelaide Cup Racing Carnival
July	Willunga Almond Blossom Festival
October	Barossa Music Festival
	Coober Pedy Horse Races
	Victor Harbor Folk & Music Festival
November	Adelaide Christmas Pageant

Sister cities (selection)

Adelaide	Austin (Texas, USA), Christchurch (New Zealand), Georgetown (Penang, Malaysia), Himeji (Japan)

Isolated Cape Adieu, South Australia.

Western Australia

Location

Western Australia occupies the western third of the continent, bordered by the Indian Ocean in the west and the Southern Ocean in the south.

Area

It is the largest state in Australia at 2 525 500 square kilometres.

Landform

The state extends from vast arable southern areas to interior semi-arid desert landscapes and the mineral-rich Great Sandy and Gibson deserts to the north. The mountain ranges are the Stirling, Kimberley and Hamersley ranges.

Population

1 876 196 (concentrated on the south-west coast), representing only 9% of the total Australian population. The large desert and semi-desert areas are unsuitable for cultivation or close settlement.

Climate

Western Australia has three broad climate divisions. The northern part is dry tropical, receiving summer rainfall. The south-west corner has a Mediterranean climate, with long hot summers and wet winters. The remainder consists of mostly arid land with desert climates.

State capital

Perth is situated on the Swan River, on the seaboard of the Indian Ocean. It is 5306 square kilometres in area and has a population of 1 341 914. Average daily hours of sunshine: 7.9.

Largest cities

Perth	1 341 914
Fremantle & environs	32 097
Boulder/Kalgoorlie	31 391
Bunbury	28 069
Geraldton	20 353
Albany	15 775
Port Hedland	13 286

Western Australian animal emblem: numbat.

Western Australian floral emblem: red and green kangaroo paw.

Industries contributing to Western Australia's gross state product

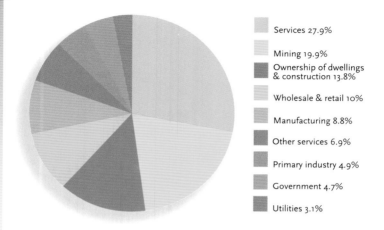

Services 27.9%

Mining 19.9%

Ownership of dwellings & construction 13.8%

Wholesale & retail 10%

Manufacturing 8.8%

Other services 6.9%

Primary industry 4.9%

Government 4.7%

Utilities 3.1%

Chief products

Agriculture:
Cattle, fruit, hardwoods, rock lobsters, wheat, wool.

Manufacturing:
Building materials, food and beverages, metal, machinery, other mineral products, petroleum products, wood products.

Mining:
Bauxite, gold, ilmenite, iron ore, nickel, oil, salt.

Main attractions
Margaret River wine and cave region, Kalgoorlie goldfields, Esperance, Kimberley and Hamersley ranges, Broome, surfing, fishing, sailing, wildflowers, Monkey Mia (dolphins), Pinnacle Desert, Bungle Bungles in the Kimberley, Wave Rock near Hyden, whale watching.

DID YOU KNOW?

Western Australia is three and a half times bigger than Texas.

Coat of arms

The present coat of arms was granted by Queen Elizabeth II in 1969. It incorporates a shield depicting a black swan, the bird emblem of the state. It is supported by two kangaroos, each holding a boomerang. The crest features an Imperial Crown surrounded by branches of kangaroo paw, the state's floral emblem.

Flag

The flag of Western Australia is based on the Blue Ensign, with the badge of the state superimposed on the right-hand side. It has a black swan within a yellow circle. This badge was granted in 1875.

Bungle Bungles, Western Australia.

Major festivals and events

January	Hopman Cup tennis, Perth
	Mandurah Festival
	Perth Vines Golf Classic
February	Festival of Perth
	Margaret River Leeuwin Estate Concert
April	Albany Festival
July	Derby Boab Festival
	Exmouth Exmo Week
August	Broome Shinju Matsuri
	Carnarvon Arts Festival
	Karratha FeNaCLNG Festival
	Newman Fortescue Festival
	Tom Price Nameless Festival
	Wyndham Top of the West Festival
September	Perth Royal Show
	Kings Park Wildflower Festival, Perth
	York Jazz Festival
October	Geraldton Sunshine Festival
November	Festival Fremantle
	Margaret River Wine Region Festival

Sister cities (selection)

Albany	Albany (USA), Fielding (New Zealand), Kessennuma (Japan)
Broome	Taichi-Cho (Japan)
Fremantle	Capo D'Orlando (Sicily), Molfetta (Italy), Wellesley (Malaysia), Yokosuka (Japan)
Perth	Houston (Texas, USA) Island of Megisti (Greece), Kagoshima (Japan), Rhodes (Greece), San Diego (USA)

DID YOU KNOW?

Wolf Creek, Western Australia, has the largest meteorite crater in Australia, 853.44 metres in diameter and 61 metres deep.

Tasmania

State capital

Hobart, on the Derwent River, is the second-oldest city in Australia and is located in the south, beneath Mount Wellington. It has an area of 936 square kilometres and a population of 194 974. Average daily hours of sunshine: 5.8.

Largest cities

Hobart	194 974
Launceston	98 352
Burnie & Devonport	78 605

Location

The island state lies 240 kilometres off the south-eastern corner of the Australian continent, and is separated from the mainland by Bass Strait.

Area

It is the smallest state in Australia, with an area of 68 331 square kilometres. The island measures 286 kilometres north to south.

Landform

Mountainous with lakes, cascades and steeply falling rivers, with vast tracts of wilderness.

Population

470 470, decentralised mostly in the south, north and northwest.

Climate

Generally temperate maritime climate with four distinct seasons. Winter can be cold and damp.

Tasmanian floral emblem: southern blue gum.

Cradle Mountain, Lake St Clair National Park, Tasmania.

Industries contributing to Tasmania's gross state product

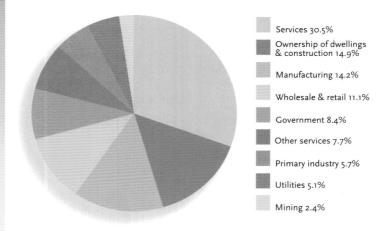

- Services 30.5%
- Ownership of dwellings & construction 14.9%
- Manufacturing 14.2%
- Wholesale & retail 11.1%
- Government 8.4%
- Other services 7.7%
- Primary industry 5.7%
- Utilities 5.1%
- Mining 2.4%

Chief products

Agriculture:
Beef, dairy products, hops, lavender, mutton, potatoes, timber, wool, fruit and vegetables.

Fishing:
Barracouta, crayfish, salmon, scallops, abalone.

Manufacturing:
Alginate, aluminium, frozen food, canned fruit, paper, pulp.

Mining:
Coal, copper, gold, iron, lead, tin, zinc.

Main attractions
Unspoiled mountain landscapes, pristine coastline, caves, historical places, Launceston and Hobart casinos, national parks, fishing, Franklin River, magnificent seascapes, Tasmanian devil, Gordon River, Port Arthur. Tasmania is known as 'The Holiday Isle', and tourism is an important industry.

DID YOU KNOW?
Tasmania's tranquil Lake St Clair is over 200 metres deep, and occupies a basin gouged out by two glaciers more than 20 000 years ago.

Coat of arms

The present coat of arms was granted by King George V in 1917. It incorporates a shield on which is depicted a ram, a sheaf of wheat and apples, representing the pastoral and agricultural industries. Also included is a thunderbolt, which represents the hydro-electric schemes. The crest consists of a red lion standing with one paw resting on a spade and pickaxe, which represent the mining industry. The shield is supported by two Tasmanian tigers. They are standing on ornamental supports above the motto *Ubertas et fidelitas* ('Fruitfulness and faithfulness').

Flag

The flag of Tasmania is based on the Blue Ensign, with the badge of the state superimposed on the right-hand side. It consists of a red lion in a white shield. This badge was chosen in 1876.

DID YOU KNOW?

To prevent convicts escaping from the penal settlement at Port Arthur, a pack of ferocious dogs guarded the Eaglehawk Neck isthmus leading to Forestier Peninsula, which was the convicts' only avenue of escape by land.

Major festivals and events

January	Cygnet Huon Folk Festival
	Hobart Summer Festival
February	Devonport Food & Wine Festival
March	Devonport Regatta
	Launceston Night in the Gorge
May	Richmond Harvest Festival
October	Burnie Rhododendron Festival
	Royal Hobart Agricultural Show
	Launceston Garden Festival
November	Deloraine Tasmanian Craft Fair
December	Sydney–Hobart Yacht Race (finish)

Sister cities (selection)

Hobart	Invercargill (New Zealand), Yaizu (Japan)
Launceston	Ikeda (Japan), Launceston (UK), Livingston (Zambia), Seremban (Malaysia)

Port Arthur, Tasmania.

Northern Territory

receives heavy rainfall for three to five months of the year; and the southern area, known as 'The Centre', has a low rainfall and no permanent rivers.

Administrative centre

Darwin is situated in Beagle Gulf on the Timor Sea, and is 1660 square kilometres in area. It has a population of 86 576. Average daily hours of sunshine: 8.5.

Chief towns

Darwin	86 576
Alice Springs & environs	36 910
Katherine	9856
Tennant Creek & environs	5634
Nhulunbuy	3719

Location

The Northern Territory occupies a huge area of the continent's north and centre. It is bordered by the Timor Sea to the north, Queensland to the east, Western Australia to the west, and South Australia to the south. It is often referred to as 'Outback Australia'.

Area

The Northern Territory comprises one-sixth of Australia's land mass and is 1 346 200 square kilometres in area.

Landform

Mostly desert and tablelands.

Population

194 221. Few people live in the vast dry areas, and almost half of the population are residents of Darwin. More than one-quarter of the people are Aborigines.

Climate

The Northern Territory lies in the torrid zone. There are two broad climatic divisions: the northern part, known as 'The Top End',

Northern Territory animal emblem: red kangaroo.

Northern Territory floral emblem: Sturt's desert rose.

Industries contributing to Northern Territory's gross state product

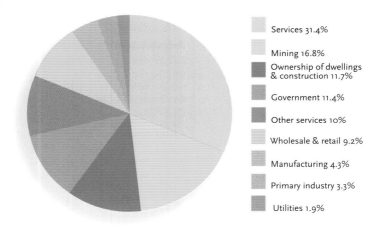

Services 31.4%

Mining 16.8%

Ownership of dwellings & construction 11.7%

Government 11.4%

Other services 10%

Wholesale & retail 9.2%

Manufacturing 4.3%

Primary industry 3.3%

Utilities 1.9%

Chief products

Agriculture:
Beef cattle, citrus fruits, lucerne, peanuts, pineapples, timber, tomatoes.

Fishing:
Fish and prawns.

Mining:
Bauxite-aluminium, copper, gold, iron, manganese, tin, uranium.

Main Attractions
Kata Tjuta National Park (Mt Olga), Kings Canyon, Standley Chasm, The Ghan (train from Adelaide to Alice Springs), Katherine Gorge, Kakadu National Park, Uluru (Ayers Rock), Devil's Marbles, Mataranka thermal pools, Litchfield National Park.

DID YOU KNOW?

Uluru (Ayers Rock) is a monolith of greyish-red arkose standing 860 metres above sea level. It is 8.85 kilometres in circumference, and is 347.3 metres above the plain.

Coat of arms

The present coat of arms was granted by Queen Elizabeth II in 1978. It incorporates a shield depicting an Arnhem Land rock painting of an Aboriginal woman. On either side there are stylised journey or path markings of the Aborigines. The shield is supported by two red kangaroos. In the forepaw of one is a true heart cockle and in the forepaw of the other is a spider conch. This all rests on a grassy mound from which grow Sturt's desert roses. The crest consists of a wedge-tailed eagle with wings splayed and its talons grasping an Aboriginal ritual stone or *Tjurunga*.

NORTHERN TERRITORY

Flag

The flag of the Northern Territory is very different from the other states' flags. Traditional Territory colours are used: black, white and red ochre. The stars on the black panel represent the Southern Cross. On the red ochre panel appears Sturt's desert rose. This flag was proclaimed in 1978.

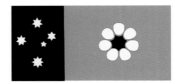

DID YOU KNOW?

Lake Eyre, 16 metres below sea level, is the lowest elevation in Australia. It is also the driest area, receiving only 8–12 millimetres of annual rainfall. Alice Springs is 609.6 metres above sea level.

Major festivals

May	Alice Springs Bangtail Muster
	Tennant Creek Cup Day
June	Katherine Barunga Sport & Cultural Festival
July	Alice Springs Camel Cup
	Darwin Agricultural Show
	Darwin International Guitar Festival
	(odd-numbered years)
August	Darwin Beer Can Regatta
	Mataranka Rodeo
September	Festival of Darwin
	Tennant Creek Desert Harmony Festival
October	Alice Springs Henley-on-Todd Regatta

Sister cities (selection)

Darwin	Ambon (Indonesia), Anchorage (Alaska, USA), Kalymnos (Greece), Xiamen (China)

Devil's Marbles, Northern Territory.

DID YOU KNOW?

Uluru (Ayers Rock) is almost at the centre of the Australian continent. As the crow flies, it is 2300 kilometres from Brisbane, 2100 kilometres from Sydney, 1900 kilometres from Melbourne, 1300 kilometres from Adelaide, 1600 kilometres from Perth, and 1450 kilometres from Darwin.

Prime ministers

Sir Edmund Barton
(1 Jan 1901–24 Sept 1903)

Alfred Deakin
(24 Sept 1903–27 Apr 1904)

John Christian Watson
(27 Apr 1904–18 Aug 1904)

George Reid
(18 Aug 1904–5 July 1905)

Alfred Deakin
(5 July 1905–13 Nov 1908)

Andrew Fisher
(13 Nov 1908–2 June 1909)

Alfred Deakin
(2 June 1909–29 Apr 1910)

Andrew Fisher
(29 Apr 1910–24 June 1913)

Sir Joseph Cook
(24 June 1913–17 Sept 1914)

Andrew Fisher
(17 Sept 1914–27 Oct 1915)

William Morris Hughes
(27 Oct 1915–9 Feb 1922)

Stanley Melbourne Bruce
(9 Feb 1922–22 Oct 1929)

James Henry Scullin
(22 Oct 1929–6 Jan 1932)

Joseph Aloysius Lyons
(6 Jan 1932–7 Apr 1939)

Sir Earle Page
(7 Apr 1939–26 Apr 1939)

Sir Robert Gordon Menzies
(26 Apr 1939–29 Aug 1941)

Sir Arthur W Fadden
(29 Aug 1941–7 Oct 1941)

John Curtin
(7 Oct 1941–5 July 1945)

Francis Michael Forde
(5 July 1945–13 July 1945)

Joseph Benedict Chifley
(13 July 1945–19 Dec 1949)

Sir Robert Gordon Menzies
(19 Dec 1949–26 Jan 1966)

Harold Edward Holt
(26 Jan 1966–19 Dec 1967)

Sir John McEwen
(19 Dec 1967–10 Jan 1968)

Sir John Grey Gorton
(10 Jan 1968–10 Mar 1971)

Sir William McMahon
(10 Mar 1971–8 Dec 1972)

Edward Gough Whitlam
(8 Dec 1972–11 Nov 1975)

John Malcolm Fraser
(11 Nov 1975–5 Mar 1983)
(caretaker prime minister from
11 Nov 1975–13 Dec 1975)

Robert James Hawke
(5 Mar 1983–19 Dec 1991)

Paul John Keating
(19 Dec 1991–2 Mar 1996)

John Winston Howard
(2 Mar 1996–)

Architects

In the early years of settlement, most buildings were primitive. It was not until Governor Macquarie came to the colony in 1810 that an extensive building programme was commenced. Gothic and Regency styles were predominant and although impressive and aesthetically pleasing, they were more suited to the European climate. In latter years, taking into account our climate and lifestyle, 'Federation' style, the forerunner to more contemporary architecture evolved, bringing a warmth and texture better suited to our conditions.

Colonial architects, planners and builders

James Blackburn 1803–54
One of Tasmania's advanced architects, he was responsible for many beautiful Gothic-style buildings of the 1830s. He designed the Yan Yean Reservoir in Victoria in 1849, and was considered to be one of the greatest engineers of that time.

Edmund Blacket 1817–83
One of our great colonial architects of churches and public buildings. His most famous building is the Great Hall of the University of Sydney, built in 1857 and considered to be the finest example of Gothic Revival style in Australia.

James Bloodsworth c. 1759–unknown
A convict brick maker who was appointed Superintendent of Buildings in 1788. He built the first permanent dwelling for Governor Phillip in 1789 – the first two-storey structure in Sydney. The foundations were unearthed in 1983.

Governor Ralph Darling 1775–1858
He introduced the Rippon Land

DID YOU KNOW?

By the mid-19th century, Francis Greenway's Georgian buildings were considered passé, and were being demolished to make way for more 'acceptable' styles. He died penniless and is thought to be buried near Maitland, New South Wales.

Regulations of 1831, which controlled allotment sizes, building alignments and street layouts. Main streets were designated 30 metres wide and secondary streets 24 metres wide.

Francis Greenway 1777–1837

In 1816 a convict named Greenway became the colony's official architect, under the guidance of Governor Macquarie. In a space of 20 years, he designed more than 40 buildings including Macquarie Lighthouse at South Head, for which he obtained his pardon.

Colonel William Light 1786–1839

The founder of Adelaide, he was responsible for the layout of the city in 1837. It is considered a fine example of a Georgian town.

Architects of the 20th century

Robin Boyd 1919–71

He was a writer as well as an architect. An influential critic of Australian aesthetics, he wrote *The Australian Ugliness* in 1960.

Philip Cox 1939–

An architect with a sound knowledge of history and a keen appreciation of the visual. His wide-ranging works include Tocal Agricultural College, New South Wales, Sydney's Star City Casino, Canberra's Bruce Stadium and the Singapore Megacentre.

Victorian Arts Centre.

Walter Burley Griffin 1876–1937

An American whose brilliant plan won first prize in the worldwide competition for the design of Australia's national capital, Canberra, in 1913. Later he and his wife designed the highly innovative Capitol Theatre in Melbourne, and in 1924 they designed the harbourside suburb of Castlecrag, Sydney.

Sir Roy Grounds 1905–81

An exponent of the new 'international' style of architecture of the 1950s, best known for his Academy of Sciences building in Canberra and the Victorian Arts Centre in Melbourne.

Harry Seidler 1923–

Contemporary Australian architect. Designed Australia Square Tower and the MLC Centre in Sydney, the Hong Kong Club, and the Australian embassy in Paris.

Jørn Utzon 1918–

The Danish architect and designer of the Sydney Opera House broke new ground in design and use of building materials. Construction began in 1959, and the Opera House was officially opened in 1973 by Queen Elizabeth II. Three Australian architects, Peter Hall, David Littlemore and Lionel Todd, took over from Utzon in 1966. In 1999 Utzon was invited back as a consultant to review the acoustics of the Concert Hall.

Aviators

Many contributed to the race to be airborne, and once it was possible, many joined another race – the race to conquer Australia's distance and isolation from the rest of the world.

Sir Reginald Ansett 1909–81

A businessman and outspoken champion of private enterprise, his companies were involved in aviation, transport, tourism and television.

Maude (Lores) Bonney 1897–1994

In the 'golden age' of aviation between 1934 and 1937 she was the first woman to circumnavigate Australia by air, the first woman to fly from Australia to England, and the first person to link Australia with South Africa by air.

John Duigan 1882–1951

In 1910 he constructed the first Australian-built aeroplane to fly.

Sir Hudson Fysh 1895–1974

Together with P. J. McGinness he founded the Queensland and Northern Territory Air Services (QANTAS) airline in 1920.

Lawrence Hargrave 1850–1915 and George A. Taylor 1872–1928

In the 1890s these two men experimented with box kites. In 1909 Taylor achieved a flight of 100 metres at Narrabeen Heads, in Sydney.

Harry George Hawker 1889–1921

Became internationally famous in 1913 for the most successful attempt to circumnavigate the British Isles in 72 hours.

Bert Hinkler 1892–1933

Known as 'The Lone Eagle', in 1928, he flew the longest solo flight from London to Darwin, in a record 16 days.

DID YOU KNOW?

Sydney International Airport is named after the famous Brisbane-born aviator, Sir Charles Kingsford Smith, who pioneered air routes from Australia across the world. His most famous plane, the *Southern Cross*, is preserved at Brisbane Airport.

Amy Johnson 1903–41

The first woman to fly from England to Australia. Her 1930 epic solo flight, in a D H Moth, took 19 days.

Sir Charles Kingsford Smith 1897–1935

Pioneer aviator. In 1928, flying the famous monoplane the *Southern Cross*, Kingsford Smith, Charles Ulm (1897–1934) and two Americans were the first men to fly across the Pacific from America to Australia. This venture included one of the longest non-stop flights ever attempted, between Honolulu and Suva (35 hours). Total flying time: 83 hours 38 minutes.

Keith Smith 1890–1955 and Ross Smith 1892–1922

Pioneered the London to Sydney air route in 1919, taking 27 days 27 minutes – total flying time for the 18 500 kilometres was 135 hours 50 minutes.

Andy Thomas 1951–

Aerodynamic scientist who headed a research program into microgravity materials processing in space for NASA. In 1996 he was named payload commander for the STS-77 and became Australia's first astronaut, completing 160 orbits of the earth.

People in business

Corporate failures, Royal Commissions, beleaguered businessmen and high interest rates was the scenario after the turbulent collapse of the stock market in October 1987. Shareholders suffered while some entrepreneurs were jailed and some went abroad. October 1997, almost 10 years to the day, saw a substantial stock market correction but without many of the subsequent problems. Over the years, Australia has been fortunate in having many well-respected businessmen and women.

Mount Tom Price, Western Australia.

142

Sir Peter Abeles 1924–99
His astute management from 1967 to 1992 enabled TNT to expand worldwide.

Dr Herbert Cole (Nugget) Coombs 1906–97
An economist, he was Governor of the Reserve Bank until 1968, and advised prime ministers as well as governments on fiscal policy in the postwar years.

Sir Warwick Fairfax 1901–87
Former chairman of John Fairfax Ltd, with interests in newspapers, magazines, TV and radio. His influence on the editorial policy of the *Sydney Morning Herald* had a great impact on Australian society.

Lang Hancock 1909–92
Discovered massive iron ore deposits in the Pilbara region, Western Australia, where he had begun the Australian iron ore mining industry in 1952–62.

Janet Holmes à Court 1943–
An exceptional businesswoman who, after the untimely death of her husband, Robert, took control of his multimillion-dollar empire, Heytesbury Holdings, with great ability and acumen.

Ian Kiernan.

Robert Holmes à Court 1937–90
Renowned for his astute business perception in assessing takeover opportunities in the heady days of the 1980s, his abortive attempts to take over BHP forced it to reassess its vulnerability.

Sir Sidney Kidman 1857–1935
He left home at 13 with a one-eyed horse called Cyclops, and five shillings (50 cents) in his pocket to become one of the largest landowners in Australian history. Some estimate that he owned nearly 495 000 square kilometres of land in the interior.

Ian Kiernan 1940–
A builder and around-the-world solo yachtsman, his 1989 vision for a cleaner environment began the Clean Up Australia movement. This is now the largest community environment organisation in Australia and its philosophy has spread to many other countries.

John Macarthur 1767–1834
A pioneer pastoralist, entrepreneur and exporter of wool to England in the early days of the colony. He and his wife, Elizabeth, made a great contribution to the wool industry by successfully breeding fine wool merino sheep.

Rupert Murdoch 1931–
An international media magnate, he became an American citizen in 1985. Chief Executive of News Corporation and Chair of Fox Inc., he owns newspaper and TV stations, and has interests in energy resources around the world.

Kerry Packer 1937–
Chair of Consolidated Press Holdings Ltd and Publishing and Broadcasting Ltd. He remains Australia's richest man, with vast commercial and rural holdings.

Dick Smith 1944–
A millionaire adventurer whose wealth emerged from a chain of electronic goods stores, for which he was the marketable front man. He is the philanthropist behind many organisations, notably the *Australian Geographic* magazine and stores.

'For gorsake, stop laughing: this is serious!'
Cartoon by Stan Cross.

Cartoonists

There has always been a recognisable Australian style of cartoon, which is an ever-popular part of the printed page.

J.C. Banks 1880–1952
Created the much-loved character of Ginger Meggs, whom he drew for 21 years.

Frank Benier c. 1923–
A highly talented traditional cartoonist whose cartoons of Henry Bolte, the premier of Victoria 1955–72, are legendary.

Stan Cross 1888–1977
An American, he created the long-running comic strip 'The Potts' in 1919. He drew for *Smith's Weekly* and in 1933 he was responsible for what is thought to be one of Australia's funniest cartoons (see above).

Eric Jolliffe c. 1907–
A postwar comic artist whose series *Witchetty's Tribe*, with its contrasts of Aboriginal and Western values, has been popular for decades.

Michael Leunig 1945–
Whimsy and sad absurdity envelop his humanoid heroes, who represent eternal innocence and truth. He enjoys cult status abroad.

Lennie Lower 1903–47
A prolific newspaper columnist and humorist of the 1930s and 40s. His collection of humorous sketches, *Here's Another*, appeared in 1932.

Emile Mercier 1901–81
A vigorous comic artist of the 1950s and 60s whose zany humour is forever remembered for its incidental details, particularly about gravy cans.

Alan Moir 1947–
A political cartoonist who prides himself on being equally unfair to all sides. His cartoons are nationally syndicated to over 100 newspapers.

George Molnar 1910–98
His cool, calculated line punctured the vanities of contemporary society, mocking its hypocrisy.

Syd Nicholls 1897–1977
His cartoon character Fatty Finn was second only to Ginger Meggs in popularity and longevity.

Bruce Petty 1929–
Widely regarded as one of the world's finest political cartoonists, his cartoons first appeared in *The Australian* in 1965.

Ron Tandberg 1943–
A political cartoonist with major newspapers. His simple line drawings make terse comments on current news stories.

Innovators

Most original ideas that succeed are usually developed from a great need to make life easier. The following are some noteworthy Australians who have proved the old adage that 'necessity is the mother of invention'.

Sir John (Jack) Brabham 1926–
Racing-car driver. He went from winning the 1948 Australian Speedway Championship in a home-made car to winning three World Grand Prix.

John Bradfield 1867–1943
Supervising engineer of the Sydney Harbour Bridge, which was begun in 1923 and completed in 1932, at a cost of £9 577 507 (equivalent to about $200 m in current terms).

William James Farrer 1845–1906
Agricultural scientist whose pioneering development in the late 1800s of early strains of wheat (particularly the

'Federation' variety), laid the foundation for the Australian wheat industry.

Sir Edward Hallstrom 1886–1970

Philanthropist, zoologist and inventor who helped develop refrigeration in Australia. His 1940s plan was for every Australian household to have a Silent Knight refrigerator.

James Harrison 1815–93

Founder of the *Geelong Advertiser*. He discovered that if ether was used to clean a metal surface, it made the metal cooler as it evaporated, thus identifying the key factor in refrigeration. Between 1852 and 1857 he experimented in a cave, eventually producing the world's first artificial ice.

Sir William Hudson 1896–1978

Commissioner in charge of the Snowy Mountains Hydro-Electric Scheme which diverts the waters of the Snowy and Eucumbene Rivers through two tunnel systems, westwards under the Great Dividing Range, to feed two inland rivers, the Murray and Murrumbidgee. The scheme provides water for irrigation and also produces electricity from seven power stations for New South Wales, Victoria, and the Australian Capital Territory.

Walter Hume 1873–1943

Inventor who disregarded conventional theories. His centrifugal painting machine led to his inventing the Hume-spun concrete pipes, an innovation of international significance; factories all over the world now make pipes by the Hume-spun method.

Sir George Julius 1873–1946

Engineer whose totalisator machine of 1913 and the fully automatic totalisator of 1932 sold worldwide.

Ben Lexcen 1936–88

One of Australia's great marine designers. He designed the famed *Australia II*, a 12-metre yacht with an incredible 'winged keel', which in 1983 won for Australia the America's Cup – the first time in 132 years that America had lost the cup.

Herbert Lysaght 1862–1940

The father of galvanised iron. He transformed urban and rural architecture with its price and availability. One of the pioneers of the Australian iron industry, he contributed to the creation of Newcastle and Wollongong as 'steel cities'.

Hugh Victor McKay 1865–1926

His 1884 invention, the stripper-harvester, not only stripped but also threshed and cleaned grain. He established many factories for reproducing the Sunshine Harvester, and revolutionised the wheat industry.

Evelyn Ernest Owen 1915–49

In the 1930s he invented the revolutionary Owen sub-machine gun.

Mervyn Victor Richardson 1894–1972

He invented the Victa rotary mower in 1952–53, which revolutionised lawn mowing for future generations.

John Ridley 1806–87

Pioneer miller and inventor, who in 1842 developed the Ridley Stripper, a machine which proved so popular that, by 1855, 30 000 had been sold.

Ralph Sarich 1938–

Inventor with many innovative projects to his credit in the fields of fuel injection and irrigation systems. He is widely known for his research in the development of the orbital combustion process engine and associated technologies.

Robert Bowyer Smith 1838–1918

Frustrated with trying to conquer the scrub on the Yorke Peninsula, South Australia, he devised a plough that could rise above stumps. The stump-jump plough revolutionised ploughing in the late 1800s.

Henry Sutton 1856–1912

Prolific innovator well ahead of

'Big Lizzie'.

DID YOU KNOW?

'Big Lizzie', invention of Mr Frank Bettrill, was built in 1914–15 at the McDonald foundry, Richmond, Victoria, to cart wool and wheat in the outback. In 1920, it was used to clear land for Australia's largest soldier settlement at Red Cliffs, Victoria. It was 10.4 metres long, 3.6 metres wide and 5.5 metres high and weighed 46 tonnes, with a normal speed of 1.6 kilometres per hour.

his time. Born in a tent on the Ballarat goldfields, at 14 years of age he invented an electric motor – later it was developed by a Belgian and called the 'gramme'. It became the basis for dynamos, the standard form of electric motors used by industry after 1871.

Headlie Taylor 1883–1957
Although self-taught, he was considered one of the greatest innovators of the industrial age and was the most prolific and persistent inventor of farm machinery in Australia. His most famous invention was the spiral auger header harvester of 1913, later to be redesigned to be self-propelled.

David Warren 1925–
He invented the prototype of the black box flight recorder in 1954. This flight memory device was rejected at first in favour of inferior imported products. Eventually, Warren's work was used as the basis for tens of thousands of black box flight recorders after his design was copied by a British firm. He received no compensation.

John Paul Wild 1923–
Radiophysicist, whose interest in and subsequent experiments on the effects of the sun's rays on the earth's surface led to the development of Interscan, a new type of radio landing-gear for aircraft. He was chair of the Commonwealth Scientific and Industrial Research Organisation (CSIRO) from 1978 to 1991.

Australia is internationally renowned for breaking new ground in many areas in the fields of science and medicine. Here are a few individuals who have made outstanding contributions.

Sir (William) Henry Bragg 1862–1942 and Sir (William) Lawrence Bragg 1890–1971
Father and son who jointly won the Nobel prize for physics in 1915. They devised X-ray crystallography, which changed the way the world studied molecular structures. This had important consequences for both medicine and metallurgy.

Sir Macfarlane Burnet 1899–1985
Virologist and immunologist. Winner of the Nobel prize for medicine, noted for his research into the control of disease, particularly poliomyelitis.

Dr Victor Chang 1936–91
He re-established the heart transplant program at St Vincent's Hospital, Sydney, in 1984 after a lapse of 10 years. Since then over 850 transplants have been performed with a five-year survival rate of just over 80%. In 1986 he and his team performed the first heart/lung transplant in Australia, and in 1990 the first lung transplant. He was murdered in 1991.

Professor Graeme Clarke 1935–
A researcher of great ability. When

he was Professor of Otolaryngology at Melbourne University in the late 1970s he was responsible for the development of the bionic ear, a cochlear implant designed to provide electrical stimulation to the inner ear to overcome profound deafness.

Sir Ian Clunies-Ross 1899–1959

Veterinary scientist and administrator and the first director of the CSIRO.

Dr Peter Douherty 1941–

He received the Nobel prize for medicine for his work in scientific research, particularly in the role of major histocompatibility complex proteins in cell medicated immunity.

Sir Edward 'Weary' Dunlop 1907–93

In World War II he was appointed commander of the Allied General Hospital in Java, in 1942. He became a Japanese prisoner of war. Through the testimony of hundreds of returning prisoners it was clear that he became their inspiration in the fight for physical and spiritual survival against the horrors of the Burma–Thailand railway prison camps.

Sir John Eccles 1903–97

Scientist who contributed greatly to the knowledge of the way nerves interact with the spinal cord.

Baron (Howard) Florey 1898–1968

Scientist and Nobel prize winner. He carried out crucial experiments in the 1930s and 40s that demonstrated the great therapeutic value of penicillin.

Reverend John Flynn 1880–1951

Founder of the world-acclaimed Royal Flying Doctor Service. In 1928, with the help of Alf Traegar's pedal radio, he began a medical service for the people of the outback.

Professor Fred Hollows 1929–93

Former chairman of ophthalmology at the University of New South Wales, he was also co-founder of the Aboriginal Medical Service. He was director of the National Trachoma and Eye Health Program, and worked extensively in Vietnam, Eritrea and Nepal establishing eye health programs.

Sister Elizabeth Kenny 1880–1952

A world-recognised nurse/ innovator. In the 1930s, with the royalties from a revolutionary stretcher she invented, she opened one of many worldwide clinics, where she achieved remarkable success in the treatment of the life-threatening disease poliomyelitis.

Dr Priscilla Kincaid-Smith 1926–

In 1968, as director of nephrology at Royal Melbourne Hospital, she was the first person to realise that renal disease was linked to long-term use of analgesics.

Dr Eric Le Page c. 1958–

Led an eight-year study of a revolutionary early warning system which can detect hearing loss years in advance. Previously, 70 per cent of hearing loss had occurred before the problem was detected, but this system meant major damage could be prevented even in new born babies.

Sir Gustav Nossal 1931–
A distinguished medical biologist. His contributions to the field of antibody formation and immunological tolerance were of worldwide significance. He was the director of the Walter and Eliza Hall Institute of Medical Research (1965–96) and the president of the Australian Academy of Science (1994–98).

Sir Marcus Oliphant 1901–
Nuclear physicist and the first president of the Australian Academy of Science. Assistant director of research at the Cavendish Laboratory in Cambridge in 1935. He is a strong opponent of nuclear weapons.

William Redfern 1774–1833
Pardoned convict who was assistant surgeon at Norfolk Island prison hospital before he was placed in charge of Sydney Hospital in 1816. In 1814 he assisted in what was said to be the first public health report in Australian history, which exposed the horrifying conditions aboard convict ships.

Dr Harry Windsor 1914–87
He pioneered and performed the first mitral valvotomy in Australia (1950), and the first aortic valve replacement, in 1963, which led to the first heart transplant in Australia in 1968.

The international acceptance of Australian literature over the past four decades has resulted in an exciting period of extraordinary diversity among Australian writers, who have made a great contribution to the way Australians perceive themselves. This modest list is just a cursory view of some past and present authors noted for their craftsmanship and originality.

Novelists and writers

Thea Astley 1925–
Novelist and three-time winner of the Miles Franklin award. Her books include *An Item from the Late News*, *It's Raining in Mango* and *Drylands*.

Murray Bail 1941–
He experimented with a new form of short story writing in the 1970s. *Contemporary Portraits and Other Stories*, *Homesickness* and *Holden's Performance* show his preoccupation with the way environment shapes identity. He won the 1999 Miles Franklin award for his novel *Eucalyptus*.

Peter Carey 1943–
Considered to be one of our finest novelists, he won the prestigious Booker Prize in 1988 and the coveted Miles Franklin award for his novel *Oscar and Lucinda*. In 1981 he wrote the movie script for *Bliss*, then came *Illywhacker*, *The Unusual Life of Tristan Smith* and *Jack Maggs*.

Professor Manning Clark 1915–91
His six-volume *History of Australia* is a valuable reference point for gaining an understanding of the forces and events which shaped Australia.

Jon Cleary 1917–
Acclaimed novelist and scriptwriter whose 1947 novel, *You Can't See Round Corners*, launched his career, which spanned stories of inner-city poverty to screenplays for Hollywood. *The Sundowners*, *The High Commissioner* and *Dark Summer* are well-known works.

Peter Corris 1942–
A skilful and sophisticated writer of detective yarns which are pithy and episodic. *White Meat* and *The Empty Beach* are a few in the series of stories about Cliff Hardy, champion-of-the-underdog investigator.

Bryce Courtenay 1933–
He enjoyed a successful advertising career before he wrote his first novel, *The Power of One*, at the age of 55. This novel became an instant bestseller and the forerunner to many more, including *April Fool's Day*, *The Potato Factory*, *Tommo & Hawk* and *Jessica*, making him Australia's bestselling author with substantial sales worldwide.

Blanche d'Alpuget 1944–
Her thumbnail descriptions of characters and atmosphere, together with her quick wit and competence, have produced engaging novels such as *Monkeys in the Dark*, *Turtle Beach* and *Winter in Jerusalem*.

Marele Day 1947–
Contemporary crime writer who uses inner-city Chinatown and Asian-populated suburbs as rich settings for her lively 'whodunits', such as *The Case of the Chinese Boxes*. Her novel *Lambs of God* was nominated for the Dublin Literary Award in 1999.

Robert Drewe 1943–
He draws ironic parallels in his short stories and novels which on the surface seem simple, but are full of inner disturbances and insecurities. *A Cry in the Jungle Bar*, *The Bodysurfers*, *The Bay of Contented Men* and *The Drowner* confirm his skill as a storyteller.

Miles Franklin 1879–1954
She wrote the satirical novels *My Brilliant Career*, *All That Swagger* and *My Career Goes Bung*. The Miles Franklin Award, a bequest from her estate, is awarded annually for a novel portraying some aspect of Australian life.

DID YOU KNOW?

The oldest daily newspaper in the Southern Hemisphere is the *Sydney Morning Herald* (1831).

Helen Garner 1942–
A writer of subtly structured novels, she is concerned with the undramatic daily encounters of modern living and the loneliness of 20th-century life. Works include *Monkey Grip*, *The Children's Bach* and *The First Stone*.

Kate Grenville 1950–
Lilian's Story, *Joan Makes History*, *Dark Places* and *The Idea of Perfection* are examples of her ingeniously conceived stories, which have a strong feminist theme and contain a touch of black comedy.

Frank Hardy 1917–94
A hard-hitting novelist and writer, his remarkable fact–fiction account of crime in *Power Without Glory* resulted in an unsuccessful libel suit against him. *But the Dead Are Many* is considered to be his masterpiece.

Robert Hughes 1938–
His ability as an art critic enabled him to compile the massive work *The Art of Australia*. His most significant work is *The Fatal Shore*, an exposé of the British policy of colonisation in New South Wales, which Hughes maintains was to expel the undesirable and not for gain and power in the Pacific, a more popular belief.

David Ireland 1927–
One of Australia's foremost novelists, he has won the Miles Franklin award three times. His works include *The Unknown Industrial Prisoner*, *The Glass Canoe*, A *Woman of the Future*, *Bloodfather* and *The Chosen*.

Elizabeth Jolley 1923–
Her novels deal not so much with characters but with the implied relationships between characters. They include *Miss Peabody's Inheritance*, *The Well*, and the trilogy *My Father's Moon, Cabin Fever* and *The Georges' Wife*.

Thomas Keneally 1935–
Won the Miles Franklin award in 1967 for his novel *Bring Larks and Heroes*. He wrote *The Chant of Jimmie Blacksmith* and *Schindler's Ark,* which won the Booker Prize and inspired Steven Spielberg's film *Schindler's List*.

Christopher Koch 1932–
One of Australia's finest writers, he pursues related themes through symbolism and imagery with care and sensitivity. Included in his works are *The Boys in the Island*, *The Year of Living Dangerously, The Doubleman* and *Highways to a War*.

Morris Lurie 1938–
Writes in a variety of genres from autobiographical to children's literature but is best known for his short stories, such as *Rappaport* and *Flying Home*. The novel *Two Brothers Running* shows his deft and economical use of words.

David Malouf 1934–
A poet and novelist, his works include *Johnno*, *Fly Away Peter*, *The Great World*, *An Imaginary Life*, *Remembering Babylon* and a collection of sensitive short stories, *Antipodes*.

Sally Morgan 1951–
An Aboriginal author and artist, her sensitive novels include the autobiographical *My Place* and *Wanamurraganya*.

Ruth Park 1926–
A skilful storyteller, her success was assured in 1947 when *The Harp in the South* won critical acclaim. Her stories deal with hard times and how ordinary people struggle to survive. Other novels include *Poor Man's Orange* and *Swords and Crowns and Rings*.

Hal Porter 1911–84
His intricately woven and studied style controlled his conscious attempts to capture the complex texture of experience. His works include the novels *A Handful of Pennies* and *The Watcher on the Cast-Iron Balcony* and the play *Eden House*.

Henry Handel Richardson 1870–1946
The pen-name of Ethel Robertson. In 1917 she began work on her masterpiece trilogy *The Fortunes of Richard Mahony*, fully published in 1930, to great acclaim.

Morris West 1916–99
He deliberately sought experiences to enrich his writing. His novels include *Children of the Sun*, *The Shoes of the Fishermen* and *The Devil's Advocate*.

Patrick White 1912–90
Considered to be Australia's greatest novelist, he was the first Australian writer to be awarded the Nobel prize for literature (1973). His publications include *The Tree of Man, Voss, The Vivisector, A Fringe of Leaves, The Twyborn Affair* and an autobiography, *Flaws in the Glass*.

Tim Winton 1960–
A prolific writer, he wrote five novels in six years. *Cloudstreet* won the Miles Franklin Award in 1992. This and *The Riders* show his preoccupation with place.

Other writers are: Dora Birtles, James Bradley, Judy Brett, Brian Castro, Bernard Cohen, Eleanor Dark, Nick Earls, Richard Flanagan, David Foster, Tom Gilling, Germaine Greer, Rodney Hall, Shirley Hazzard, Xavier Herbert, Donald Horne, Janette Turner Hospital, Ion Idriess, George Johnston, Fiona McGregor, Drusilla Modjeska, Frank Moorhouse, Brenda Niall, Katharine Susannah Prichard, Steele Rudd, Mandy Sayer, Christina Stead, Randolph Stow, Kylie Tennant, Christos Tsiolkas, Archie Weller, Amy Witting and Beth Yahp.

Playwrights

Richard Beynon 1925–99
An actor and TV writer as well as a playwright, in 1957 he wrote *The Shifting Heart*, regarded as one of the first plays to address homegrown Australian intolerance towards immigration.

Alex Buzo 1944–
A satirist of Australian morals and manners, he wrote the plays *Martello Towers* and *Norm*

and Ahmed, and the novel *The Search for Harry Allway*.

Jack Davis 1917–
He saw first-hand the injustices tribal Aborigines suffered, and his subsequent plays *The Dreamers* and *No Sugar* suggest that dependency and pessimism can only be broken by a change in the Aborigines' view of themselves.

Sumner Locke Elliott 1917–91
An actor and a writer for radio. There was a public storm over censorship of language when his play *Rusty Bugles* was produced in 1949. His novel *Careful, He Might Hear You* was made into a film in 1983.

Ray Lawler 1921–
Playwright and actor. His play *Summer of the Seventeenth Doll*, regarded as an Australian classic, challenges mateship and toughness and broke new ground in Australian theatre in 1955.

Louis Nowra 1950–
A prolific writer of plays, screenplays and novels. His epic style of writing borders on black comedy and is concerned with timeless questions about human motivations and passions. *Inner Voices, The Precious Woman* and *Cosi* are three of his plays and *Misery of Beauty* and *Red Nights* are among his novels.

Hannie Rayson 1957–
A freelance journalist, editor, playwright and scriptwriter, her plays include *Room to Move* and *Hotel Sorrento*. She presents characters who struggle with changing attitudes, cultural belonging, loyalty and betrayal.

Alan Seymour 1927–
A theatre critic, he wrote for the stage and TV, drawing frequently on life in the 1940s. His *The One Day of the Year*, a benchmark play, questioned the traditional veneration of Anzac Day. Other plays include *Swamp Creatures* and *A Break in the Music*.

David Williamson 1942–
Internationally acclaimed playwright. His raucous, fast-moving plots are witty and recognisable, and his plays include *Don's Party, The Removalists, The Club, Emerald City* and *Brilliant Lies*. He wrote the screenplays for *Gallipoli* and *Phar Lap*.

Other playwrights are: Janis Balodis and Peter Kenna.

Poets

Bruce Dawe 1930–
Poet and novelist whose work reinforces the simple truths in a world of confused morals. *No Fixed Address*, and *This Side of Silence* are statements of his crusading zeal.

C.J. Dennis 1876–1938
He was known as 'the laureate of the larrikin' because he wrote a series of verse stories told in slang. One of these was the bestseller of World War I, *The Song of a Sentimental Bloke*.

Rosemary Dobson 1920–
A love of art and antiquity reflects her conviction of the supremacy of Art over Time. She captures moments of existence in word paintings that show a sharp awareness of the joy of life over mortality, such as in *The Greek Coins*.

Geoffrey Dutton 1922–98
Part of the Angry Penguins group, this versatile writer's easy reflective lyrics marked by strong word pictures, in *Antipodes in Shoes* and *Night Flight and Sunrise*, celebrate his joy and love of nature.

Dame Mary Gilmore 1865–1962
Poet, writer and social worker who championed the underdog. Among her works are *The Passionate Heart*, *Old Days, Old Ways* and *Battlefields*.

Gwen Harwood 1920–95
Her fluid narrative and colloquial tone made her distinctive lyrical poetry impressive and compelling. Works such as *Night and Dreams* and *The Lion's Bride* reinforced her view that life could be exquisitely rhapsodic yet sharp with the pain of memory.

Dorothy Hewett 1923–
With romantic vigour and frankness she pursues a quest for self-discovery that is both liberating and restraining. Her poems include 'What About the People!' and 'A Tremendous World in her Head'.

A.D. Hope 1907–
Noted for his sarcastic wit and precise expression. His poetry deals with disillusionment with human nature, blended with compassion. His many works include *The Wandering Islands*, *The Drifting Continent* and *Antechinus*.

John Kinsella 1963–
His intense and lyrical poetry depicts the light, heat and dryness of the desert landscape, particularly in *The Bird Catcher's Song* and *Night Parrots*.

Ruby Langford (Ginibi) 1934–
She paints a graphic picture of her life of disappointments and hardships and her constant struggle to survive in both black and white cultures. Although her writing is brutally frank, it contains much humour. *Real Deadly* and *Don't Take Your Love to Town* express her feelings of exclusion.

Henry Lawson 1867–1922
One of the most widely acclaimed Australian writers, his ballads and stories depict the nobility and humour found in ordinary folk facing hardships. Most famous are the selection of poems *In the Days When the World was Wide* and the short-story collection *Joe Wilson and his Mates*.

Les Murray 1938–
Successful poet and verse-novelist whose subjects are compelling and convincing. His works include *The Vernacular Republic*, *Lunch and Counter Lunch* and *Subhuman Redneck Poems*.

Oodgeroo of the tribe Noonuccal (formerly Kath Walker) 1920–93

An Aboriginal poet who expressed her feelings powerfully and with passion. Her collections include *My People, Father Sky and Mother Earth, Stradbroke Dreamtime* and *Then and Now* (see p. 5).

A.B. 'Banjo' Paterson 1864–1941

Qualified solicitor, war correspondent in the Boer War and remount officer in World War I. This much-loved poet concentrated on the humorous and exciting side of life in the early part of the 20th century. His works include the bush ballads *The Man from Snowy River* and *Clancy of the Overflow*, which made him the toast of the countryside in 1895. These are perhaps the best-known poems in Australian literature. He is believed to have written the words to *Waltzing Matilda*.

Dorothy Porter 1954–

An exponent of her craft, her witty, finely honed lyrics reflect her keen interest in mythology, nature and the arts. Her poems 'The Night Parrot', 'Driving Too Fast', and 'The Bison' are sensuous, colourful, full of sharp imagery and are fine examples of her skill.

Kenneth Slessor 1901–71

Considered one of Australia's finest poets, his writings and in particular his war poems were powerful and thought-provoking. They include *Five Bells* and *Beach Burial*.

John Tranter 1943–

One of Australia's most significant contemporary poets, his poetry is abstract, obscure and experimental, displaying wit and skill. His works include *Parallax, Crying in Early Infancy* and *Dazed in the Ladies Lounge.*

Judith Wright 1915–

Leading poet and author whose sensitive and powerful works include *Woman to Man, The Cry for the Dead* and *Born of the Conquerors.*

Theatre

For many years, theatre in Australia seemed to be a pale reflection of its British counterpart. All this changed in 1954 when the Elizabethan Trust was established to promote and subsidise the profession in Australia. It created an exciting and flourishing national theatre. Great personalities of early Australian theatre included:

Dame Judith Anderson 1898–1991

An Adelaide actress, she won the prestigious Donaldson Award in 1948 for most distinguished actress in the American theatre. She performed overseas for most of her career and in latter years made guest appearances in soap operas in the USA.

Oscar Asche 1871–1936

Actor and playwright. Author of the Orient-inspired musical *Chu Chin Chow.*

Bert Bailey 1868–1953
Formed the Bert Bailey Dramatic Company in 1912, and was the most successful exponent of hayseed comedies such as *On Our Selection* and *Golden Shanty*. (See also **Films**.)

Dame Doris Fitton 1897–1985
An actress and director, she opened the Sydney Independent Theatre Company in 1930. In 1948 she produced the play *Rusty Bugles*, breaking new ground in the theatre by placing greater emphasis on realism and social criticism.

Joseph Bland Holt 1853–1942
Australia's greatest actor/manager. He was hailed as the 'Monarch of the Melodrama' after his spectacular production of *Riding to Win*, featuring a cycle race and a lake on stage.

Nat Phillips 1883–1923 and **Roy Rene 1891–1954 ('Stiffy and Mo')**
A vaudeville team of the 1920s and 30s, they scandalised and delighted audiences with their bawdy humour. Many of Mo's sayings are still quoted, such as 'Strike me lucky!' and 'You little trimmer!'

Nellie Stewart 1858–1931
An evergreen musical comedy star and favourite pin-up of the 1890s. She sang the ode 'Australia' at the grand ball after the opening of Federal Parliament in Melbourne on 9 May 1901. Her career spanned 67 years.

J.C. Williamson 1835–1913
Theatrical entrepreneur whose company dominated Australian theatre for almost a century. He imported many famous performers, such as Anna Pavlova and Sarah Bernhardt. The original company folded in 1982.

When the Elizabethan Theatre Trust produced the controversial plays, Summer of the Seventeenth Doll *(1955),* The Shifting Heart *(1957) and* The One Day of the Year *(1961), significant milestones were reached. These 'new wave'*

DID YOU KNOW?

Hobart is the home of Australia's oldest surviving theatre – The Theatre Royal in Campbell Street, Hobart which opened in 1837. The first live theatre entertainment took place in an especially prepared hut in Sydney Cove in 1789. In 1796 the first playhouse opened in Bligh Street, Sydney. The first performance in Adelaide was 1838 at the Adelaide Tavern in Franklin Street and in Melbourne at the Pavilion in 1841.

plays not only promoted Australian playwrights but also local Australian actors. Some notable artists to emerge in the 60s were:

Gordon Chater 1922–
A versatile character actor, famous for his role in *My Name's McGooley*. In 1984 he starred in the Australian play *The Elocution of Benjamin Franklin* in the USA.

Colleen Clifford 1898–1996
This grand lady of theatre was much admired. Over her long career (she was still working in her 90s) she performed on radio, on the stage, in films and on TV.

Ruth Cracknell 1925–
Doyenne of the stage and screen, her unique ability to re-create dramatic characters, as well as her perfect timing in comedy roles, brings accolades from far and wide. Outstanding roles include Maggie Beare in *Mother and Son* (TV), Rose in *Spider and Rose* (film) and lead roles in *A Little Night Music* and *She Stoops to Conquer* (theatre).

Ron Haddrick 1929–
A distinguished actor, he trained and performed with the Royal Shakespeare Company. Notable performances were as Jack in *The Club* and James Tyrone in *Long Day's Journey into the Night*.

Barry Humphries 1934–
An international star, he created the character Dame (now Mrs)

Ruth Cracknell.

Edna Everage, housewife from Moonee Ponds, in 1958. Through his many characters he satirises suburban life and values.

John McCallum 1918– and **Googie Withers 1917–**
Long-standing husband-and-wife team of superstar proportions. They epitomised the 'golden age' of drawing-room comedy of the 1950s and 60s.

Leo McKern 1920–
He joined the Old Vic company, London, in 1946, and has many fine acting roles to his credit, the most notable being the crusty barrister Horace Rumpole, of the British TV series *Rumpole of the Bailey*.

John Meillon 1934–89
One of the best-loved and greatest actors of Australian film, TV, stage and radio. He appeared

in *They're a Weird Mob, The Fourth Wish* and *The Picture Show Man*. His last film appearance was in *Crocodile Dundee II*.

Keith Michell 1928–

Actor of outstanding ability. He has won many international awards for his stage and screen performances, most notably his starring roles in *Man of La Mancha, Cyrano de Bergerac* and *The Six Wives of Henry VIII*.

June Salter 1932–

She began her career in radio theatre in the 1940s and has since gained the respect of her peers and audiences for her performances in theatre and on TV. These include the TV series *The Mavis Bramston Show* and the plays *Crown Matrimonial* and *The Cocktail Hour*.

Leonard Teale 1922–94

He had a wonderfully modulated voice and his career in film, TV, theatre, cabaret, recordings and radio, including over 15 000 radio serial episodes, spanned 40 years.

Other artists of note are Terence Donovan, Judi Farr, Noel Ferrier, Maurie Fields, Reg Livermore, Max Phipps, Gwen Plumb, Sean Scully and Byron Syron.

Artists of the 1980s and 90s

Robyn Archer 1948–

Actor, writer and director, she has toured widely at home and overseas. Her 18 full-length

Sandy Gore.

works for the theatre include *Songs from Sideshow Alley* and *Cafe Fledermaus* as well as her one-woman show *A Star Is Torn*. She has recorded nine albums including *The Pack of Women* and the internationally acclaimed *Robyn Archer Sings Brecht, Vol. 1 and 2*.

John Bell 1940–

Foremost Australian Shakespearian actor and director and co-artistic founder of the Nimrod Theatre, Sydney, where he directed many Shakespearian plays as well as introducing David Williamson's plays to Sydney. He is presently director of the Bell Shakespeare Company.

Max Cullen 1940–

Well-known character actor whose 'lived-in' look has graced many theatre productions and TV mini-series, as well as films.

These include *Sunday Too Far Away*, B*oundaries of the Heart* and *Kiss or Kill*. He believes that good acting should always look like an accident.

Jon Ewing c. 1940–

His vast experience, natural aptitude and intense dedication have enabled this versatile actor and theatre director to be outstanding in his field.

Sandy Gore c. 1949–

She began her career in 1969 and has extensive experience in all facets of drama. Impressive examples of her work are roles in *Summer of the Seventeenth Doll* and *Medea* (theatre), *Brides of Christ* (TV) and *Evil Angels* (film).

Melita Jurisic

This versatile actress of stage, TV, radio and screen performed the lead role in *The Tale of Ruby Rose*, which won an international critics' prize at the Venice Film Festival in 1987. Other outstanding performances include Kattrin in *Mother Courage* and Nora in *A Doll's House.*

Garry McDonald 1948–

An actor in comedy and satire, he breathed life into the character of 'the little Aussie bleeder' Norman Gunston, the naive interviewer who bewildered celebrities worldwide. His role as Arthur in the TV series *Mother and Son* with Ruth Cracknell will also never be forgotten.

Angie Milliken 1968–

Her role as Louise Coleman in the film *Act of Necessity* brought her to the attention of producers and her career has since embraced theatre, films and TV. An innovative and sensitive actress, she appeared as Susanna Hall in the play *The Herbal Bed* and Edie in *Redemption*.

Robyn Nevin 1942–

An acclaimed actress who has an impressive list of roles in film, stage and TV productions. These include the films *Careful, He Might Hear You* and *Emerald City*. Her stage performances include *A Streetcar Named Desire* and *Who's Afraid of Virginia Woolf?* She is now artistic director of the Sydney Theatre Company.

Angie Milliken.

Barry Otto.

Barry Otto c. 1943–
A respected actor of TV, film and theatre fame. He has starred in *Bliss*, *Strictly Ballroom* and *Cosi* (films) and *The Marriage of Figaro* and *Barrymore* (theatre).

Pamela Rabe c. 1963–
One of the country's most sought-after actresses for film and stage. She has a long list of roles, from Shakespearian heroines to abandoned adolescents. Her theatre credits include *A Little Night Music* and *Private Lives*. She also starred in the film *The Well* and *The Leaving of Liverpool* (TV).

John Waters 1945–
An actor of stage and screen, he is memorable for his roles in *They're Playing Our Song* and the musical based on the life and times of John Lennon, *Looking Through a Glass Onion*. His TV appearances include *Rush* and *Play School*.

Jacki Weaver 1947–
This bubbly, multi-talented actress has throughout her long career graced the theatre, film and TV to great applause.

David Wenham 1965–
This versatile actor of film, theatre and TV has an extensive repertoire of characters. He memorably played Diver Dan in ABC TV's *SeaChange* and won international critical acclaim as the pathological killer Brett Sprague in the film *The Boys*.

Richard Wherrett 1940–
He has distinguished himself with many of the country's leading theatre and opera companies. His unusual ability and wide experience have enabled him to direct some fine stage productions and top-drawer musical films and operas since 1979.

Other artists of note are Paul Capsis, Nicholas Eadie, Rodney Fisher, Julie Forsyth, Frank Gallacher, Paul Goddard, Hugh Jackman, Barrie Kosky, John O'May, John Polson and Damian Rice.

Radio

In 1918 Ernest Fisk of Wahroonga, a suburb of Sydney, picked up the first historic wireless broadcast from the Marconi station in Wales. It wasn't until the early 1920s that radio became not only a practical proposition but also an important means of mass communication. In 1932 the Commonwealth government combined all licence-funded A-class stations to form the ABC (Australian Broadcasting Commission, now Corporation).

B-class stations were commercial stations. Pioneers of radio included the following:

George Edwards 1886–1953

An actor/producer, radio pioneer and personality of the 1930s. His best-known radio serial, about the farmers of Snake Gully, was 'Dad and Dave'. Other serials were 'Search for the Golden Boomerang' and 'Courtship and Marriage'.

Ted Howell 1902–86 and Therese Desmond c. 1909–c. 1959

A husband-and-wife team who in the 1930s popularised Fred and Maggie Everybody, characters in the first Australian radio program to be recorded.

Sir Charles Moses 1900–88

His famous 'synthetic' cricket broadcasts of the Australia/ England Test Series of 1934, and his pioneering commentary of the historic landing of aviatrix Jean Batten on her arrival at Mascot airfield, Sydney from Britain in 1934, are legendary. He later became general manager of the ABC.

Then came 'The Golden Age of Radio'. In the 1940s and 50s radio captivated a vast audience and was the medium of the imagination. It was the era of quiz shows and high drama sprinkled with a large helping of variety programs. Popular shows were 'Lux Radio Theatre', 'Amateur Hour', and 'The Dulux Show'.

'Andrea' (Dorothy Gordon Jenner) 1890–1985

Considered the grand duchess of broadcasting, in the 1950s she became the top-rating, irascible and indomitable commentator of daytime radio. Her call sign was 'Hullo, mums and dads'.

Queenie Ashton 1903–99

One of the most-loved actresses in Australian show-business history, and together with Alastair Duncan, Muriel Steinbeck, Owen Weingott, Lynn Murphy and others, popularised long running serials such as 'Blue Hills', 'Doctor Paul', 'When a Girl Marries' and 'Portia Faces Life'.

Jack Davey 1907–59

A popular and jovial personality of talk and quiz shows of the 1940s and 50s. His famous greeting, 'Hi ho everybody', was known Australia-wide. In his last year of work he completed 682 shows.

Bob Dyer 1907–84

An early radio personality from 'The Last of the Hillbillies' show who made the transition to TV without difficulty. (See also **Television**.)

Bobby Limb 1924–99

A variety performer and band leader who, at times, performed in seven different shows a week. When Jack Davey died, Limb was invited to host 'The Dulux Show' and 'The Mobil Show', which involved performing before live audiences throughout Australia.

In the early 1960s radio was left far behind by the new medium, television. However, with the explosion of the Beatles' music it suddenly became a young person's medium for rock and pop. Music charts of the 'Top Ten' became essential and DJs such as Ward (Pally) Austin, John Brennan, Phil Hunter, Mike Walsh, Tony Murphy, John Laws Bob Rogers, Ken Sparkes, Bill Gates, Bob Francis, Tommy Hannan and the 'Good Guys' (Phil Halderman, John Mahon, John Fryer, Ian McRae, Guy Burgess) became the new stars.

Bob Francis 1938–

A popular personality who, in his 30-year association with 5AD, has contributed greatly to Adelaide radio. Currently presents the night program on 5AA.

Bill Gates c. 1945–

In the 1960s he recognised the unique harmony of the group which now bears his initials – the Bee Gees. He also devised a complete sound selection system which is used throughout ABC radio.

Caroline Jones 1938–

One of Australia's most respected broadcasters, she is well-remembered for her ABC programs 'City Extra' and 'The Search for Meaning'.

Ron Moss 1959– and Marius Webb 1943–

Innovative presenters of the progressive ABC 2JJ AM radio station (which later became 2JJJ FM) playing rock 'n' roll music pitched solely at huge teenage audiences.

Rod Muir 1941–

He returned from America in the early 1970s with a tight-format approach to rock music programs with which he rejuvenated flagging radio stations. His 'Room to Move' developed a fanatical audience. He commenced innovative FM radio, and in 1979 was awarded one of the first two commercial licences in New South Wales.

Bob Rogers 1927–

Phenomenally popular in the 1960s, he and John Laws were 'famous enemies' vying for top radio ratings. Now well into his 70s, his career is still on a roll. He recently signed a contract which will see him presenting his popular radio program well into the new century.

> **DID YOU KNOW?**
>
> **The first radio transmitting and receiving station in Australia was built near Pennant Hills, Sydney, in 1912.**

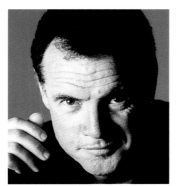

Mike Carlton.

The introduction of FM radio in 1974 gave high-quality reproduction, and in the 1980s challenged the ratings of conventional AM radio. Listeners were enticed back to new AM talkback formats with personalities such as Margaret Throsby, Bob Maumill, Jeremy Cordeaux, Mike Carlton, John Laws, Alan Jones, Ron Casey and John Raedler.

Phillip Adams 1939–

With a wide-ranging career in journalism, advertising, radio, film and TV, he is well equipped to chair numerous advisory bodies concerned with the performing arts. He produced the films *The Adventures of Barry McKenzie* and *Don's Party* and hosts 'Late Night Live' on ABC Radio National.

Mike Carlton 1946–

He began his chequered career as a cadet broadcast journalist with the ABC. His natural talent and often wicked sense of humour

took him from ABC foreign correspondent to TV producer and presenter of current affairs programs. His radio programs on both national and commercial stations are noted for their succinct commentaries and pithy observations and draw a loyal following of fans.

Jeremy Cordeaux 1945–

With over 30 years in radio, TV and print media, he is one of the most highly regarded media presenters. In recent years he has won four gold medals from the International Radio Festival of New York for 'The Best Talk/Interview Program Host in the World'. He presently hosts 5DM's morning show in Adelaide.

Andrew Denton c. 1960–

A rare type of quick wit and off-beat humour with uncanny timing enables him to do and say almost anything, anywhere, anytime to the acceptance of legions of fans. A prolific writer and presenter of TV shows such as *The Money or the Gun*, *Live and Sweaty* and *The Topic of Cancer*, he has broken new ground by giving acceptance to previously taboo subjects. He now hosts his own breakfast show on 2MMM, Sydney.

Geraldine Doogue c. 1943–

A renowned journalist and broadcaster who approaches the complexity of often unaddressed ethical, spiritual and religious issues with an infectious optimism, humour and warmth,

John Laws.

John Laws 1935–
He began his career in country radio in Victoria in 1955. One of the first rock DJs, he has since presented top-rating talkback shows, syndicated nationwide.

Ian MacNamara 1947–
Affectionately known as 'Macca', he is the host of the highly successful 'Australia All Over' ABC radio program. He is the epitome of the 'dinkum Aussie'.

appealing to a diverse audience. *Compass* and her more recent Radio National 'Life Matters' programs have pioneered media coverage of major social changes in our society.

Jon Faine 1956–
He has a professional background in law and a keen nose for a good story. He joined the ABC and presented the 'Law Report'. Now a morning presenter with 3LO in Melbourne, he enjoys the constant task of investigating stories of immediate interest to devoted listeners of his show.

Keith Martyn c. 1940– and Jeff Sunderland c. 1944–
A well-known breakfast radio duo since 1986, they are the anchors for the enormously popular 'Keith and Sundo Show' on 5AD, Adelaide. These 'ordinary blokes', with an extraordinary sense of humour, present a kaleidoscope of news, contests, weather and relaxing music to thousands of avid fans.

Neil Mitchell 1951–
A former editor and journalist, he has dominated Melbourne radio since 1990. His family-based talkback is the voice exposing controversial issues affecting the community at large. He was judged the best radio talkback personality in Australia in 1997.

Doug Mulray 1945–
A fearless radio and TV non-conformist. Considered to be the 'Sultan of Radio' in the 1980s, he set his own agenda for black comedy, stretching convention to the limit. He is presently with 2WS Drivetime.

Keith Martyn and Jeff Sunderland.

Clive Robertson 1945–
This lateral thinker, with his pseudo-pedantic attitude, often confuses not only his colleagues but his unsuspecting guests and talkback callers as well. However, he does have a natural and outrageous sense of humour which endears him to thousands of listeners.

Howard Sattler 1945–
He has been reporting on local, national and international current affairs and human interest stories for over 30 years. Synonymous with controversy, he is enquiring, persistent, provocative and opinionated but is conscious of his responsibilities, and campaigns strongly for victims of crime and poverty and for the underprivileged.

Margaret Throsby 1942–
She joined the ABC in 1967, and was the first woman announcer to read a news bulletin on ABC radio. She was

Clive Robertson.

also the first woman to present a national news bulletin on ABC TV. She currently presents the morning show on ABC Classic FM.

Other radio personalities are Barry Bissell, Angela Catterns, Mike Gibson, Wendy Harmer, Gael Jennings, Alan Jones, Amanda Keller, Terry Laidler, Bob Maumill, Phil O'Neil, Mikey Robbins, Ron Sparks and Stan Zemanek.

Neil Mitchell.

Howard Sattler.

In 1956, radio and picture shows were pushed aside for the first exciting glimpse of TV in Australia. It was new and riveting. Families without TV camped outside stores, the kids in pyjamas, to watch this incredible new medium. Home-grown producers were quick to realise there were huge audiences who were enthralled with the adventures of seemingly ordinary folk. Over the next two decades, viewing of shows such as Bellbird, No. 96 *and* Skippy *and the action-packed dramas* Homicide, Matlock Police *and* Division 4 *became nightly rituals, as viewers became more demanding.* The Mavis Bramston Show *and* The Naked Vicar Show *stretched satirical convention to previously unacceptable limits, while weekly servings of* Six O'clock Rock *and* Bandstand *had the teenage population gasping for more. Personalities included:*

Del Cartwright c.1927–
She set the agenda for good housekeeping for the 'little woman' who stayed home in the 60s. Apart from cooking, sewing and gardening demonstrations, her program influenced women's fashions and general buying patterns.

Hector Crawford 1913–91
Affectionately known as 'The Silver Fox', he was the pioneer of TV drama in Australia. As head of Crawford Productions he produced more than 2000 hours of shows extending over a period of 25 years. He gave the public what they wanted, hence the popularity of shows such as *Matlock Police*, *Homicide* and *The Sullivans*.

Bob Dyer 1907–84
An early radio and TV personality. With his wife, Dolly, he set a record for the longest-running TV show, *Pick-a-Box*, 1957–71. His 'Howdy customers', 'Tell them Bob sent you' and 'The money or the box' became household sayings. (See also **Radio**.)

Bruce Gyngell 1929–
The first person to appear on Australian TV (TCN Channel Nine, Sydney). The first words spoken were 'Good evening, ladies and gentlemen. Welcome to television'. He has held executive positions with the Seven and Nine networks and helped to set up SBS.

Graham Kennedy 1934–
Generally referred to as 'The King'. In 1957 he became the outrageous compere of the extremely popular *In Melbourne Tonight*, which ran until 1969.

Ernie Sigley 1940–
At 16 he compered Melbourne's first live TV show, *Teenage Mail Bag*. Later he was the anchor for the long-running *The Ernie Sigley Show*. He and Denise Drysdale formed an immensely popular double act and are fondly remembered for their hit tune 'Hey Paula'.

Other artists of early TV included: Noeline Brown, Maggie Dence, Gordon Chater, Carol Raye, Gordon Boyd, Abigail, Leonard Teale and Johnny O'Keefe.

By the early 70s, black-and-white TV was viewed by 98% of the population. In 1975, colour TV began, which widened the horizons. The variety shows Young Talent Time, In Melbourne Tonight, and The Mike Walsh, Don Lane and Paul Hogan Shows all became immensely popular. As well, the ground-breaking This Day Tonight, with Bill Peach, was the forerunner of current affairs programs of the future.

Lorraine Bayly 1939–
An actress of stage and screen, she played Grace Sullivan in the period piece The Sullivans which ran for seven years, and the lead female role in Carson's Law.

James Dibble 1923–
A much-respected newsreader on ABC radio and TV. For over 25 years his voice was a familiar one in Australian homes.

Bert Newton 1938–
Since television began in Australia, he has been a favourite with viewers,

celebrities and critics alike. With his twin talents as a natural comedian and sophisticated compere, his remarkable career has been recognised by an incredible number of awards, including 15 Logies (6 gold).

Mike Walsh 1938–
From being a country radio announcer in the 1960s he made inroads into daytime TV, previously a woman's domain, to become the host of the long-running and popular The Mike Walsh Show.

Mike Willesee 1942–
At 22 he was the youngest-ever fully accredited political correspondent in Canberra. He hosted many current affairs programs in the 1970s and 1980s.

Johnny Young 1945–
He delighted thousands of children and parents around Australia in the 1970s and 80s with the long-running children's talent show Young Talent Time. In 1990 he was admitted to the Golden Logies Hall of Fame.

Other artists of the 1970s included Ross Higgins, Tony Bonner, Lynda Stoner, Rowena Wallace and Stuart Wagstaffe.

DID YOU KNOW?
The first television station in Australia opened in 1956 as TCN Channel 9, Sydney.

In 1980 ethnic television began broadcasting on a permanent basis through SBS. By 1983 there were 50 commercial channels and ABC services were available through more than 80 transmitters. Some very fine period pieces came out of this era, Rush, Sara Dane, The Restless Years, Carson's Law *and* Come in Spinner, *to name just a few. The blockbuster* Sale of the Century *quiz show appeared. However, some of the most popular shows were the soapies.* Neighbours, Sons and Daughters *and* A Country Practice *were enormously popular, both in Australia and abroad.*

Tony Barber 1940–
He was for many years the smiling, genial host of the popular quiz show *Sale of the Century*. He began his career as the 'Cambridge whistler' on a TV cigarette commercial in 1969.

Bill Collins 1934–
Australia's amiable 'Mr Movies' is a journalist and cinema historian. He is an authority on motion pictures, particularly those of Hollywood's 'Golden Years'.

Noni Hazlehurst 1954–
This fun-loving and sensitive actress has notched up many successes in film and TV. She is known for her appearances on *Play School* and as co-host of *Better Homes and Gardens*.

David Salter 1947–
An executive producer, his back-room career has embraced print journalism, lecturing and

Bananas in Pyjamas.

producing, writing and directing some of the most thought-provoking programs over the last two decades. *This Fabulous Century*, *The Australians* and *Media Watch* are some of his creations.

Other artists of the 1980s include Paul Cronin, Derryn Hinch, Clive James, Kylie Minogue, Jason Donovan, Lorrae Desmond, Rachel Friend, Shane Porteous, Craig McLachlan and Ross Symonds.

The 1990s have heralded incredible choice. Pay TV has become a reality, even though a great percentage of viewers remained unconvinced. Unfortunately, the battle for ratings in mainstream TV has become paramount and management has been inclined to favour tried and true formulas, seeking instant success, high ratings and hence revenue. As a consequence, new material has tended to be stifled. Budget cuts in other areas mean that high-class dramas like those of the 1980s have been bypassed for 'infotainment' programs and the decade has been dominated by sports and 'How to' shows.

Bananas in Pyjamas

Starting life as a nursery rhyme in 1972, the characters became regulars on ABC's *Play School* in the 1980s and in 1991, B1 and B2 branched out with their own show. They are currently seen by over 100 million viewers in 69 countries and the show is translated into many languages. Renowned for their phrase, 'Are you thinking what I'm thinking, B1?' 'I think I am, B2!'

Don Burke 1948–

A horticulturist, his very popular *Burke's Backyard*, with its theme 'Give me a home among the gum trees', has revitalised thousands of amateur gardeners.

John Clarke c. 1943–

This ex-pat Kiwi is a natural comic with a po-face. His infamous interviews with straight man Brian Dawe on *A Current Affair* had viewers quietly chuckling at the truth behind the fearless observations.

Ernie Dingo 1956–

Has a sense of fun and playfulness that endears him to many. He began his career with the Middar Aboriginal Dance Theatre in Western Australia, and a part in the 1986 Bruce Beresford film *The Fringe Dwellers* assured his success. He is the host of the popular *Great Outdoors* TV show.

John Doyle and Greig Pickhaver ('Roy and HG')

This duo has mastered the art of coupling outrageous comedy with 'in your face' commentary, pushing everything to the limit. They host weekend sports on ABC youth radio Triple J and have made several series for ABC TV.

Elizabeth (Liz) Hayes c.1956–

From a regional newspaper reporter in Taree to a top TV journalist, her career has been varied and extremely successful. For 10 years she co-hosted the *Today* show and is presently an international reporter with *60 Minutes*.

Brian Henderson 1931–

He began his career in radio but soon made his name in TV as host of the popular music show *Bandstand*. His most noteworthy position in recent years has been newsreader for the Nine Network.

Steve Liebmann c.1949–

He began his media career while still at high school and over the past 30 years has distinguished himself as a news journalist, presenting and commenting on the news with numerous radio and TV stations in Sydney and Canberra. With his extensive knowledge and warm approach he is the extremely successful co-host of the long running *Today* show.

Ray Martin 1944–

As a journalist he clocked up more than a million miles when he was a reporter for

Tony Martin.

60 Minutes. From 1985 to 1993 he was the genial host of the popular *Midday Show* and fronted *A Current Affair* until 1998.

Tony Martin 1956–
Utterly professional, his complex portrayal of characters such as Happy in *Death of a Salesman* (theatre), Neddy Smith in *Blue Murder*, Detective Bill McCoy in *Wildside* (TV) and Detective-Sergeant Steel in *The Interview* (film) makes his work extremely convincing and compelling.

Norman 'Nugget' May 1928–
With his famous sporting exclamation 'Gold! Gold! Gold!' of the 1980s, this veteran radio and television commentator has covered eight Olympic Games and nine Commonwealth Games since his first, the Perth Empire and Commonwealth Games (as they were then called) in 1962. A Games without 'Nugget' would be 'like a pie without sauce'!

Bruce McAvaney c. 1948–
Considered 'The Master Sportscaster' he started his media career in 1976 at Radio 5DN calling horse races. Since then, with his keen sense of timing and great sporting knowledge, he has hosted hundreds of major sporting events nationally and internationally, including the Olympic Games in Atlanta, Seoul, Barcelona and Nagano. He presently fronts sporting telecasts on Channel 7 in Melbourne.

Catherine McClements 1965–
Major roles in the films *Weekend with Kate* and *Redheads* resulted in enthusiastic recognition for her extraordinary talents as well as awards. She played the character of Rachel Goldstein in *Water Rats* with great verve.

Lisa McCune 1971–
Born in Perth, Western Australia, she came east in 1983 to become famous and steal the hearts of millions of viewers as policewoman Maggie Doyle in the long-running *Blue Heelers*.

Catherine McClements.

Mike Munro.

Ian 'Molly' Meldrum 1946–

The guru of the Australian rock scene and TV pioneer with *Countdown*, many Australian bands owe their success to his promotion of them. His high profile enables him to have entrée to first-class international performers.

Mike Munro 1954–

Since 1971 his talents as an investigative journalist have enabled him to participate in top-rating shows such as *60 Minutes*. Although he has a reputation as a pushy, 'foot-in-the-door' interviewer, he can also be very genial. He presently hosts *A Current Affair* and *This Is Your Life*.

Peter Phelps 1960–

One of our best-known actors, he has appeared in dozens of films, TV shows and theatre productions. He currently appears as Senior Constable Peter Church in *Stingers* (TV).

Daryl Somers 1952–

Born into a show-business family, his break came when he appeared on *New Faces*, attracting the attention of the Nine Network. He was the host of the long-running *Hey Hey It's Saturday* show.

Gerald Stone 1933–

As creator of Australia's *60 Minutes*, he is credited with launching the careers of such TV stars as Ray Martin, Jana Wendt and George Negus. American-born, he arrived in Australia in the early 1960s, rising to national prominence as one of the original reporters on the ABC's groundbreaking *This Day Tonight*. He served as both a newspaper and TV correspondent in Vietnam and wrote a book about that conflict, *War Without Honour*, which was highly influential in the anti-war movement.

Sigrid Thornton 1959–

One of Australia's most experienced actors, she stars in many films now regarded as classics. Her measured portrayal of feisty but charming leading ladies is legendary in films such as *The Man from Snowy River* and

Peter Phelps.

The Light Horsemen, as well as the mini-series 1915 and All The Rivers Run. Her performance as Laura Gibson in the TV show SeaChange helped the ABC to its first top-rating show.

Jana Wendt 1956–
A journalist who joined the 60 Minutes Team in 1982. She became a leading TV host/reporter, recognised by her sultry voice, which belied the relentless tenacity with which she conducted her interviews. She now hosts Dateline on SBS.

Other artists of the 1990s include Paul Barry, Roger Climpson, Brian Deakin, Alex Dimitriades, Denise Drysdale, Rebecca Gibney, Lisbeth Gorr, Kerri-Anne Kennerley, Dylan Lewis, Peter Luck, Paul Lyneham, Paul McDermott, Maxine McKew, Indira Naidoo, Brian Naylor, George Negus, Laurie Oakes, Kerry O'Brien, Margaret Pomeranz, John Safran, Rob Sitch, David Stratton, Ken Sutcliffe, Gary Sweet, Magda Szubanski, Jim Waley, Max Walsh, Helen Wellings and John Wood.

Films

In 1908, when the pioneer film producer Raymond Longford realised that there may be a future for films in Australia, little did he know how successful the Australian film industry would be. Although the going has not always been smooth, the film industry in the 1990s is testament to the persistence of those involved in the industry over the last century.

Take 1 Silent films and early talkies 1898–1935

Bert Bailey 1868–1953
He is famous for his role as Dad, the genial patriarch in On Our Selection, a feature film comedy based on Steele Rudd's characters. (See also **Theatre**.)

Lottie Lyell 1890–1925
She was Australia's first film star and appeared in many of Raymond Longford's films. She starred in The Silence of Dean Maitland and played Doreen in The Sentimental Bloke.

Arthur Tauchert 1877–1933
C.J. Dennis chose this former vaudeville actor to play the title role in The Sentimental Bloke. He was the most popular screen actor of the 1920s.

George Wallace 1895–1960
A very popular comedian of the Depression era. His most famous film was Gone to the Dogs.

Take 2 The talkies 1935–70

Peter Finch 1916–77
Film and theatre actor of West End fame. He appeared in 51 films, including Charles Chauvel's The Rats of Tobruk, Robbery Under Arms and Network, in a career that spanned more than 30 years.

Errol Flynn 1909–59
Swashbuckling Hobart-born actor, notorious on and off the screen. His debut film was in the role of

Fletcher Christian in Charles Chauvel's *In the Wake of the Bounty.* He moved to Hollywood and became a legend.

Chips Rafferty 1909–71
An actor and producer, he epitomised all that was decent in the typical Australian bushman. He appeared in *The Rats of Tobruk* and *Forty Thousand Horsemen,* achieving international status.

Take 3
1970–91

Ray Barrett 1927–
In 1958 his successful tour with Margaret Rutherford in *The Happiest Days of Our Lives* was the turning point of his career. For over 40 years he has enjoyed an international career and recently returned to Australia to star in James Bogle's film *In the Winter Dark.*

Bryan Brown 1947–
This very popular, devil-may-care actor is noted for his down-to-earth character portrayals of ordinary heroes who are up against the odds. His films include *Breaker Morant* and *Two Hands.*

Judy Davis 1956–
A sensitive and compelling actress, she played the starring role in the film *My Brilliant Career* and from there her future was assured. She brings a complete understanding and clarity to her screen roles.

Colin Friels 1953–
Hard-hitting, convincing and intelligent, he starred in the films *Monkey Grip, High Tide* and *Mr Reliable* among many others. He was the knockabout larrikin of the TV series *Water Rats.* His latest role as Macbeth in the stage production of the play shows his versatility.

Mel Gibson 1956–
This suave international superstar rose from receiving $400 for his first movie role, in *Summer City,* to some $20 million for his *Lethal Weapon* series. His post-holocaust ex-cop role in the *Mad Max* trilogy began his rise to stardom and he triumphed at the 1996 Oscars with *Braveheart.*

John Hargreaves 1946–96
This warm-hearted and popular actor played lead roles in the films *The Removalist, Don's Party, My First Wife, Emerald City,* and *Country Life.*

Chris Haywood 1949–
A distinguished actor who is constantly in demand. With over 50 top-rating TV series and more than 30 films to his credit, he has demonstrated the ability to play a character with conviction and truth. *The Cars that Ate Paris, Newsfront, Golden Braid* and *Janus* (TV) are fine examples of his work.

Paul Hogan ('Hoges') 1940–
He clambered down the rungs of the Sydney Harbour Bridge to become a multimillion-dollar film producer when in the 1980s, in partnership with John Cornell, he produced and starred in the *Crocodile Dundee* series.

Wendy Hughes 1950–
A film actress internationally acclaimed for her performances in *Newsfront, Careful, He Might Hear You* and *Boundaries of the Heart.*

Bill Hunter 1939–
Able and sensitive character actor whose versatility allows him to portray a bent politician one day and an outback yobbo the next with equal conviction. Films include *Strictly Ballroom, The Adventures of Priscilla, Queen of the Desert* and *Muriel's Wedding.*

Nicole Kidman 1967–
Her talent was obvious from the age of 15, and among her many outstanding performances are the films *Dead Calm, Emerald City, Flirting, To Die For* and *Portrait of a Lady.* She starred with her husband, Tom Cruise, in Stanley Kubrick's final film, *Eyes Wide Shut.*

Sam Neill 1948–
A high-profile international actor of great ability who returns regularly to Australia to star in films such as *The Piano, Sirens* and *Country Life.* He worked in the US blockbusters *Jurassic Park* and *Event Horizon* to name a few.

Jack Thompson 1940–
A rugged and convincing actor, his undoubted ability has won him roles in the films *Sunday Too Far Away, Breaker Morant, The Man from Snowy River, The Sum of Us* and *Under the Lighthouse Dancing.*

Charles 'Bud' Tingwell 1923–
A legendary figure who has made a huge contribution to radio, film, television and theatre over a career spanning almost six decades. With approximately 70 films and TV appearances to his credit, he also directed many favourite TV shows such as *The Sullivans* and *The Box* and appeared in films including *Breaker Morant, Puberty Blues* and *Malcolm.* He recently played the astute retired lawyer in the very successful film *The Castle.* His latest role is Bishop Guiart in the TV production *The Violent Earth.*

Hugo Weaving 1960–
An experienced actor of theatre, TV and film, his ability to take risks caused an enormous stir at the 1991 Cannes Film Festival for his sensitive portrayal of a blind photographer in the film *Proof.* In 1994 to tremendous acclaim he played Mitzi, the flamboyant and outrageous drag queen, in *The Adventures of Priscilla, Queen of the Desert.*

Toni Collette.

Matt Day and Frances O'Connor.

performances which are truthful and impassioned and often overridden by a gutsy menacing violence which leaves the audience chilled. *Romper Stomper* and *L.A. Confidential* are two of his most memorable films.

Recently he has starred in *The Interview*, *The Matrix* and *Bedrooms and Hallways*.

Take 4
1990s

Cate Blanchett 1972–
A rare talent, her meteoric rise to stardom has been phenomenal. This gifted artist has many stage performances to her credit and has starred in films including *Oscar and Lucinda*, *Paradise Road*, *Thank God He Met Lizzie* and *Elizabeth*.

Toni Collette 1972–
She fast-tracked to international fame as the gormless heroine in *Muriel's Wedding* and has since appeared in *Emma*, *The Velvet Goldmine*, *The Boys* and *The Sixth Sense* among many others.

Russell Crowe 1954–
Well on the way to becoming an established international star, his trademark of believable character acting produces

Matt Day c. 1974–
He acts on instinct and has shrugged off previous boy-next-door roles to play more telling and rugged parts in *Kiss or Kill* and *Sugar Factory*.

Rachel Griffiths c. 1972–
Fiery and articulate, this most competent actress has made very successful inroads into the British film industry. The sidekick in *Muriel's Wedding*, she is now playing harsher, more earthy roles in dramas such as *Jude* and *Among Giants*. She gained an Academy Award Nomination for her role in *Hilary and Jackie*.

Jacqueline McKenzie c.1974–
Dedicated and focused, vibrant and emotional, she has managed to carry off the weightiness of the role of Joan of Arc in the Sydney Theatre Company production. Her films include *Under the Lighthouse Dancing* and *Deep Blue Sea*.

Ben Mendelsohn c. 1972–
He believes that Australia has more to offer than the glitz of Hollywood. His ability to portray roles as diverse as the sensitive producer in *Cosi* and the tough guy in *Idiot Box*,

Ben Mendelsohn.

assures him a position among the group of young actors going places.

Miranda Otto 1973–

Since the 1995 film *Love Serenade* her career has gained a life of its own. Consistency, dedication and natural talent landed her prestigious roles in *Doing Time for Patsy Cline* and *The Well*. Recently she has attracted international attention and won coveted roles in *The Thin Red Line* and *In the Winter Dark*.

Guy Pearce 1974–

Once a handsome heartthrob in TV's *Neighbours*, this rising star rode the bus as a drag queen in *The Adventures of Priscilla, Queen of the Desert*. This was the springboard for landing a career-making role as a self-righteous, intelligent detective in *L.A. Confidential* in Hollywood in 1997.

Richard Roxburgh 1971–

Shot to prominence when he played Hamlet to great applause at Sydney's Belvoir Street Theatre in 1995. His ability to involve the audience in his versatile approach to acting has won him lead roles in the films *Doing Time for Patsy Cline, Thank God He Met Lizzie, Mission Impossible II* and the period piece *Passion*, in which he plays the famous Australian composer Percy Grainger.

Geoffrey Rush 1950–

Although he writes, directs and acts in plays, TV and films, his first love is theatre. He was thrust into the international spotlight when he played the demanding role of David Helfgott in the movie *Shine*, for which he received an Oscar. Since then, this unassuming, intelligent actor has gone on to win roles in *Les Miserables, Elizabeth* and *Shakespeare in Love*.

Noah Taylor 1972–

An enigmatic character who, although aloof and

Miranda Otto.

unpredictable, brings to his roles a genuine insight and understanding. His performances in *The Year My Voice Broke, True Love and Chaos* and *Shine* won him a role in *There Are No Fish in Heaven*, filmed in the USA.

Aden Young 1973–
Well rehearsed and researched, he has a maturity, focus and cleverness which is rare in someone of his age. *Black Robe, River Street, Under Heaven* and *Cousin Bette* are some of his most notable films.

Other artists of the 1990s are Claudia Karvan, Heath Ledger, Frances O'Connor, Sacha Horler, Maya Stange and Sophie Lee.

Film-makers

Gillian Armstrong 1950–
Revered in the industry, her success in directing *My Brilliant Career* gained international recognition. Then followed *Starstruck, Mrs Soffel, The Last Days of Chez Nous, Little Women* and *Oscar and Lucinda,* to name just a few.

Bill Bennett c. 1957–
Although he had vast experience in TV and film in the late 70s, it was the 1984 film *A Street to Die* which won him international fame. His unique approach of fusing documentary and drama creates an exciting unpredictability of narrative which, although spontaneous, is still controlled and has

direction. *Backlash, Spider and Rose, Malpractice, Kiss or Kill* and *In a Savage Land* are some of his films.

Bruce Beresford 1940–
He has made more films and broken more ground, both artistically and commercially, than anyone else in the industry. He established himself in the 1970s with films such as *The Adventures of Barry McKenzie, Breaker Morant* and *The Fringe Dwellers*. He has worked in Hollywood and has many notable films to his credit such as *Crimes of the Heart, Driving Miss Daisy* and *Black Robe*.

Russell Boyd 1944–
A cinematographer, he has made some of the most famous Australian feature films, such as *Picnic at Hanging Rock,* which won a British Oscar. This film captured the imagination of audiences worldwide and set a mood for other films to follow. His later films include *Gallipoli, Crocodile Dundee, Blood Oath* and *Liar Liar.*

Tim Burstall 1929–
He pioneered the 'new wave' films of the 1970s. His work includes *Alvin Purple, Eliza Fraser, Attack Force Z, Kangaroo, The Naked Country* and *Slate, Wyn and Me.*

Jane Campion 1954–
New Zealand-born director with a most poetic and unique talent who has won numerous international awards. *An Angel At My Table, Sweetie, The Piano, The Portrait of a Lady* and *Holy*

Smoke illustrate her mastery of the visual image.

Charles Chauvel 1897–1959
The most accomplished film-maker of the 1920s and 30s, he made films with a distinctly Australian flavour, including *Jedda*, *In the Wake of the Bounty* (starring Errol Flynn), *Forty Thousand Horsemen* (which is regarded as the first truly great Australian film), and *The Rats of Tobruk*.

Rolf de Heer 1951–
Born in Holland, a childhood spent in Sumatra has coloured the perception of this sensitive and explorative writer-director. His many successes include *Bad Boy Bubby*, *The Quiet Room* and *Dance Me to My Song*, all of which he says 'push boundaries of both form and content'.

Laura Jones 1951–
One of the leading screenwriters in the international film industry. Her acute observations and ability to transform a story into strong visual images have her constantly in demand. Her films include *The Well*, *High Tide*, *The Portrait of a Lady* and *The Shipping News*.

Byron Kennedy 1952–83 and George Miller 1945–
This was a highly successful production team, breaking new ground with the *Mad Max* series. *Mad Max* (1979) and *Mad Max 2* (1981) became the most imitated films of the 1980s. Kennedy Miller produced the television drama *The Dismissal,* but tragically, in 1983, Kennedy was killed in a helicopter crash. Miller continued and in the next 10 years directed *Twilight Zone*, *Mad Max Beyond Thunderdome* and *The Witches of Eastwick*, and co-produced *The Year My Voice Broke, Dead Calm, Lorenzo's Oil* and the *Babe* series.

Raymond Longford 1878–1959
Australia's most successful director of silent films, he independently developed the use of close-ups to great effect, particularly in *The Silence of Dean Maitland*. He directed the silent cinema classics *Mutiny on the Bounty* and *The Sentimental Bloke*.

Pat Lovell c. 1932–
A dynamic film producer and perfectionist who enjoys a challenge, she is responsible for the box-office hits *Picnic at Hanging Rock, Monkey Grip* and *Gallipoli*.

Baz Luhrmann 1960–
He hit the big time with *Strictly Ballroom*, an adaption of a musical play he had developed for the stage.

Baz Luhrmann.

Another blockbuster followed: an 'urban' version of Shakespeare's *Romeo and Juliet*. His word-song 'Everybody's Free (to Wear Sunscreen)' was a chart winner.

Phillip Noyce 1950–

He struck a new screen reality when he directed *Newsfront*, where he moulded fictional footage with film of actual events from the 1950s. Other works to his credit are *Heatwave* and *Dead Calm*, and for TV *The Dismissal* and *Cowra Breakout*. In 1988 he became one of the 'Gum Leaf Mafia' (expatriates in Hollywood) and made *Blind Fury, Patriot Games* and *The Saint*.

Fred Schepisi 1939–

An acclaimed director with a larrikin air and a rare wit. He left school at 15 and learnt his craft 'from the ground up'. He became a dynamic force in the industry with films such as *The Devil's Playground* and *The Chant Of Jimmie Blacksmith*. He has since directed *Roxanne, Evil Angels, The Russia House* and *IQ*.

John Seale 1944–

He began his career in 1962 as a camera assistant and is now a top cinematographer. In 1975 he assisted Russell Boyd with filming *Picnic at Hanging Rock*. His successes include *Careful, He Might Hear You* and *The Empty Beach*. He moved to the USA, and filmed *Mosquito Coast, Children of a Lesser God, Rain Man, Dead Poets Society* and *The*

English Patient, for which he won an Oscar in 1997.

Dean Semler 1943–

A cinematographer whose pictures are distinguished by their sweeping vision of often unspoiled and unforgiving backgrounds. *Steam Train Passes* was his first film, then his big break came with *Mad Max 2*. From then on he filmed *The Lighthorsemen* and *Dead Calm* and won an Oscar for his work on Kevin Costner's blockbuster movie *Dances with Wolves*. Recent films include *Waterworld*.

Nadia Tass 1956–

She began her career in theatre as both an actor and director. Ably assisted by her cinematographer–screen writer husband, David Parker, she directed the film *Malcolm* in 1986, which astonished and charmed audiences of the day. She also directed *The Big Steal* in 1989 and *Amy* in 1997.

Peter Weir 1944–

He emerged from the 1970s as the country's leading director, with films such as *The Cars that Ate Paris* and *Picnic at Hanging Rock*. In 1982 he realised a burning ambition when he directed *Gallipoli,* which was a major success and won nine AFI awards. *The Year of Living Dangerously* was his last Australian film of the 1980s. *Witness, Mosquito Coast, Dead Poets Society, Green Card, Fearless* and *The Truman Show* were all made in the USA.

Rock music

The 1950s, 60s and 70s

Although popular rock in these decades was often influenced by overseas trends, Australia evolved its own kind of music. Extraordinarily popular at home but not generally well known abroad, bands and artists who made it in the 1970s burst on to the international stage, opening the eyes of the world. Their music was not in the mould – it was different and experimental and its sound became clearly recognisable as typically Australian.

Bands of influence

The Bee Gees

Teenagers in the 1960s, this Brisbane trio has been hugely successful over four decades. With a unique vocal harmony and maturity beyond their years, their fame followed them to the USA. There they pioneered disco in the 1970s with the hit 'Staying Alive' from the soundtrack of the movie *Saturday Night Fever* which had sales of over 30 million. They were inducted into the world's Music Hall of Fame in 1997.

Billy Thorpe and the Aztecs

A raucous band of the 1960s and 70s. 'Most People I Know (Think That I'm Crazy)' was an Aussie classic and Thorpe was indisputably a rock'n'roll hero. He is now a serious songwriter and author.

Billy Thorpe.

Daddy Cool

An energetic and courageous band, they stormed onto the rock scene of the 1970s with their jovial and post-hippy music, making a significant breakthrough. Under the leadership of guitarist Ross Wilson, their main hit was 'Eagle Rock'. Wilson later went on to form the 1980s band Mondo Rock.

The Easybeats

One of the earliest rock group exports. In 1966 this strong, energetic band hit the Top 10 in the UK with 'Friday on My Mind' and 'Sorry'. The band established George Young and Harry Vanda, as a prolific song writing duo who later produced AC/DC.

Little River Band

Glenn Shorrock was lead singer and the band was wildly successful in the USA with well-produced, catchy mainstream rock hits such as 'Help is on its Way' and 'Reminiscing'. In the 1980s, with John Farnham as lead singer, they resurfaced briefly with 'Down on the Border'.

Radio Birdman

This six-piece outfit exploded out of the inner city regions of Sydney with their own kind of 'blitzkrieg' rock and brought the crowds to their feet. *Radio Appear* was considered the seminal Aussie rock LP of the 1970s. Disbanded but regrouped in 1996 with the album *Ritualism.*

The Saints

They have the reputation of being the first band in the world to release a punk rock album (even before the Sex Pistols). EMI Records UK heard about it and independently signed them to their label. Their biggest hit was '(I'm) Stranded'.

Sherbet

With Daryl Braithwaite as lead singer they were extraordinarily successful in the 1970s. They topped the UK charts with 'Howzat'.

Skyhooks

With prominent members Shirley Strachan and Red Symons, this band began a new rock culture in the 1970s. They developed a truly Australian style with powerful vocals and guitar. There were huge sales of their hits 'Living in the Seventies', 'Horror Movie' and 'Ego (is not a Dirty Word)'.

Solo artists

Col Joye 1938–

He began his career with Johnny O'Keefe in 1958 and helped introduce a new and exciting kind of music to the teenagers of the time, who had just experienced their first taste of TV. His best-known hits are 'Sixteen Candles' and 'Bye Bye Baby'.

Olivia Newton-John 1948–

Popular vocalist since 1965. With her intrinsic charm and sweet 'girl-next-door' vocals, she made world charts with her song 'Banks of the Ohio'. Success increased with her lead role in the US film musical *Grease.* A song from the movie 'You're the One that I Want', sung with John Travolta, was huge. Other smash hits include 'I Honestly Love You' and 'Physical'.

Johnny O'Keefe 1935–78

Known as the Boomerang Kid, his career began in 1956 with the volatile and charismatic, action-packed TV show 'Six o'clock Rock', which introduced rock music to thousands of screaming teenagers. Smash hits included 'She's My Baby', 'Shout' and 'Move Baby Move'.

Helen Reddy 1942–

A most successful vocalist in Australia, but her breakthrough came in the USA in 1972 with 'I am Woman', which became the theme song for the women's liberation movement worldwide.

Normie Rowe 1947–

At 17 he was crowned Australia's first 'King of Pop', becoming enormously popular with his innovative and raucous brand of music. His career was interrupted by Army service in

Vietnam. Now performing in musicals and the cabaret circuit, he is a tireless worker for Vietnam veterans and handicapped children.

John Paul Young 1953–

In 1975 he had tremendous success with 'Yesterday's Hero', then he rocketed to the top of the European charts with 'Love is in the Air' in 1978. He successfully re-recorded this hit song in 1995 for the soundtrack of *Strictly Ballroom*.

The 1980s

This was a time when Australian bands were making their mark overseas, and because of their different sound, the world couldn't get enough. Many performers signed with big international labels which recognised the popularity of this unique Aussie sound. At home, bands attracted huge followings.

Bands of influence

AC/DC

One of the world's most popular and longest-running bands, their aggressive assault on the rock scene has had a huge influence over the past 20 years. They enjoyed worldwide success in 1979 with their explosive hard rock album *Highway to Hell*. After the tragic death of lead singer Bon Scott the band almost disbanded, but they carried on with UK vocalist Brian Johnson and enjoyed phenomenal success in 1980 with the comeback album *Back in Black*.

Air Supply

Essentially 'middle of the road', they enjoyed an exceptional following in the UK and USA and had a record-breaking seven consecutive hits on five top international charts. Hits included 'The One that You Love' and 'Lost in Love'.

The Angels

Charged with their screaming guitars and aggressive lead singer Doc Neeson, their thunderous and athletic hard rock stage show was still attracting huge audiences after 20 years. Hits include 'Shadow Boxer', 'Dogs are Talking' and 'Take a Long Line'.

The Black Sorrows

Diverse, original and with a soulful sound, they are based around front man Joe Camilleri. (He was in Jo Jo Zep and the Falcons in the late 1970s.) The Sorrows still enjoy a wide following and their hits include 'You've Got Me in the Shape I'm In', 'Harley and Rose' and 'Last One Standing for You'.

Cold Chisel

Their lively blues-influenced style was typical Aussie rock. From 'Khe Sanh' and 'Cheap Wine' to *Teenage Love* they were always a top-class band with fans clamouring for more. Although the band broke up in 1980, Don Walker, Jimmy Barnes and Ian Moss have gone on to enjoy prolific solo careers. They reunited in 1998 for the album *The Last Wave of Summer*.

Icehouse.

singer/songwriter Iva Davies, the hits 'I Can't Help Myself', 'Crazy', 'Great Southern Land' and 'Electric Blue' assured their success.

Crowded House

Enjoying unparalleled success for a decade, this extraordinarily creative group, with its easy anecdotal style and collective sense of humour, were huge in the UK and USA and hit the top time and time again. 'Mean to Me', 'Private Universe' and 'Don't Dream It's Over' were just a few of their hits. Together with their lead singer/songwriter Neil Finn, they bowed out in a nostalgic farewell concert on the steps of the Sydney Opera House (1997) to applause from thousands of devoted fans.

Divinyls

With mainstays Chrissie Amphlett and Mark McEntee, this brash, diverse and controversial band continually topped national and international charts. Chrissie is renowned for her raunchy presentation of hits, which include 'Science Ficton' and 'Pleasure and Pain'. In the early 1990s, they went huge worldwide with 'I Touch Myself'.

Icehouse

Originally called Flowers, this band was a curtain-raiser to the acceptance of high-tech synthesised bands as authentic Aussie rock. Based around lead

Mental As Anything

A popular five-piece outfit performing purely for fun, wowing three generations of fans with their quirky pop style. Always mixed with a dash of good humour, their favourite hits are 'If You Leave Me, Can I Come Too?' and 'Live It Up'.

Noiseworks

Fronted by Jon Stevens they played typical 1980s rock, thoughtful and creative, bringing a weightiness to their act. Because of their diversity, they attracted a wide range of audiences with hits such as 'No Lies' and 'Hot Chilli Woman'.

Rose Tattoo

With diminutive lead singer 'Angry' Anderson, they had the reputation of being the loudest band in Australia at the time.

Mental As Anything.

Remembered for their hits 'Bad Boy for Love' and 'We Won't Be Beaten'.

The 1990s

For better or worse, popular rock is transient. There is always pressure from overseas companies to produce music attracting huge audiences which in turn make huge profits. Today, there are dozens of aspiring Aussie bands, but few of these are being sponsored even though Australia is the eighth largest music market in the world. Unlike in the 1970s and 80s, the large record companies tend to 'play safe', investing in recognised and proven groups. However, despite the international demand and fickle market, Australian bands, on the whole, are continuing to play their own kind of music – still clearly identifiable, still Australian.

Bands of influence

Baby Animals
A hard rock band falling under the same influences as the Divinyls. Brazen and flagrantly unreserved, major international success came with their debut album *Baby Animals* and the hit 'Early Warning'.

Human Nature.

Hunters and Collectors.

Dave Graney and the Coral Snakes
Although some in the industry are mystified, since the 1970s Graney has produced a unique and diverse type of work he considers to be rock'n'roll. He has a broad audience of devoted fans and has several albums, including *The Devil Drives*. He was crowned 'King of Pop' in 1996.

Hoodoo Gurus
Constantly touring, this lively power-pop rock'n'roll four-piece produced catchy hook-laden songs, making them a definite favourite amongst Aussie punters. Their debut album was *Stoneage Romeos*. They consolidated their career in the 1990s with a compilation album, *Electric Soup*.

Human Nature
Highly successful vocal quartet whose big break came when they were selected by Michael Jackson to join his European tour, giving them massive exposure. Their debut album, *Telling Everybody*, went platinum in less than three weeks. It was followed by *Counting Down* and the hit 'Cruel'.

Hunters and Collectors

The spectacle of this rough-edged rock band astonished UK audiences in the 1980s. With their musical diversity they had extraordinary success with 1990s hits such as 'Where Do You Go', 'We the People' and 'Throw Your Arms Around Me'. Their singer/songwriter Mark Seymour enjoys a respectable solo career.

INXS

Always successful nationally, they broke worldwide in 1987 with the album *Kick*. They went on to become one of the world's most awesome and popular bands and Australia's most successful international act of all time. Smash hits include 'I Need You Tonight', 'The Devil Inside', 'Burn for You' and 'New Sensation'. Their lead singer, Michael Hutchence, died tragically in 1997. They had been together for 20 years.

Midnight Oil

With their energetic and politically motivated lead singer, Peter Garrett, this forthright band burst onto the rock scene with a powerful force. Extremely popular since the 1980s and enjoying a cult following, their hits include 'Power and the Passion' and 'Beds are Burning' from their platinum albums *10, 9, 8, 7, 6, 5, 4, 3, 2, 1, Diesel and Dust* and *Redneck Wonderland*.

Regurgitator

A totally different band which combines scratchy grinding funk melodies with hip-hop and synth-pop disco. Always

Regurgitator.

refreshing, their sounds and lyrics range from heavy metal to touches of the Orient. *Unit* won Best Album at the 1998 ARIA awards.

Savage Garden

The combination of Darren Hayes (singer) and Daniel Jones (writer) went from a couple of lads playing local Brisbane gigs to megastars on the world scene in the space of just over 12 months. They set the standard for pop music for the next decade with 'I Want You', 'To the Moon and Back' and

Savage Garden.

The Screaming Jets.

'Truly, Madly, Deeply'. Their self-titled album had a record run on top of the charts for 14 consecutive weeks and they scooped the pool at the 1997 ARIA Awards with a record-breaking 10 awards.

The Screaming Jets
They hit instant fame in 1991 with the smash hit 'Better'. They are the untamed boys of Aussie rock with their wild and spectacular stage show. From Newcastle, New South Wales, they tour extensively in the USA and UK with cult followings. Their hits include 'Helping Hand', 'Sad Song' and a cover of Nick Cave's 'Shiver'.

silverchair
After five years of phenomenal success, this trio of Novocastrians, with their obscure grunge-rock, are still at the top. With more maturity

and sense of purpose they have found a new sound, blending futuristic noises with classical influences to create an unusual, electrifying blend. Their albums include *Pure Massacre*, *Freak Show* and *Neon Ballroom*, which contains the hit 'Anthem for the Year 2000'.

TISM (This Is Serious Mum)
A quirky pop band who poke savage fun at just about anything. They keep a gruelling schedule, maintaining a carefully crafted incognito presence playing to sell-out concerts. Their lead singer-songwriter goes under the pseudonym Ron Hitler-Barassi! Hit songs include 'Greg, the Stop Sign!' and 'He'll Never be an Ol' Man River'.

The Whitlams
The brutal dynamics between founder-members Tim Freedman, Stevie Plunder and Andy Lewis drew crowds from

silverchair.

The Whitlams.

You Am I.

the start to hear their mixture of tidy jazz-pop melodic funk. After Plunder died the band wrote *Eternal Nightcap* as a tribute to him. It was spearheaded by the tragicomic ballard 'No Aphrodisiac', which was ARIA song of the year in 1998.

Yothu Yindi

With an unusual mix of traditional dance and strong rock rhythms, this award-winning Aboriginal band brought to the attention of the world the passions and frustrations of their people. The *Tribal Voice* album, from which came the single 'Treaty', pushed them to the top of the charts. Then came 'Djapana', 'Freedom' and the *Bercuta* album, with the hit 'Super Highway'.

You Am I

A Sydney three-piece who came to prominence in 1993 with their first album *Sound as Ever*. In 1995 they set a precedent by debuting at No. 1 on both the mainstream and alternative charts with their sophomore release *Hi Fi Way*, gaining international recognition. Their album *Hourly, Daily* was released in 1997 to critical acclaim. Frontman Tim Rogers also enjoys a successful solo career.

Yothu Yindi.

Merril Bainbridge.

Solo artists of the 1980s and 90s

Christine Anu c. 1973–

Born in the islands of the Torres Strait, her music is a weave of many different threads – her background of an idyllic island existence, her foray into indigenous dance and her life in the harsh city. There are traces of funk, soul, hip-hop, reggae and dub in her music. Her debut album *Stylin' Up* was certified gold and yielded the hit songs, 'Island Home' and 'Party'. She recently played Mimi in the rock musical *Rent* to great acclaim.

Tina Arena 1967–

From 'Young Talent Time' popette to hugely successful international star, her *Don't Ask* debut album notched up 50 weeks on top of the charts. The record-breaking multi-platinum hit singles 'Chains' and 'Burn' were both huge internationally.

Merril Bainbridge c.1970

It was the pop tune 'Mouth' that rocketed her to prominence domestically and internationally. Her follow-up single 'The Garden' confirmed her popularity, particularly with younger audiences.

Jimmy Barnes 1956–

The gravel-voiced lead singer of the legendary Cold Chisel has the well-earned title of wild man of Australian rock. Since the demise of Cold Chisel he has pushed his own brand of music, writing and singing popular rock tunes to a loyal and fanatical audience. There are huge sales of anything that bears his name. *Bodyswerve* was his first post-Chisel album, then came *Freight Train Heart, Soul Deep* and *Two Fires*. His top hits include 'Working Class Man', 'Stone Cold' and 'Lover'.

Nick Cave 1957–

Evolving from the dynamic Melbourne punk culture of the late 1970s, this confronting and outrageous singer/songwriter and author, with his band The Birthday Party, played a mixture of extreme demonic music and sombre, moody works to huge European audiences. With his current band The Bad Seeds, his brutal narratives, often considered harrowing and intimidating, continue to break new ground. His 1997 hit album was *The Boatman's Call*.

Kate Ceberano 1966–

Her sultry vocal ability, embodying a great natural style

and range, enable her to travel from pop to jazz to funk with ease. Her hit singles include 'You've Always Got the Blues', 'Let You Down', 'Bedroom Eyes' and 'Pash'.

Richard Clapton c. 1946–

A singer/songwriter and considered the 'Godfather' of Aussie rock. Collaborating with Cold Chisel and INXS, his classic hits like 'Girls on the Avenue', 'I am an Island' and 'Glory Road' have spanned three decades and attract enormous attention. A brand-new generation of fans are stomping to 'Distant Thunder' and 'Angel Town'.

John Farnham 1949–

A hugely successful 1960s teen idol, he became 'King of Pop' when he was 17 with the hit 'Sadie, the Cleaning Lady'.

Natalie Imbruglia.

He reclaimed his career in the 1980s fronting the Little River Band. They parted and his solo career took him from pop idol to national icon with enormous success. His powerful and technically capable voice is considered one of the best ever produced in Australia. The powerful *Whispering Jack* album of the 1980s from which comes the record-breaking single 'You're the Voice', attracted mega followings. Other hits include 'Chain Reaction', 'Touch of Paradise' and 'Every Time You Cry' (with Human Nature).

Natalie Imbruglia 1975–

Her meteoric rise to international fame after the debut album *Left of the Middle* and its instant-classic single 'Torn' was nothing short of breathtaking. Her easy postmodern guitar pop and charismatic openness assure this dedicated artist a place in the post-grunge music scene.

John Farnham.

Paul Kelly.

Paul Kelly 1955–

A sensitive singer/songwriter whose lyrics, coupled with simple, hypnotic music, reflect down-to-earth detail in simple word pictures of heroes who do ordinary things. His sensitivity, warmth and understanding of human nature and the darker side of modern living entitles him to be called 'The poet of the common man'. *Comedy*, *Gossip* and *Post* are outstanding examples of his work. He won Most Popular Artist ARIA award in 1997 as well as the prestigious honour of being inducted into the Hall of Fame. His album *Songs of the South* went double platinum and he has since released *Words and Music*.

Ed Kuepper c. 1952–

Since the early 1970s, when he played blistering punk rock with the primordial band The Saints, his career has had many detours. Sometimes it is prickly guitar rock moderated with jazz and at other times it embraces disco/folk. His album *Frontierland* exposed the many facets of his extraordinary ability.

Richard Lowenstein 1960–

Among the new wave of international film-makers of the 1970s, he pioneered and perfected the technique of video filming. He made videos for famous rock bands such as INXS and Cold Chisel as well as the Aussie cult film *Dogs in Space*.

Wendy Matthews 1960–

A back-up singer through the 1980s, in the early 90s she was Australia's premier female artist. The huge hits 'Émigré', 'Lily' and 'The Witness Tree' are all fine examples of her work.

Kylie Minogue 1968–

Her meteoric rise from soapie star to top international recording artist in the late 1980s was extraordinary. After topping the charts with a cover of the hit 'Locomotion', she had 10 hit singles worldwide. Songs penned by the team of Stock, Aitken and Waterman included 'I Should be so Lucky' and 'Better the Devil You Know', and became incredible hits, particularly with teenagers in the UK. Her 1998 album *Impossible Princess* spawned the hits 'Did it Again' and 'Some Kind of Bliss'.

Archie Roach.

Archie Roach 1956–

Aboriginal singer/songwriter with a rare ability to convey the deep emotions and hurt of his people. His debut album *Charcoal Lane* is widely regarded as one of the most compelling in Australian recording history. Other albums include *Jamu Dreaming*, *Looking for Butter Boy* and *Gondwana*.

Other artists of the 1990s are Peter Andre, Daryl Braithwaite, Deborah Conway, Diesel (Mark Lizotte), Grace Knight, Jenny Morris, Max Sharam, Vika and Linda, and Weddings Parties Anything.

Country music

For years this type of music was marginalised. Country singers were forced to travel constantly, honing their craft in a thousand tin-roofed halls of a thousand country towns to small but enthusiastic audiences. When rock'n'roll emerged in the 1950s, country was relegated to the backblocks of popular music and only a few remaining travelling performers such as Smoky Dawson, Rick and Thel Carey, Reg Lindsay, Tex Morton, Buddy Williams and Slim Dusty kept it

alive. Then came an awakening of interest. Radio programs broadcasting out of Tamworth in the late 1960s became extremely popular and an excitement in the air indicated a revival. The result was an astonishing expansion of popularity and the Tamworth Country Music Festival was born. Country music now has a following of 38% of the population over 18 and the new wave of contemporary musicians have the crowds enthralled.

James Blundell 1965–

He was a stockman who could sing, but this photogenic, talented country boy became one of the hottest acts in country music, breaking down urban barriers and attracting huge audiences with songs such as 'Kimberley Moon', 'Touch of Water' and 'Way Out West'. Lately he has changed direction slightly, with hits such as 'Amsterdam Breakfast' having less of a country twang.

James Blundell.

Troy Cassar-Daley.

Colin Buchanan 1964–

Born in Ireland, his break came when John Kane of The Flying Emus was convinced that 'Galahs in the Gidgee' was a classic, and became his mentor. Success was instantaneous. With wry and often witty observations, his songs reflect the lives and emotions of rural and urban folk who take it on the chin regardless of what is dealt out to them. 'Hard Times', 'Edge of the Kimberley' and 'The Measure of a Man' are songs telling of the 'real' Australia.

The Bushwackers

Born of the pub-rock era of the 1970s, their aggressive, uncompromising approach to traditional folk music draws huge crowds. Over 30 years musicians have come and gone, the band has broken up, re-formed and been revitalised but under the big stick of frontman

Dobe Newton, the band proved, with their *Oz Rock Salute* album, that they are still a force to be reckoned with. Their latest album is *No Nuts 'Til Monday*.

Troy Cassar-Daley c. 1968–

His talent was obvious from the time he began busking in the streets of Tamworth at the age of 12. In 1997 and 1998 the CMAA voted him entertainer of the year. He describes his music as 'country with attitude – more risqué'. His songs deal with timeless themes with strong influences drawn from his Aboriginal-Maltese background. 'Dream Out Loud', 'Beyond the Dreaming' and 'True Believer' assure his superstar status.

Graeme Connors 1955–

The 'quiet achiever' of country music, his writing reflects a strong sense of time and place. From his tongue-in-cheek 'I'm Married to My Bulldog Mac' to 'The Road Less Travelled', his remarkable and engaging stage presence has built up a huge following.

The Crosby Sisters

Jodie and Kelly are considered Australia's foremost harmony

The Crosby Sisters.

Slim Dusty.

duo. Although their roots are in traditional country, their refreshingly versatile music enables them to cross musical boundaries with ease. *Coming on Strong* is up there with the best in country music.

Smoky Dawson 1913–
A legendary figure for more than 70 years, this doyen of country music has attracted remarkable praise for the years of joy he has brought to both young and old. He has been involved in TV, Broadway musicals, radio, stage and screen production, song and script writing and rodeo. With his wonder horse Flash, he featured in TV advertising jingles. One of his biggest hits, 'Old Khancoban', came in 1988 from his album *High Country*.

The Dead Ringer Band
The ability to survive, combined with mental and physical strength bound by strong family ties, is the essence of this incredibly talented band. Made up of two generations of the Chambers family, their music is a reflection of life as they see it – raw, down to earth, unpretentious and truthful. Their single 'I am the Only One', from the highly acclaimed album *Living In The Circle* was top of the country charts for a record 15 weeks.

Slim Dusty 1927–
From an optimistic farm boy who dreamed of writing and singing country music, he has become a prolific recording artist, selling over 5 million units on the domestic market. Known as 'the historian of the bush', his songs have reflected the changing face of Australia for well over 50 years. He has recorded 96 albums. A worldwide hit was 'Pub With No Beer', in 1957.

Gina Jeffreys 1968–
Called the 'Golden Girl' of country, this singer/songwriter is at the forefront of

The Dead Ringer Band.

contemporary country music. Her exceptional vocal talents cover country, blues and folk music with overtones of an exciting rock beat. From the moment she won the prestigious Star Maker award in 1991, her career has been unstoppable. *The Flame* album surpassed platinum and her *Up Close* crossed over the barrier between country and mainstream, taking No. 1 position on the national country charts. A recent single was 'Somebody's Daughter'.

Lee Kernaghan 1959–

In the early part of his career he travelled around the country singing and writing songs reflecting life as he saw it. However, his fruitful songwriting partnership with Garth Porter in 1986 created a special type of magic which rushed him to the top with ferocious energy. His appeal to huge crowds both in the country and the city has earned him the reputation of single-handedly moving country music towards the 21st century. The recent album *Hat Town* went platinum.

Tania Kernaghan c. 1964–

Coming from one of Australia's most prolific musical families and possessing a remarkable voice, her debut album *December Moon* and the subsequent *Dancing on Water* and *Dunroaming Station* assured her recognition as one of the finest female country singers.

Anne Kirkpatrick 1952–

From an early age she has been immersed in music and the travelling life. The daughter of Slim Dusty and Joy McKean, this gifted singer has a unique style. Her album *Cry Like a Man* contained a collection of hard-hitting, truthful and evocative songs.

Reg Lindsay 1929–

This appealing down-to-earth showman has toured every inch of the continent over the past 40 years, gathering a huge following wherever he has appeared. His trademark is his voice, once described as rich, mellow and like fine wine – it keeps on getting better. He is now taking time out to relax a little. Hits include 'July, You're a Woman', 'Silence on the Line' and 'Armstrong'.

Jimmy Little 1937–

The gentleman of Australian country music, he has thoroughly earned this reputation with a magnificent career spanning over 40 years. His smooth, mellow voice and intimate and warm performances have built up an incredible affection between legions of fans and performer. 'Royal Telephone', 'I Love You Because', 'Baby Blue' and 'Yorta Yorta Man' are his major successes.

John Williamson 1945–

His perception and deep understanding of human nature allows this Aussie balladeer to write enormously popular

John Williamson.

songs which strike a chord in most of us. 'Old Man Emu' was the first of many great hits. Others include 'True Blue', 'Cootamundra Wattle', 'Mallee Boy', 'Goodbye Blinky Bill', 'Rip Rip Woodchip' and 'Pipedream'.

Popular music

Hundreds of talented musicians have contributed over the years to the music scene. Names such as June Bronhill, Rhonda Burchmore, Peter Dawson, Jon English, Paul Grabowsky, Rolf Harris, Nancye Hayes, Kamahl, Ricky May, Gladys Moncrieff, Patsy Ann Noble and Jill Perryman evoke memories of fantastic performances, which have sometimes changed the direction of music in Australia.

Peter Allen 1944–92
Born in Tenterfield, New South Wales, this internationally renowned songwriter and performer has been immortalised in the musical *The Boy from Oz*. The nostalgic 'I Still Call Australia Home' is probably his best-known song, along with 'I Go to Rio', 'Tenterfield Saddler' and 'Don't Cry Out Loud'.

David Atkins 1955–
He has danced professionally for more than 20 years. With remarkable ability and enormous energy he has choreographed and danced in hugely successful shows such as *Dancing Man, Hot Shoe Shuffle* and *Little Shop of Horrors*.

Don Burrows 1928–
A jazz musician whose distinguished career spans more than 40 years. He excels with flute, saxophone and clarinet and is renowned for his special interest in children's music and his command of Latin American music.

David Campell 1973–
Actor, singer and cabaret performer. His major break-through performance came with his role as Tim in the musical *Only Heaven Knows* at the Sydney Opera House. His appearance at the New York Cabaret Convention led to a series of cabaret performances in that city. He played to sell-out houses and to standing ovations. He was given the role of Marius in the Sydney production of *Les Miserables* in 1997/98 and sang with his father, Jimmy Barnes, at the NRL Grand Final in 1998.

Tommy Emmanuel.

Tommy Emmanuel 1955–
Regarded as one of the world's finest guitarists, his music is an integration of blues, rockabilly and bluegrass interspersed with classical and Spanish flamenco. Hits include 'Guitar Boogie', 'Terry on the Turnpike', 'Determination' and 'The Journey'.

Adam Garcia 1974–
High-energy performer who won the coveted role of dance-floor romeo Tony Manero in the recent stage version of *Saturday Night Fever* in London's West End.

Todd McKenney c. 1968–
Inspiring all-round performer and choreographer whose energy and stage presence in starring roles in the musicals *Crazy for You* and *The Boy from Oz* have dazzled audiences.

James Morrison 1962–
A world-famous virtuoso jazz musician and a brilliant technician with startling originality. His natural sense of humour and his ability to play 16 instruments, excelling at trumpet and trombone, makes him a highly sought-after performer. Hits are 'Men Are Dangerous', 'Two the Max' and 'Hot Horn Happening'.

Dein Perry 1959–
Creator of the stage phenomenon *Tap Dogs*, performed by the harsh, steel-hard boots-and-all dance troupe which also gave us *Steel City*. Their energy and volatility, reflecting their Newcastle origins, have mesmerised audiences worldwide.

Marina Prior 1964–
A feisty opera singer who went from busking in the street in 1983 to the lead role of Mabel

Todd McKenney in **The Boy from Oz.**

James Morrison.

tremendous success in *Les Miserables* and was the voice that gave *The Phantom of the Opera* a spirit all of its own. He has performed as Higgins in *My Fair Lady* and as Archibald Carew in *The Secret Garden* and has released several highly successful albums.

Other popular artists are Julie Anthony, Debra Byrne, Nathan Cavaleri, Geoff Harvey and The Seekers.

Classical music

Cultural isolation from Europe in the late 19th century affected our music greatly. Few home-grown musicians or composers achieved levels expected of them. It wasn't until the Leipzig-trained Alfred Hill and Percy Grainger returned from Europe that a new level of technical professionalism was achieved and accepted.

John Antill 1908–86
Composer and former assistant musical director for the ABC. His ballet *Corroboree* is based on snatches of tunes gleaned from the music of the Aborigines at La Perouse, Sydney.

Don Banks 1923–80
Leading Australian composer and teacher, specialising in the composition of electronic music. In the 1950s he established the Australian Music Association in London, which introduced Australian composers and performers to the international circuit.

in *The Pirates of Penzance*. Then came *Camelot* and the prestigious female lead of Christine in *The Phantom of the Opera*. She has starred in numerous productions, including *Les Miserables* and *The Merry Widow*.

Geraldine Turner 1951–
Not only has this versatile actress performed in many facets of film, TV and theatre, she has sung and danced across the stage of many popular musicals, including *Anything Goes*, *Sweeney Todd* and the 1997 production of *Cabaret*.

Tommy Tycho 1928–
He migrated from Hungary in 1951, bringing with him the twin gifts of genius and excellent training. He is highly acclaimed as a superb conductor, composer, arranger and virtuoso pianist.

Anthony Warlow 1962–
With his glorious baritone voice with a tenor reach, he had

Richard Bonynge 1930–
An opera conductor, he was the vocal coach for Joan Sutherland; they married in 1954. His conducting debut was with the Santa Cecilia Orchestra in Rome in 1962. He was the musical director of the Australian Opera from 1975 to 1986, and is renowned for his interest in the lesser-known operas of the 18th and 19th centuries. (See also **Opera**.)

Brenton Broadstock 1952–
As a composer and educator, he has made a significant and diverse contribution throughout his career. He is one of Australia's most frequently performed composers and is best known for his symphonies, compositions for brass band, wind and other chamber ensembles, musical theatre and vocal pieces. His music is performed by national and international artists and orchestras. His works include his first symphony *Towards the Shining Light* and his third symphony *Voices of the Fire*. He is the 1999 recipient of the Australia Council's prestigious Don Banks Music Award.

Nigel Butterley 1935–
A contemporary composer specialising in music for string quartets, he won the prestigious Italia Prize for *In the Head the Fire*, a musical work for radio. His music has often been inspired by poetry and architecture.

Stuart Challender 1947–91
A Tasmanian, he began his musical career at the age of five. He was guest conductor of many of the world's great orchestras, including the Chicago Symphony Orchestra. He was considered to be a master of the large symphony, and was chief conductor of the Sydney Symphony Orchestra.

Sir Eugene Goossens 1893–1962
An Englishman, he became the resident composer and conductor of the Sydney Symphony Orchestra and co-director of the New South Wales Conservatorium of Music in 1947. He was the SSO's greatest single influence, changing it from a city orchestra to one which was world class. He turned Sydney into a mecca for the world's finest artists.

Percy Grainger 1882–1961
A pianist and composer of world fame, he gave concerts as a child and at the age of 11 continued his musical studies in Germany. His irreverent and uninhibited approach to the piano delighted his audiences everywhere. His most famous compositions are *Shepherd's Hey* and *Country Gardens*.

Slava Grigoryan 1976–
Born in Khazakstan, he was raised in Melbourne from the age of five and was taught guitar by his violinist father. He toured extensively overseas from the age of 12, receiving standing ovations and many awards. His work is 'expressive and daring'

and his brilliant performances as a classical guitarist receive international acclaim.

Michael Kieran Harvey 1961–
A piano virtuoso who has won international acclaim, including the Ivo Pogelorich International Piano competition, 1993, USA and the Debussy Gold Medal in Paris 1996. He has played with most of the world's greatest orchestras, notably the Concertgebouw Orchestra in Amsterdam.

Sir Bernard Heinze 1894–1982
A powerful musical administrator who virtually controlled the classical musical scene in the 1940s and 50s. He was director of the New South Wales Conservatorium of Music and music adviser to the ABC, and he was responsible for all the states having their own symphony orchestras. He trained thousands of young musicians, and his music examination methods became the foundation for music exams today.

Alfred Francis Hill 1870–1960
A gifted violinist, at 15 he studied at the Leipzig Conservatorium. Through his innovative work he co-founded the New South Wales State Conservatorium of Music in Sydney in 1897, which represented a significant advancement in Australian music.

Eileen Joyce 1912–91
Born in the Tasmanian bush, she grew up in Kalgoorlie and later became an international concert pianist. By 1950 she had the widest following of any concert pianist in England.

Elena Kats-Chernin 1957–
Born in Russia, she received her classical training in Moscow, Sydney and Hanover. In 1994 she settled permanently in Australia and became a full-time composer. She enjoys international acclaim, her music being described as 'complex and academic but beautiful and full of fun'.

Festival Centre, Adelaide.

Joseph Post 1906–72
One of the most experienced and respected of Australia's conductors, his characteristic brisk, down-to-earth intensity was highly regarded. He was the original director of the Elizabethan Opera Company, associate conductor of the Sydney Symphony Orchestra, and a director of the New South Wales Conservatorium of Music.

Karin Schaupp.

Karin Schaupp c.1975–
German-born Karin is regarded as 'the poet of the guitar'. Her meticulous interpretation of Spanish masterworks and an incredible technique, coupled with poignant artistry, make her a major new talent on the national and international stage.

Peter Sculthorpe 1929–
Talented contemporary composer. From 1965 to 1967 he wrote 'Sun Music I–IV' based on the Australian landscape. Other works include the operas *Rites of Passage* and *Quiros,* and the vocal-orchestral works *Child of Australia* and *Great Sandy Island.* In 1997 he collaborated with the Aboriginal Islander Dance Theatre on a Festival of the Dreaming Project.

Margaret Sutherland 1897–1984
She pioneered new music in the first half of the 20th century when Australian composers experienced public indifference and a profound sense of isolation. She wrote some of the country's most original and striking works. All her life she promoted Australian music, especially in the field of education.

John Williams 1941–
One of the world's leading classical guitarists, his music possesses a distinctive clarity of tone. At the age of 12 he studied with the world-famous guitarist Andres Segovia, after which he toured extensively. In 1979 he formed the jazz-orientated group Sky.

Malcolm Williamson 1931–
A prolific composer, he was appointed Master of the Queen's Musick in 1975. His best-known works are the music for Robert Helpmann's ballet *The Display* and the opera *English Eccentrics,* which premiered at the Aldeburgh Festival in England.

Roger Woodward 1942–
An acclaimed pianist, he studied in London and Warsaw and made his debut with the Warsaw National Philharmonic Orchestra in 1967. His wide repertoire ranges from Beethoven and Chopin to Australian contemporary music.

Simone Young 1962–
Regarded as one of the most highly talented conductors of her time, she makes guest appearances conducting orchestras worldwide. She broke new ground in 1993 when she became the first female conductor of the all-male Berlin Philharmonic Orchestra. She is musical director designate of Opera Australia.

Ballet

In 1938 Edouard Borovansky established his renowned ballet company in Melbourne. Before this, overseas companies enjoyed great success in Australia but the local artists were viewed with some degree of apathy. His company was a pioneering force for the next two decades, with local artists and productions of high quality. In 1962 a new national company was formed, The Australian Ballet under the artistic direction of Peggy van Praagh. This, together with subsidies from the federal government in the 1970s, enabled Australian ballet to at last become recognised worldwide.

[Throughout the text the Australian Ballet is abbreviated to AB, the Sydney Dance Company to SDC and the Australian Dance Theatre to ADT.]

Early artists

Margaret Barr 1904–91
A protégé of Martha Graham of New York, she was an imaginative and independent dancer, choreographer and teacher.

Edouard Borovansky 1902–59
Czech-born, he came to Australia as a dancer with Anna Pavlova in 1926. In 1938 he returned and the following year founded the Borovansky Ballet Company in Melbourne. This company was the nucleus of the present AB.

Kelvin Coe 1946–92
A foundation member of the AB, he and Marilyn Rowe-Maver were the first Australians to compete in the Moscow International Ballet Competition, in 1973.

Sir Robert Helpmann 1909–86
Born in Adelaide, he danced his way to fame in 1933, partnering Dame Margot Fonteyn at Sadler's Wells Ballet. He created the first all-Australian ballet, *The Display*, in 1964.

Marilyn Jones 1940–
Widely considered to be Australia's greatest prima ballerina, she was acclaimed for her interpretation of the great classics.

Laurel Martyn 1916–
Her distinguished career spanned more than half a century. She danced with the famed Sadler's Wells Ballet, and for 30 years was director of the Victoria Ballet Guild.

Garry Norman 1951–
An inspired dancer, his elevation to soloist and a principal dancer with the AB was meteoric. He toured the world extensively and is now teaching at the Royal Ballet School.

Colin Peasley 1934–
His background in theatre, TV, classical ballet and modern dance has developed his extraordinary ability to recreate character roles. He is presently the Manager of Education Programs with the AB.

Dame Margaret Scott 1922–
She danced with Sadler's Wells Ballet in London (1940–52). She became a founding director of the AB School in 1964, and retired in 1990 after more than fifty years' association with ballet.

Dame Peggy van Praagh 1910–90
A dancer and ballet mistress with Sadler's Wells Ballet, she became the founding artistic director of the AB, which encouraged and established the careers of many young talented dancers.

Garth Welch 1936–
A distinguished ballet virtuoso, choreographer and highly innovative teacher of abstract dance over many years. His contribution to the ballet scene and encouragement to students have been invaluable.

Contemporary artists

Vicki Attard c. 1967–
An accomplished principal artist with the AB whose inspired performances in the title role of *Giselle* and the lead roles of Odette in *Swan Lake* and Cio-Cio-San in *Madame Butterfly* were highly praised.

Stephen Baynes 1954–
After a distinguished international career he was appointed resident choreographer with the AB in 1995. His works include *Rococo Variations*, *Beyond Bach* and *Shadow in the Facet,* which was set to the music of Ravel.

Lisa Bolte c. 1975–
Studying abroad, but initially training in Sydney, she joined the AB and in 1993 was promoted to principal artist. She has danced lead roles in *Onegin, Romeo and Juliet* and *Theme and Variations*.

Miranda Coney 1966–
A principal artist with the AB, her extensive repertoire, which includes the lead roles in *Romeo and Juliet* and *The Sleeping Beauty* has placed this Perth-born artist at the top of her profession.

Maina Gielgud 1945–
Determination and energy marked her years as artistic director of the AB (1983–96).

Steven Heathcote 1965–
Born in Perth, he has toured extensively. His vast classical

repertoire has gained for him principal dancer status with the AB, where he has performed lead roles in *Swan Lake*, *La Sylphide*, *The Sleeping Beauty* and *Spartacus*.

Greg Horsman 1963–

A former principal artist in the AB, he became a senior principal dancer with the English National Ballet in 1994.

David McAllister 1963–

With an extensive repertoire, his performances are inspiring. He is a principal artist with the AB and his outstanding solo roles include those in *Equus* and *Don Quixote*.

Paul Mercurio 1963–

A multi-talented dancer and choreographer whose strong sense of theatre and unconventional approach to dance compelled him to break with classical ballet. He joined the SDC and has danced in more than 30 productions. He shot to stardom with the film *Strictly Ballroom* but then has returned to the SDC and performed to great acclaim in his own piece *Dancing with The Clown*, celebrating the company's 20th anniversary.

Graeme Murphy 1950–

Melbourne-born, he became the artistic and choreographic director of the SDC in 1976. With his great talent and unusual approach, over the years he has become the inspiration for young dancers to break away from the classical mould, creating exciting and innovative dance.

Stephen Page 1960–

A descendant of the Munaldjali clan (Queensland), his dance career began with the SDC where he danced and choreographed pieces such as *Mooggrah* and *Late Afternoon of a Faun*. He became principal choreographer of the Bangarra Dance Theatre and his works included *Ninni* and *Ochres*. His first commission for the AB was *Alchemy* in 1996.

Bill Pengelly 1956–

Versatile choreographer with wide experience whose classical training as a dancer began in Queensland. He moved to the SDC, where he made the transition from

Steven Heathcote in **Spartacus**.

dancer to dance master and honed his skills as a teacher, coach and repetiteur. He is now artistic director of the ADT.

Marilyn Rowe 1946–
The first ballerina to reach the pinnacle of her profession having trained only with the AB. In 1973, together with Kelvin Coe, she won a silver medal in Moscow. She became a director of the AB school in 1999.

Gailene Stock 1946–
In 1962, at the age of 16, she was the youngest member of the fledgling AB. She toured extensively and is currently director of the Royal Ballet School.

Ross Stretton c. 1950–
A dancer who has always been driven by creativity and passion. He began his career in Australia but joined the American Ballet Theatre, eventually becoming assistant director. He was appointed artistic director of the AB in 1997.

Justine Summers c. 1974–
A talented dancer whose training embraced both classical and modern dance. She is now a principal artist with the AB.

Meryl Tankard c. 1957–
Highly creative and inventive dancer who is renowned for giving 'new life' to the dance. She was artistic

Justine Summers, Damien Welch and Vicki Attard in Divergence.

director of the ADT from 1993 to 1999 and is recognised as an international choreographer who pushes the boundaries of contemporary dance.

Damien Welch c. 1972–
Brother of Stanton and a principal artist with the AB, he tours extensively and was one of six Australian dancers who worked with Twyla Tharp in New York on *The Storyteller* for the Melbourne Festival.

Stanton Welch 1967–
Son of renowned dancers Marilyn Jones and Garth Welch, his classical background and individual style have led him to choreograph such highly acclaimed works as *Divergence* and *Madame Butterfly*. He was appointed resident choreographer at the AB in 1995.

Other dancers of note are Li Cunxin, Beth Dean, Paul De Masson, Adam Marchant, Lisa Pavane and Roslyn Watson.

Opera

Opera has always been popular in Australia, and eisteddfods and aria competitions foster the aspirations of young singers. The tendency in the past has been to disregard local talent in favour of overseas singers and productions; singers were expected to have European training before they were recognised. Great Australian singers of the early part of the century were:

Florence Austral 1894–1968
She stood supreme among world sopranos. Her great vocal ability to evoke strong emotion enchanted audiences and was unparalleled. She battled for many years with multiple sclerosis.

John Brownlee 1900–69
A world-famous operatic baritone who was encouraged in his career by Dame Nellie Melba and sang duets with her in the early 1900s.

Dorothy Helmrich 1889–1984
The first Australian to achieve worldwide recognition as a lieder singer, she founded the Arts

Council movement in Australia in 1943 to enable the youth of the nation to experience music and the arts.

Gertrude Johnson 1894–1973
A coloratura soprano, she was a pupil of Melba. She founded the National Theatre Movement in 1934, which produced operas with all-Australian casts.

Marjorie Lawrence 1909–79
A brilliant soprano, she made operatic history in Europe by riding a horse into the flames on stage as Brünnhilde in *Der Ring des Nibelungen,* as Wagner intended. In 1941 she contracted poliomyelitis but made many wheelchair appearances.

Dame Nellie Melba 1861–1931
Her voice was acclaimed everywhere for its purity and silvery brilliance of tone. Gounod coached her in the role of Juliet in his opera *Romeo et Juliette,* and Puccini chose her to play Mimi in his *La Bohème* in 1900.

In 1934 the National Theatre Movement was established, and in 1951 Clarice Lorenz set up the National Opera in Australia. The Australian Elizabethan Theatre

Madame Butterfly.

Trust was formed in 1956, and now with government and private funding Australian opera is at last highly regarded internationally. Artists of the mid to late 20th century include:

Robert Allman 1927–
A principal baritone of world renown, his ability and sensitivity enable him to create wonderful dramatic characters such as Tonio in *Pagliacci*.

Maroochy Barambah c. 1955–
An Aboriginal singer with a remarkable contralto range. In the early 1990s she defied the white establishment when they said black opera singers did not exist in Australia. She stunned everybody as one of the stars of the award-winning opera *Black River*, then came her performance as Maria in *Porgy and Bess*, a role which blazed the trail for other Aboriginal singers of the 90s.

Cheryl Barker c. 1960–
Studying and honing her craft under Dame Joan Hammond, her beautiful soprano voice and outstanding talent have won her many prestigious roles, such as Mimi in *La Bohème*, Violetta in *La Traviata* and Cio-Cio-San in *Madame Butterfly*. Now based in London, she makes regular appearances throughout Britain as well as at the Royal Opera House, Covent Garden.

Heather Begg 1933–
A New Zealand-born mezzo soprano with an international career spanning nearly 40 years. Well known for her extensive repertoire of character roles, such as Flora in *La Traviata* and Mother Marie in *Dialogues of the Carmelites*.

Harold Blair 1924–76
An Aboriginal tenor, he was born at Cherbourg Station, Queensland, and was the first of his race to achieve international fame singing opera. His natural flair and clear tenor voice, nurtured in church choirs, placed him on the world stage in the 1940s.

Joan Carden 1937–
A soprano, and one of the most remarkable singers to emerge in Australia. Her international performances were highly acclaimed; in 1971 she returned home and began a long association with national opera, with singing engagements all over Australia.

Peter Coleman-Wright 1959–
A seasoned performer of huge international standing, his musical range is astounding. He has been

Cheryl Barker.

described as having a consistently beautiful voice, unforced and passionate, which allows this baritone to dominate the world stage. He recently returned home to play the hero of Britten's *Billy Budd*, which has become a signature role.

Marie Collier 1927–71
A dramatic and flamboyant soprano, her greatest triumph came in 1964 when she stood in for Maria Callas in *Tosca* at Covent Garden, taking 14 curtain calls and 20 minutes of applause. She fell to her death from her apartment window in London in 1971.

Dame Joan Hammond 1912–96
A soprano, she upheld the traditions of Nellie Melba and Florence Austral and reigned supreme in prima donna roles. She toured the world extensively and was noted for her superb singing in the role of *Tosca*.

Yvonne Kenny 1951–
A leading soprano, she appears regularly in operas around the world as well as performing with famous orchestras in Europe. She has topped the classical music charts with popular opera and song selections for ABC Classics.

Yvonne Kenny.

Moffatt Oxenbould 1943–
He was appointed artistic director of Opera Australia in 1984. His great vision has been responsible for the development of many young performers, designers and directors.

Graham Pushee c.1955–
Much sought-after because of his unusual counter-tenor voice, he has appeared in most of the famous opera houses of the world to sell-out audiences. He has an extensive repertoire, including the title role in Handel's *Julius Caesar* and Andronico in Handel's *Tamerlano*.

Donald Shanks 1940–
A bass baritone from Brisbane who has been singing

DID YOU KNOW?

Opera Australia begins preparation for future seasons five years in advance. In general terms a new production could cost between $1 million and $1.5m (1999).

Cleopatra and Julius Caesar.

professionally with Opera Australia since he was 24. His versatility spans dramatic, comic and *bel canto* styles, and his roles include many from the works of Wagner and Verdi. He is in great demand overseas.

John Shaw 1924–
A baritone, he began his international career as Rigoletto at Covent Garden in 1958. He is renowned for his roles as Iago in *Otello* and Scarpia in *Tosca*.

Dame Joan Sutherland 1926–
The foremost soprano of our age and one of the greatest operatic artists of all time. Her husband and coach, conductor Richard Bonynge, recognised the potential of her voice, and together they resurrected some of the seldom-sung major *bel canto* roles in opera. She retired in 1990.

Neil Warren-Smith 1929–81
A leading principal bass singer with a refreshing comic talent who sang with Opera Australia for 25 years.

Art

The Dreaming is an Aboriginal philosophy explaining the origins of the universe. It embraces people, animals and landscape as part of a harmonious whole. Ancient Aboriginal art, spanning tens of thousands of years, reflected this theme. There are many cave paintings and rock carvings of great significance still in existence. The modern resurgence of Aboriginal art, incorporating new forms, continues this rich tradition and philosophy.

For early European painters in Australia, the new land was so strange that they found it difficult to reproduce a true likeness of their surroundings. Convict painters, such as Joseph Lycett, John Eyre and Thomas Watling, and artists among the free settlers who arrived as early as 1830 produced bland images more reminiscent of the gentler landscape of their homeland than the harsher landscape of Australia.

Abram-Louis Buvelot 1814–88
Swiss-born, he excelled in painting the elusive colours of light in the Australian landscape. He brought to Australia the traditions of European landscape painting. He profoundly influenced young artists of the 1860s and 70s by encouraging them to paint outdoors.

Charles Conder 1868–1909
A surveyor, he met Tom Roberts in a Sydney wine bar in 1888 and returned with him to Melbourne where he spent

The Sunny South *by Tom Roberts.*

two years painting at the artists' camp. His paintings include *The Departure of the S.S. Orient* and *A Holiday at Mentone* (both 1888).

John Glover 1767–1849
He arrived in Tasmania in 1831, aged 64. He recognised the differences and subtleties of light in Australia, which is evident in his paintings *Patterdale Farm* (c. 1840) and *Glover's House and Garden* (1840).

Sir Hans Heysen 1877–1968
Emigrated with his parents from Germany, and settled in Hahndorf, South Australia. He remained completely unaffected by the popular theories of the day, and had a single-minded devotion to one ideal: capturing the beauty and majesty of the Australian landscape. A notable example is *Summer* (1909).

Frederick McCubbin 1855–1917
Inspired by the landscape around Melbourne, more than any painter before him he understood the Australian

bush. His paintings frequently told of the hardship of the pioneers: *Down on his Luck* (1889), *The Wallaby Track* (1896) and the three-panel work *The Pioneer* (1904).

Sir Bertram Mackennal 1863–1931
A prolific sculptor, in 1888 he completed the panelling for Government House in Melbourne. His most famous works are *Circe* (1893) and a marble bust of Dame Nellie Melba (1899).

Conrad Martens 1801–78
A watercolourist, he left England in 1832 and after sailing around the world for three years settled in Sydney. His main paintings are *Sydney* (1857) and *The Viaduct Lithgow* (1876).

Max Meldrum 1875–1955
A former pupil of Frederick McCubbin, he caused a sensation in art circles by challenging the Heidelberg School's theories. His ideas of

Shearing the Rams *by Tom Roberts.*

strict tonal painting were promoted through his own art school, which he began in 1913. One of his most famous works showing tonal theory is *Portrait of the Artist's Mother* (1913).

Tom Roberts 1856–1931
The 'father' of Australian landscape painting. A pupil of Buvelot and influenced by French Impressionism, he recognised the subtle effects of changing light on colour. He and Frederick McCubbin started the now-famous painting camps outside Melbourne, and together with Arthur Streeton and Charles Conder were the first Australian painters to capture the spirit and colour of the Australian landscape. They became known as the Heidelberg School of Australian Impressionism. His paintings include *Bailed Up* (1895), *Shearing the Rams* (1890) and *Breakaway* (1891).

Sir Arthur Streeton 1867–1943
Revered as the painter who 'fixed the images of his country', he was an official World War I artist and his works are displayed in the Australian War Memorial in Canberra. His most noted paintings include *Fire's On, Lapstone Tunnel* (1891) and *The Purple Noon's Transparent Might* (1896).

During the first part of the 20th century post-impressionism came to prominence. The many influences resulted in a kaleidoscope of differing styles, which gave rise to the Modern Movement in Australia. Experiments with texture and colour allowed artists to be less restricted. They became aware of the vastness of the desolate landscape, the intimidating urban scene and the hostility of war.

Arthur Boyd 1920–99
Along with artists such as Albert Tucker, Sidney Nolan, John

Perceval and Danila Vassilieff, he belonged to the 'Angry Decade' of 1937–47 which disliked the complacency of Australian society. Works include *The Butterfly Man* (1943), *Wimmera Landscape* (1950), *Figure in Landscape* (1961) and *Landscape at Murrumbeena* (1987).

Judy Cassab 1920–

Born in Vienna, she migrated to Australia with her husband after World War II. She is best known as a portrait painter in an abstract and impressionist style. Her portraits of the royal family were hung at the Royal Academy, London, in 1962.

Grace Cossington Smith 1892–1984

Together with Roland Wakelin and Roy de Maistre, she established the Modern Movement in Sydney. Her painting *The Sock Knitter* (1915) was the first modern painting by an Australian to be exhibited in Australia.

Sir William Dobell 1899–1970

His finest works were portraits such as *Margaret Olley* (1948) and *Dame Mary Gilmore* (1957). He won the Archibald Prize in 1943 with the controversial portrait *Joshua Smith.* Other work includes *The Boy at the Basin* (1932) and *The Billy Boy* (1943).

Sir Russell Drysdale 1912–81

He was born in England into a family whose members had been among the pioneer pastoralists of Australia. *Two Children* (1946), *The Rabbiters* (1947) and *Sofala* (1947) are among his best-known works which capture the desolation and colour of the outback.

The Rabbiters *by Russell Drysdale.*

Sali Herman 1898–1993
Swiss-born, he migrated to Australia in 1937. He is best known for his paintings of the early slums and tenements of Sydney, particularly the Paddington, Kings Cross and Woolloomooloo areas. Typical of his works are *Potts Point* (1957) and *Colonial Castle* (1958).

Norman Lindsay 1879–1969
A controversial and multi-talented artist whose works included woodcuts, watercolours and etchings. Well-known pieces are *Pollice Verso* (1907) and *The Crucified Venus* (1907). He wrote and illustrated the children's book *The Magic Pudding* (1918).

Albert Namatjira 1902–59
A full-blooded member of the Arrernte tribe, his watercolours of Central Australia became very popular in the 1950s and 60s. He handled European techniques with great skill.

Sir Sidney Nolan 1917–92
One of the most distinguished Australian painters of the century, he often painted series which together captured a changing mood or action. *Paradise Gardens,* consisting of 1320 paintings, was given by Sir Sidney to the Victorian Arts Centre and is permanently housed there. Other examples are *Pretty Polly Mine* (1948) and the *Ned Kelly* series (1956).

Margaret Preston 1875–1963
A prolific painter, she was a forthright modernist who had an instinctive feel for colour. Later in her career she was influenced by Aboriginal art and carvings. Her works include *Implement Blue* (1927) and *Gum Blossoms* (1927).

Lloyd Rees 1895–1988
He was a fine draughtsman with a unique vision of the Australian landscape, yet often his works recall the dreamlike qualities of the light and colour of Tuscany. Among his paintings are *The Road to Berry* (1946) and *A Tribute to France* (1968).

By the 1960s, abstract art was sweeping the world. Young artists rebelling against the accepted art of the time began to create unrestricted. From their need to be aggressively Australian, their works became more textured and experimental, using mixed media and pieces created from the discarded items of a consumer society. Regional galleries emerged and exhibitions and lectures led to greater patronage, increasing appreciation of contemporary Australian art.

Peter Booth 1940–
His dark landscapes and monstrous figures, painted with strong colour thickly applied (impasto), create a menacing and melancholic theme – the artist's response to his perception of a holocaustic world. Pieces include *Crowd in a Snowstorm* and *Laughing Man with Bag on Head.*

John Coburn 1925–
An abstract painter, among his works are *Power Game* (1968),

and the design for the 'Moon and Sun' curtains for the Sydney Opera House in 1973.

Ken Done 1940–
This multi-talented artist and designer has held over 50 one-man shows at home and abroad. His arresting freedom in design and courageous individuality reflect his willingness to experiment with movement, energy and vibrant colour.

Ken Done.

Sam Fullbrook 1922–
Recognised as a supreme colourist, he is one of Australia's best draughtsmen. A maverick in the art world, he now lives in Ohio, USA. His works include *Girl and Fruit* (1967) and *The White Heifer* (1985).

Rosalie Gascoigne 1917–99
Using familiar inanimate objects, she assembles patterns and grids to form simple designs which evoke a sense of 'place' from the material which has been gathered. *Grass Rack* (1977), *Icon* (timber and paper, 1981) and *Rose Red City* (1981), display her unusual talent.

Robert Juniper 1929–
An artist of poetic spontaneity, his background as an industrial designer and graphic artist led him to paint. Influenced by the philosophy of Sam Fullbrook, he enjoys the process of simplifying and abstracting images and colour into refined versions of the original concept. *Crabs and Aubergines* and *Me from Sara's Point of View* are among his works.

Robert Klippel 1920–
Considered to be one of Australia's greatest modern contemporary sculptors, his *Steel and Bronze* sculpture (1961) is exhibited in the Art Gallery of New South Wales.

Emily Kame Kngwarreye c. 1916–96
An exceptional artist who bridged the gap between traditional and contemporary art. Although distinctly Australian, her style jumped barriers between black and white perceptions of landscape, allowing all to relate to her work. The series *Shimmering* shows her genius.

Colin Lanceley 1938–
He tries to produce in his collage paintings a deep sense of belonging, and melds sculpture and painting into one poetic art form. *Pianist, Pianist* (1965), *The Fall of Icarus* (1985) and *The Song of a Summer Night – Lynn's Garden* (1985) are among his well-known works.

Ginger Riley Munduwalawala 1937–
With extraordinary insight, his

bold patterning and startling juxtaposition of colour vibrate across the canvas in a unique visual display. Always incorporating the Aboriginal icons of Ngak Ngak, the sea eagle, and Garimala, the serpent-creator, his paintings range from landscapes of his mother country to a Melbourne football ground. *Home Ground* and *AFL Football* are fine examples of his work.

Trevor Nicholls 1949–

A painter of considerable experience, he has lectured in art in most states of Australia. He has held many individual exhibitions, and was chosen to represent Australia at the 1990 Venice Biennale.

Margaret Olley 1922–

Interiors and still life are her forte. With a well-developed sense of colour, harmony, place and time, she has ignored the fickleness of the art world and concentrated on her open-minded approach to the familiar and intimate, striving for perfection with her 'unerring placement of objects'. Her works include New Guinea canvasses of the 1950s and the 'yellow room' paintings of the last three decades, including *Rushcutter's Bay* and *Still Life*.

John Olsen 1928–

A landscape painter who depicts the emotions, his *Salute to Five Bells* (1973) is in the Sydney Opera House.

Ron Robertson-Swann 1941–

Influenced by the internationally renowned sculptor Anthony Caro, Robertson-Swann's works are imposing and controversial. Mainly constructed from found metal objects, his large-scale outdoor welded abstracts include the machine-like sculpture *Big Red*. He makes a strong personal statement that challenges the conventional definition of sculpture.

Bill Robinson 1936–

From his painstaking web of brushstrokes he creates a rich vision of surreal rainforests and glowing beachscapes. Although recognisably Australian, he sees his subjects from a different perspective, establishing an almost spiritual illusion of the seemingly ordinary. Examples are *The Jellyfish Ring* and *Creation Landscape Earth and Sea*. He won the 1996 Archibald Prize with *Self Portrait Stunned Mullet*.

Jeffrey Smart 1923–

Part of the modern movement as it emerged in Adelaide, he is a leading exponent of urban imagery. A widely travelled artist with an international reputation, he employs motifs derived from the urban environment as devices to highlight the sense of 'human dislocation in an alien, inhuman domain', which gives his work a haunting quality. His paintings include *Cahill Expressway*, *Truck and trailer heading into a city*, *The Oil Drums* and *Corrugated Gioconda*.

Tim Storrier 1949–

A contemporary abstract painter, he is an exponent of still life. His works include *Moonstick, Box*

Fireworks mark the opening of the Olympic Stadium at Homebush Bay, Sydney, in 1999.

and Berry: Still Life with Fire (1976) and *Isolation* (1977).

Judy Watson 1959–
Rejecting the values of the transient art culture, her paintings *On the Tail of the Horse* and *Self Portrait as a Little Girl* reveal a naive child-like quality which exposes her highly personalised view of life. A wall of 74 of her etched zinc panels is featured in Bunjilaka, the Aboriginal Centre at the new Melbourne Museum.

Brett Whiteley 1939–92
An uninhibited and polished draughtsman who tried to express in his paintings 'life force and its insoluble conflicts'. His works include *The Christie Series* (1964), *The Big Orange – Sunset* (1974) and *The Balcony* (1975).

Fred Williams 1927–82
Born in Melbourne, he painted works which simplified and abstracted the Australian landscape. Examples include *Sapling Forest* (1962) and *Waterfall Polyptych* (1979).

Sport

Australia is a very enthusiastic sporting nation; we love our sport, whether watching it or playing it. In 2000, one of the most exciting events in sport will take place on our shores – the Sydney Olympic Games – and the country is gearing up to show the world just how colourful and vibrant Australia is. Over the years there have been countless sporting legends who have excelled in literally hundreds of different sports.

Tennis
Lawn tennis was first introduced in the 1870s and the first Australian championship was in 1905. The first Davis Cup challenge was issued in 1906.

Tennis has become one of Australia's most popular sports. The following list names some of the top players:

1900–40s

Norman Brookes
Jack Crawford
Harry Hopman
Gerald Patterson
Adrian Quist

1950s–70s

Mal Anderson
John Bromwich
Evonne Cawley (Goolagong)
Ashley Cooper
Roy Emerson
Neale Fraser
Lew Hoad
Rod Laver
Ken McGregor
John Newcombe
Tony Roche
Ken Rosewall
Frank Sedgman
Margaret Smith Court
Wendy Turnbull

1980s–2000s

Pat Cash
Jelena Dokic
Scott Draper

South Australian Road Cycling Champion Rachael Linke.

Annabel Ellwood
Kerri-Anne Guse
Lleyton Hewitt
Rachel McQuillan
Mark Philippoussis
Nicole Pratt
Patrick Rafter
Sandon Stolle
Jason Stoltenberg
Todd Woodbridge
Mark Woodforde

Cricket

The first organised match was held in Sydney in 1803. The Australian Club was formed in 1826 and the Melbourne Cricket Club in 1838. International cricket began in 1861. Famous players include:

1900–30s

W.W. Armstrong
Don Bradman
Bill Hunt
M.A. Noble
Bill O'Reilly
W.H. Ponsford
Hugh Trumble
Victor Trumper

1950s–60s

Ian Craig
Richie Benaud
Wally Grout
Neil Harvey
Lindsay Hassett
Bill Lawry
Ray Lindwall
Keith Miller
Bob Simpson

1970s–2000s

David Boon
Allan Border
Greg Chappell
Ian Chappell

Ian Healy
Merv Hughes
Dennis Lillee
Geoff Marsh
Rod Marsh
Craig McDermott
Glenn McGrath
Mark Taylor
Shane Warne
Mark Waugh
Steve Waugh

*Bridge to Bridge water-ski race,
Hawkesbury River, New South Wales.
Russell Kinred and Mark Nicholson.*

Golf

Australians have more public golf
courses per head of population
than any other nation. The
game was first played in the
1870s and in 1890 the first
established golf club was at
Falstaff Gardens in Melbourne.
Notable players include:

1920s–40s
Jim Ferrier
Joan Hammond
Joe Kirkwood
Norman von Nida
Ivo Whitton
1950s–70s
Bruce Crampton
Bruce Devlin
Edwina Kennedy
Kel Nagle
Jack Newton
Peter Thomson

1980s–2000s
Robert Allenby
Stuart Appleby
Ian Baker-Finch
Roger Davis
Steve Elkington
David Graham
Bradley Hughes
Graham Marsh
Greg Norman
Craig Parry

Peter Senior
Bob Shearer
Craig Spence
Jan Stephenson
Karrie Webb

Swimming

Because of our wonderful
climate and beautiful beaches,
Australians have always loved
swimming. Swimming racing
gained international fame when
the 'Australian crawl' (now
called freestyle) was introduced
in the 1890s. Famous
swimmers include:

1900–30s
Frank Beaurepaire
Dick Cavill
Fred Cavill
Andrew 'Boy' Charlton
Claire Dennis
Fanny Durack
Annette Kellerman
Barney Bede Kieran
Freddy Lane
Bill Longworth

1940s–60s
Kevin Berry
Gary Chapman
Lorraine Crapp

John Devitt
Dawn Fraser
Jon Henricks
John Konrads
Ilsa Konrads
Lynn McClements
Linda McGill
John Marshall
Ian O'Brien
Murray Rose
David Thiele
Mike Wenden
Bob Windle

1970s–80s

Duncan Armstrong
Clifford Bertram
Neil Brooks
Brad Cooper
Lisa Curry
Michelle Ford
Shane Gould
Gail Neal
Des Renford
Jon Sieben
Beverley Whitfield
Tracey Wickham

1990s–2000s

Rebecca Brown
Daniel Kowalski
Grant Hackett
Michael Klim

Australia's Hockeyroos versus China, 1997.

Susie Maroney
David O'Brien
Susan O'Neill
Kieren Perkins
Samantha Riley
Shelley Taylor-Smith
Ian Thorpe
Tammy van Wisse
Joseph Walker

Australian Football League (AFL)

Devised in 1858 by cricketers as a form of exercise in their off-season, Australian Rules Football has now become one of the most popular spectator sports in Australia. The AFL has inducted 15 legends into its Hall of Fame:

Roy Cazaly (played 1910–27)
Gordon Coventry (1920–37)
Bob Pratt (1930–46)
Haydn Bunton (1931–41)
Jack Dyer (1931–49)
Dick Reynolds (1933–51)
John Coleman (1949–54)
Ted Whitten (1951–70)
Ron Barassi (1955–77)
Graham 'Polly' Farmer (1956–60)
Bob Skilton (1956–71)
John Nicholls (1957–74)
Ian Stewart (1963–75)
Leigh Matthews (1969–85)
Peter Hudson (1969–80)

National Rugby League (NRL)

The first Kangaroo team toured England in 1908–09 and won their first Test in 1911–12. The Kangaroos have won the World Cup eight times out of the 11 tournaments played. Some greats of the game and the years they played are:

Basketballer Shane Heal.

Herbert 'Dally' Messenger
(1908–13)
Duncan Thompson (1911–25)
Frank Burge (1911–27)
Harold Horder (1912–26)
Dave Brown (1930–41)
Vic Hey (1933–49)
Clive Churchill (1951–63)
John Raper (1957–73)
Ken Irvine (1958–72)
Reg Gasnier (1959–67)
Graeme Langlands (1962–76)
Keith 'Golden Boots' Barnes
(1963–70)
Ron Coote (1965–78)
Arthur Beetson (1966–81)
Bob Fulton (1965–79)
Tom Radonikus (1976–85)
Wally Lewis (1978–92)
Mal Meninga (1978–94)
Peter Sterling (1978–)
Allan Langer (1986–99)
Laurie Daley (1987–)
Ricky Stuart (1988–)
Brad Fittler (1989–)

Rugby Union

Rugby Union began to be
played in Australia in 1864. The
first Wallabies team won gold at
the 1908 London Olympics.
They won the World Cup
Grand Slam tour in 1984,
defeating England, Scotland,
Wales and Ireland and in 1991
and 1999 won the World Cup
championships. Some great
names from the last three
decades are:

David Campese
Mark Ella
Nick Farr-Jones
Michael Lynagh
Andrew Slack

Soccer

Although the game was played
as early as 1880, it only gained
prestige and popularity when
the Australian team, the
Socceroos, qualified for the
first time in the World Cup
finals. In later years the
Socceroos reached the finals
of the Seoul, Barcelona and
Atlanta Olympics. Some of
Australia's soccer legends are:

Atti Abonyi
Mark Bosnich
Branko Buljevic
Alan Davidson
Craig Johnston
Harry Kewell
John Kosmina
Eddie Krncevic
Jim MacKay
Peter Ollerton
Jack Reilly
Jimmy Rooney
Paul Wade
Johnny Warren
Harry Williams
Peter Wilson
Charlie Yankos
Ned Zelic

Boxing

Bare-knuckle fights were staged as early as the 1790s but the rules were standardised in 1912. Some of this century's greats and the years of their glory are:

Bill Squires (1906–8)
Jerry Jerome (1913)
Les Darcy (1914–17)
Colin Bell (1921)
Billy Grime (1926–7)
Ambrose Palmer (1932–8)
Vic Patrick (1941–6)

Tommy Burns (1941–7)
Dave Sands (1945–52)
Jimmy Carruthers (1948–54)
Johnny Famechon (1964–70)
Rocky Galtellari (1965–7)
Lionel Rose (1966–70)
Tony Mundine (1972–6)
Rocky Mattioli (1977–80)
Jeff Fenech (1985–93)
Barry Michael (1985–7)
Lester Ellis (1985)
Joe Bugner (1986–)
Jeff 'Hitman' Harding (1989–94)
Grahame 'Spike' Cheney (1988)
Kostya Tszyu (1995–)

Melbourne Cup

This is the richest racing event in Australia. The race began in 1861 when the immense wealth from the goldfields created the climate for a race such as this. Archer was the first horse to win the Melbourne Cup. Some past winners are:

1930 Phar Lap
1931 White Nose
1932 Peter Pan
1933 Hall Mark
1934 Peter Pan
1935 Marabou
1936 Wotan
1937 The Trump
1938 Catalogue
1939 Rivette
1940 Old Rowley
1941 Skipton
1942 Colonus
1943 Dark Felt
1944 Sirius
1945 Rainbird
1946 Russia
1947 Hiraji
1948 Rimfire
1949 Foxzami
1950 Comic Court
1951 Delta
1952 Dalray
1953 Wodalla

1954 Rising Fast
1955 Toparoa
1956 Evening Peal
1957 Straight Draw
1958 Baystone
1959 Macdougal
1960 Hi Jinx
1961 Lord Fury
1962 Even Stevens
1963 Gatum Gatum
1964 Polo Prince
1965 Light Fingers
1966 Galilee
1967 Red Handed
1968 Rain Lover
1969 Rain Lover
1970 Baghdad Note
1971 Silver Knight
1972 Piping Lane
1973 Gala Supreme
1974 Think Big
1975 Think Big
1976 Van Der Hum
1977 Gold and Black

1978 Arwon
1979 Hyperno
1980 Beldale Ball
1981 Just a Dash
1982 Gurner's Lane
1983 Kiwi
1984 Black Knight
1985 What a
     Nuisance
1986 At Talaq
1987 Kensei
1988 Empire Rose
1989 Tawrrific
1990 Kingston Rule
1991 Let's Elope
1992 Subzero
1993 Vintage Crop
1994 Jeune
1995 Doriemus
1996 Saintly
1997 Might and
     Power
1998 Jezabeel
1999 Rogan Josh

Track and field athletics

This is a term embracing a variety of sporting activities. The first club was the Sydney Amateur Athletic Club, formed in 1872. Here are some past medal winners.

1890s–1930s
Jean Coleman
Jack Donaldson
Edwin Flack
Jack Metcalf
Decima Norman
George Parker
Thelma Peake
Stan Rowley
Eileen Wearne
Anthony Winter
Joan Woodland

1940s–60s
George Avery
Raelene Boyle
Theo Bruce
Maureen Caird
Nor Crocker
Betty Cuthbert
Ralph Doubell
Herb Elliott
Noel Freeman
Graham Gipson
Kevan Gosper
Leon Gregory
Hec Hogan
Marjorie Jackson
Brenda Jones
Pam Kilborn
Joyce King
Jenny Lamy
John Landy
Allan Lawrence
David Lean
Betty McKinnon
June Maston
Marlene Mathews
Fleur Mellor

Peter Norman
Chilla Porter
David Power
David Stephens
Shirley Strickland
John Winter

1970s–80s
Don Baird
Peter Bourke
Raymond Boyd
Ron Clarke
Robert de Castella
Debbie Flintoff-King
Graham Haskell
Gary Honey
Susan Howland
Kerry Junna-Saxby
Tony Manning
Gail Martin
Lisa Martin-Ondieki
Rich Mitchell
Glynis Nunn
Gary Parsons
Lowrie Peckham

1990s–2000s
Nicole Boegman
Dean Capobianco
Louise Carney
Darren Clark
Jane Flemming
Tim Forsyth
Cathy Freeman
Melinda Gainsford-Taylor
Anne Manning
Steve Moneghetti
Nova Peris-Kneebone
Kyle Vander-Kuyp

Australian Olympic medals

Games	Gold	Silver	Bronze	Total
1896 Athens	2	0	0	2
1900 Paris	3	0	4	7
1904 St Louis	0	0	0	0
1908 London	1	2	1	4
1912 Stockholm	2	2	2	6
1920 Antwerp	0	2	1	3
1924 Paris	3	1	2	6
1928 Amsterdam	1	2	1	4
1932 Los Angeles	3	1	1	5
1936 Berlin	0	0	1	1
1948 London	2	6	5	13
1952 Helsinki	6	2	3	11
1956 Melbourne	13	8	14	35
1960 Rome	8	8	6	22
1964 Tokyo	6	2	10	18
1968 Mexico City	5	7	5	17
1972 Munich	8	7	2	17
1976 Montreal	0	1	4	5
1980 Moscow	2	2	5	9
1984 Los Angeles	4	8	12	24
1988 Seoul	3	6	5	14
1992 Barcelona	7	9	11	27
1996 Atlanta	9	9	23	41

Paralympics

The first Paralympics were held in 1960 and they have since been held every four years, usually in the same country as the Olympic games of that year. Australia has been very successful in these games and has produced some very fine athletes, winning 24 gold medals in the 1992 Barcelona Paralympics and 42 gold in the 1996 Atlanta Paralympics.

DID YOU KNOW?

The mascots for the Sydney Olympics are a kookaburra, a duck-billed platypus and an echidna. The platypus and the echidna are monotremes and the world's only egg-laying mammals.

1901   Australia wins cricket Test match against England. In one game M.A. Noble takes seven wickets for 17 runs, and Hugh Trumble a hat-trick.

1903   First car race in Australia. Dick Cavill wins every men's freestyle event at Australian swimming championships.

1904   First Australian Open golf championship held at Botany, New South Wales.

1905   First Davis Cup entry by Australasia. Norman Brookes reaches finals at Wimbledon.

1906   Bondi Surf Bathers' Life Saving Club is formed.

1907   First Davis Cup win to Australasia. Norman Brookes is the first non-British tennis player to win Wimbledon (singles, doubles and mixed doubles). Rugby League begins.

1908   First Australian Surf Carnival held at Manly, New South Wales. H.D. McIntosh builds Sydney Stadium to promote world boxing. Australia wins gold at London Olympics for Rugby Union. Davis Cup final here for first time; Australasia beats USA 3–2.

1909   Australian Rugby Union team, now called Wallabies, beats England 25 to 5 games.

1910   Frank Beaurepaire tours Europe, winning all 48 swim races in which he competes.

1911   Second Kangaroo Rugby League team tours England and wins Test, a feat not repeated until 1963. Australian Pro Golf Association formed.

1912   All-round sportsman 'Snowy' Baker buys Sydney Stadium and establishes championship conditions in Australian boxing. Australia wins two gold medals at Stockholm Olympics.

1913   'Dally' Messenger, 'master of Australian Rugby League', retires. Middleweight Jerry Jerome becomes first Aborigine to hold the title of national boxing champion.

1914   Norman Brookes wins men's singles at Wimbledon.

1916   Les Darcy becomes Australian heavyweight boxing champion.

DID YOU KNOW?

Sir Donald Bradman, who turned 90 in 1998, made his first century in cricket at the age of 12 at Bowral High School (New South Wales). He was the first living Australian to be honoured with having his portrait on an Australian postage stamp.

1917	Annette Kellerman makes world-record dive of 28 metres. Les Darcy dies in USA.
1919	Australian Imperial Force rowing team wins Royal Henley Peace Regatta; the trophy becomes the King's Cup.
1922	Gerald Patterson wins Wimbledon men's singles.
1924	Australia wins three gold medals at Paris Olympics. Speedway racing is inaugurated at Maitland, New South Wales.
1926	Sydney Showground speedway opens. Roy Cazaly becomes folk hero of Australian Rules football; the cry of 'Up there Cazaly' passes into the language.
1927	First meeting of 'electric hare racing' at Epping, New South Wales. Fred Cavill, who experimented with and developed new swimming techniques, dies.
1928	Australia wins one gold medal at Amsterdam Olympics. Don Bradman plays his first cricket Test match. Hubert Opperman wins French Bol d'Or 24-hour cycling event.
1929	Sydney–Perth Trans-Continental Air Race; Geoffrey de Havilland makes fastest time in Gypsy Moth. Norman 'Wizard' Smith breaks Australian land speed record.
1930	Phar Lap wins Melbourne Cup at 11/8 on, shortest odds in history of Cup. Bradman sets world record in first-class cricket for a single innings with a score of 452 runs. Bradman's aggregate of 974 runs in five tests against England sets world record average (which still stands) of 139.14.
1932	Phar Lap dies in USA in controversial circumstances. Walter Lindrum sets world record in billiards. 'Bodyline' cricket Test series begins. Australia wins three gold medals at Los Angeles Olympics.
1933	England regains the Ashes after controversial 'Bodyline' cricket tour. Jack Crawford wins men's singles at Wimbledon.
1934	C.W.A. Scott and T. Campbell Black win Melbourne Centenary England–Australia Air Race. Australia wins the Ashes in England.
1935	Adrian Quist and Jack Crawford win Wimbledon doubles title.
1936	Don Bradman appointed Australian cricket captain. Lionel van Praag wins first world speedway title. Water-skiing begins in Australia.
1937	First Australian women cricket team tours England.
1938	Bathurst's Mount Panorama racing circuit completed. Peter Whitehead of England wins Grand Prix at Bathurst, New South Wales.
1939	Australia wins Davis Cup for first time.
1945	First Sydney–Hobart yacht race.
1946	Sydney Turf Club introduces photo-finish cameras. Horace Lindrum wins world snooker championship.
1947	Jim Ferrier wins US professional golf championship title. John Marshall wins every Australian men's freestyle championship.

1948   Australia wins two gold medals at London Olympics. Don Bradman retires from test cricket with an aggregate of 6996 runs made in 52 tests (average 99.94).

1949   Don Bradman is knighted. Dave Sands wins Empire middleweight boxing title.

1950   Jockey Rae 'Togo' Johnstone wins four of the five England classic horse races in one season. Adrian Quist and John Bromwich win Wimbledon doubles title. John Marshall's sensational swimming establishes four world freestyle records in US national championships. Clive Churchill captains Australian Rugby League team's victory against England.

1951   Frank Sedgman wins US men's singles tennis title.

1952   Australia wins six gold medals at Helsinki Olympics. Ken Rosewall and Lew Hoad (both aged 17) win Wimbledon men's doubles. Jimmy Carruthers is Australia's first world boxing champion.

1953   Lew Hoad and Ken Rosewall retain Davis Cup.

1954   Golfers Peter Thomson and Kel Nagle win Canada Cup. Peter Thomson wins British Open golf tournament. Jimmy Carruthers retires undefeated from world boxing. John Landy becomes the second man to break the four-minute mile a few weeks after Roger Bannister of England. Bannister beats Landy at Vancouver Commonwealth Games (the first race where two men break the four-minute mile). Clive Churchill captains Australia's World Cup Rugby League team in France. 'Gelignite' Jack Murray wins Redex Motor Trial.

1955   Arthur 'Scobie' Breasley begins a horse-racing record of 100 winners each season.

1956   First Olympic Games held in Southern Hemisphere take place in Melbourne. Australia wins 13 gold medals; swimmers broke 18 world records. Lew Hoad beats Ken Rosewall for men's singles title at Wimbledon. Peter Thomson wins the British Open golf tournament, first man to win the event three years in succession.

1957   Ian Craig captains Australia's cricket team in Johannesburg.

1958   Herb Elliott runs his first sub-four-minute mile in 3 minutes 59.9 seconds. Marlene Mathews sets world records for running 90 metres and 200 metres. Richie Benaud, great all-rounder, captains Australian cricket team.

1959   Racing driver Jack Brabham becomes world Grand Prix champion. John Konrads wins all men's freestyle swimming events in Australian championships.

1960   Australia wins eight gold medals at Rome Olympics. Neale Fraser beats Rod Laver at Wimbledon. Australia plays the West Indies in the only cricket Test ever tied. Kel Nagle wins British Open golf championship in its centenary year.

1961   Heather McKay is national squash champion.

1962   Australia wins 17 gold medals in Perth Commonwealth Games. Dawn Fraser becomes first woman swimmer to break

60 seconds for 100 metres freestyle. Rod Laver wins 'Grand Slam' of world tennis (Australian, French, Wimbledon and US titles). Stewart Mackenzie wins Henley Diamond Sculls for the sixth time. Reg Gasnier is appointed Australia's youngest-ever Rugby League Test captain (at age 23).

1963   Margaret Court is first Australian to win Wimbledon women's singles title. Ken Hiscoe wins all world squash titles. Australian netball team wins world championship in London. Kangaroos win World Cup.

1964   Lake Eyre, South Australia, is the venue for world land and water speed records by Donald Campbell. First official world surfing championship held at Manly, won by 'Midget' Farrelly. Australia wins six gold medals at Tokyo Olympics. Dawn Fraser becomes only swimmer ever to win gold medals in three successive Olympic Games. Roy Emerson wins Wimbledon men's singles.

1965   Linda McGill is first Australian to swim English Channel. Long-distance runner Ron Clarke breaks 11 world records. Bill Lance sails single-handed around Cape Horn. Geoff Hunt is national squash champion at age 17. Peter Thomson wins British Open golf tournament for fifth time (second only to H. Vardon, six times). Roy Emerson wins Wimbledon men's singles for third successive year.

1967   Australia wins Admiral's Cup for yachting. Roy Emerson becomes Australian singles tennis champion. George Moore wins English Derby on Royal Palace. Australia wins Davis Cup for fourth successive time.

1968   Australia wins five gold medals at the Mexico Olympics. Australian Iron Man titles introduced; Barry Rodgers wins inaugural. Boxer Lionel Rose wins world bantamweight title. Rod Laver becomes first player to win two 'Grand Slams' in world tennis. Nat Young wins world surfing championship.

1969   Boxer Johnny Famechon wins world featherweight title. Margaret Court wins 'Grand Slam' of tennis.

1970   John Newcombe wins men's singles at Wimbledon. Judy Trim wins world championship in ladies' standard pistol shooting. Ken Rosewall wins US open tennis championship. Barry Rodgers wins Iron Man title for third time.

1971   Wayne Jones is first Australian to water-ski over 160 kilometres an hour. Ken Rosewall wins world tennis championship. Roy Emerson and Rod Laver win men's doubles at Wimbledon. Evonne Goolagong, the first Aborigine to play at Wimbledon, wins women's singles championship. Australian netball team wins world championship in Kingston, Jamaica.

1972   Australia wins eight gold medals at Munich Olympics. Shane Gould becomes first woman to hold all five world freestyle swimming records at once. Joe Meissner becomes the first non-Japanese world karate champion.

1973   Margaret Court wins her fifth US tennis singles championship. Heather McKay wins her 14th Australian women's squash title.

1974   Evonne Goolagong wins Australian women's open tennis title. Australia qualifies for World Cup soccer final for the first time.

1975   John Newcombe beats Jimmy Connors for Australian men's open tennis title. Des Renford becomes 'King of the Channel' with his 10th English Channel crossing since 1970. Australian netball team wins world championship.

1976   Controversy over Raelene Boyle's disqualification for two 'false' starts at Montreal Olympics.

1977   Women's bowls team wins gold medal in world bowls titles. Rocky Mattioli wins world junior middleweight boxing championship. Trainer Bart Cummings has his sixth Melbourne Cup win with the horse Gold and Black. World Series Cricket is launched. Australia and England commemorate 100 years of Test cricket. Heather McKay wins her 16th British squash championship.

1978   Tracey Wickham takes only world record set at Edmonton Commonwealth Games. Australian women's cricket team wins second World Cup tournament in India. Ken Warby sets world water speed record. Edwina Kennedy, aged 19, becomes British women's amateur golf champion. Wayne 'Rabbit' Bartholomew becomes world professional surfing champion.

1979   Jack Newton wins Australian Open golf tournament. Australian netball team shares win in world championship in Spain.

1980   Australia wins two gold medals at Moscow Olympics. Geoff Hunt wins his seventh Australian open squash title. Greg Norman wins Australian Open golf championship. Alan Jones wins world Formula One driver championship. Grant Kenny wins both junior and senior Iron Man titles at age 16. Des Renford swims English Channel three times in 10 days to regain title of 'King of the Channel' (16 crossings in all). Gary Sutton wins world amateur point score for 50-kilometre cycling.

1981   David Graham wins US Open golf championship. Australian women's cricket team wins third World Cup tournament in New Zealand. Jan Stephenson wins women's world golf championship in Japan.

1982   Australia wins three gold medals at Commonwealth Games in Brisbane. Bob Shearer wins Australian Open golf championship. Kangaroo Rugby League team wins all matches against British Isles and France for the first time.

1983   *Australia II* wins America's Cup after USA held it for 132 years. Davis Cup victory for Australia. Grant Kenny wins fourth Iron Man title. Australian netball team wins world championship.

1984   Australia wins four gold medals at Los Angeles Olympics. Peter Brock wins Bathurst 1000 car race for eighth time. The Wallabies Rugby Union team is undefeated and completes a 'grand slam' by defeating England, Scotland, Wales and Ireland in four Tests. Mark Ella is first Aborigine to become captain of Australian Rugby Union team; on tour of UK he scores tries against England, Wales, Scotland and Ireland in the one season (a record). Brett Wing becomes fastest man in world for barefoot water-skiing, his brother Robert becomes fastest man in world for backward barefoot water-skiing. Grant Kenny wins Iron Man title for fifth time.

1985   Inaugural Australia Games held. Jeff Fenech (aged 20) wins IBF world junior bantamweight title. Barry Michael wins IBF world junior lightweight title. Australian women's bowls team wins three gold medals at world bowls titles.

1986   Robert de Castella wins Boston Marathon. Australia wins 40 gold medals at Edinburgh Commonwealth Games. For the second time running, the Kangaroo Rugby League team is undefeated in tour of British Isles and France. Men's eights win world championship rowing. Australia wins men's world cup hockey. Greg Norman wins British Open golf championship. Kerry Saxby sets world record in Moscow for walking (10-kilometre track).

1987   Wayne Gardner wins World 500cc Motorcycle Championship. Cricket World Cup, played in India and Pakistan, is won by an Australian team for the first time. Pat Cash becomes first Australian to win Wimbledon in 17 years. Adrian Ferguson wins singles sculls world title. Trevor Hendy wins Iron Man title.

1988   Kay Cottee becomes first woman solo sailor to circumnavigate the globe. Australia wins three gold medals at Seoul Olympics. Jeff Fenech becomes first boxer in history to win three world titles without a defeat. Trevor Hendy wins world Iron Man title.

1989   Australian cricket team regains the Ashes in England. Clifford Bertram (aged 68) is oldest man ever to swim English Channel. Wayne Gardner wins inaugural 500cc motorcycle Grand Prix at Phillip Island, Victoria. Barton Lynch wins world surfing championship. Stephen Pate wins world professional cycling championship. Ian Dipple wins world water-ski championship. Kerry Saxby sets world record for three-kilometre indoor walk. Jeff Fenech successfully defends his WBC world featherweight boxing crown. Jeff 'Hitman' Harding takes WBC world light/heavyweight title.

1990   Vicki Roycroft is world champion lady show jumper. Susie Maroney (aged 15) becomes youngest and fastest Australian to swim the English Channel. Trevor Hendy wins Iron Man title. Stephen McGlede wins world 50-kilometre amateur cycling point score. Pam Burridge wins world surfing championship.

1991   Shelley Taylor-Smith is world marathon swimming champion. Richard Marsh wins inaugural surf championship. Susie Maroney swims record breaking double crossing of English

Channel. Ian Baker-Finch wins British Open golf championship. Simon Fairweather wins world archery title. Australian women's netball team wins world championship. Australian women's hockey team wins World Cup. Wallabies have historic win in Rugby Union World Cup. David O'Brien becomes men's world swimming champion.

1992 Australia wins Rugby League Ashes. Australia wins seven gold medals at Barcelona Olympics. Disabled skiers win gold for first time in Winter Paralympics; 37 gold medals won in Summer Paralympics. Wallabies tour UK and defeat Ireland, Wales and the invitational side, the Barbarians. Mark Woodforde and Todd Woodbridge ('The Woodies') win world doubles tennis championship. Wayne Gardner retires from 500cc motorcycle racing. Scott Sunderland wins Mazda Alpine Tour (cycling). Steve Elkington wins Australian Open golf championship. Trevor Hendy wins all world Iron Man titles since 1988.

1993 Greg Norman wins British Open golf title. Australia retains the cricket Ashes. Wallabies beat Springboks in historic Rugby Union test series. Jeff Harding holds WBC world light/heavyweight title, regained in 1992. Lester Ellis wins WBF world welterweight title. Women's hockey team wins the Champions Trophy for sixth time. Michelle Jones becomes world champion triathlete. Pauline Menczer wins world surfing championship.

1994 Jeff Malcolm wins WBF welterweight championship. Grahame 'Spike' Cheney retains WBC welterweight title. Garry Parsons breaks world record for 1000-metre track run. Rebecca Brown breaks world record for 200-metre breaststroke. Australia wins World Series cricket, defeating South Africa in finals. Allan Border retires from international cricket. Miles Stewart wins men's and Rina Bradshaw wins women's world indoor triathlon championships. Mick Doohan wins World 500cc Motorcycle Championship. Australian women's hockey team

DID YOU KNOW?

The medals for Australian Rules Football in the various states are:
South Australia – W.A. Magarey, awarded first in 1898
Western Australia – Sandover introduced in 1921
Victoria – Brownlow introduced in 1924
Tasmania – William Leitch
Queensland – J.A. Grogan
New South Wales – The Phelan

wins World Cup. Kangaroos win Rugby League Ashes against England. Craig Parry wins Australian Masters golf for second time. Australia wins 71 gold medals at Commonwealth Games in Canada. Rugby Union's Mal Meninga retires. Wallabies beat All Blacks to retain Bledisloe Cup. Robert Allenby is Australian Open golf champion. Trevor Hendy is the most successful Iron Man in the world, winning four world titles. First Cannonball Run through centre of Australia.

1995   Australia retains the cricket Ashes. Kostya Tszyu wins junior welterweight IBF boxing championship. Australian cricketers beat West Indies and win Frank Worrell trophy after 20 years. Mick Doohan wins his second World 500cc Motorcycle Championship. Steve Elkington wins US golf championship. Kangaroos win Rugby League World Cup. Michael King wins Iron Man title. Michelle Martin wins world squash championship. Greg Norman wins Australian Open golf.

1996   Swimmer Tammy van Wisse is first person to conquer Bass Strait. Mick Doohan wins 500cc Motorcycle Championship for third time. 'The Woodies' win doubles title at Wimbledon for fourth consecutive time. Miles Stewart becomes world champion triathlete. Paul Patterson wins world surfing championship. Lone sailor David Dicks circumnavigates globe. Jane Crafter wins ladies' World Masters golf. Emma George sets world record in pole vault. Australia wins nine gold medals at Atlanta Olympics. Troy Corser wins world Super Bike championship. Darryn Hill wins world sprint title (cycling). Craig Lowndes (aged 22) is the youngest driver to win Bathurst 1000. Layne Beachley wins women's world surfing championship. Louise Sauvage becomes world's best track Paralympian.

1997   Kirstie Marshall is first Australian to win a world snow skiing championship. Kostya Tszyu retains IBF world junior welterweight title. Australia wins cricket Test series against both West Indies and South Africa. 'The Woodies' win Australian Open tennis doubles. Susie Maroney becomes first person to swim from Cuba to USA. Peter Brock, a nine-time Bathurst 1000 winner, announces his retirement. Mick Doohan wins 500cc Motorcycle Championship for fourth time. Cathy Freeman wins world 400-metre championship. Karrie Webb wins second British Open golf title. Australia retains the cricket Ashes. Cyclist Shane Kelly wins third consecutive world championship one-kilometre time trial. Patrick Rafter wins US Open tennis. Larry Perkins wins Bathurst 1000 for sixth time. Sarah Fitz-Gerald is women's world squash champion. Zali Steggall wins women's slalom world cup. Australia wins World Cup women's cricket. Shane Warne gets his 500th first-class wicket. Louise Sauvage wins Boston Paralympics marathon.

1998   Ian Thorpe wins 400-metre freestyle world swimming championship. Controversial cricket Test win to Australia against South Africa. Greg Norman wins Greg Norman Holden International. Bradley Hughes wins Australian Masters golf and sets new record. Shane Warne takes his 300th Test wicket (a record). Ian Thorpe breaks two world records for 400-metres freestyle. Karrie Webb wins Australian Ladies Masters golf. Tammy van Wisse breaks two world records, swimming 40 kilometres in 9 hours 7 minutes 12 seconds (50 laps of Bondi Beach). Louise Sauvage wins Boston wheelchair marathon. Susan O'Neill holds 29 national titles, beating Sir Frank Beaurepaire's record. Susie Maroney sets world ocean swimming record from Mexico to Cuba (197 kilometres in 38.5 hours). Hockeyroos win Ladies World Cup for second time. Shelley Taylor-Smith wins her fifth Manhattan marathon swim. Wallabies beat All Blacks and win Bledisloe Cup. Patrick Rafter wins Canadian Open tennis. Racing trainer T.J. Smith dies. With 10 gold medals, Susan O'Neill becomes greatest gold medal winner in 68 years. First Test cricket win in Pakistan in 39 years; Mark Taylor becomes most successful Test captain in history. Greg Chambers wins Australian Open golf. Cricket scandal over alleged payments by illegal bookmaker. Mick Doohan wins fifth consecutive World 500cc Motorcycle Championship. Wicketkeeper Ian Healy breaks world record with 156 dismissals. Mark Taylor achieves record-equalling innings when he matches Bradman's greatest Test score of 334, but retires nobly not out on equal score. Kostya Tszyu wins interim WBC super-lightweight boxing championship.

1999   Mark Taylor and Ian Healy retire from international cricket. Zali Steggall wins women's slalom skiing, becomes our first alpine world champion. Grant Hackett breaks 200-metre freestyle world record. Samantha Riley betters Sir Frank Beaurepaire's 80-year-old record with 33 Australian breaststroke titles. Layne Beachley is first surfer in 15 years to claim consecutive world championships. Karrie Webb wins Golf Titleholders Championship in USA and becomes world's number one woman golfer. Tony Lockett of the Sydney Swans passes Gordon Coventry's record of 1299 career goals in AFL football. The women's Hockeyroos win world championship trophy against Korea. Australian cricket team wins World Cup Series. Wallabies defeat England in Rugby Union Centenary Test. Ian Thorpe breaks three world records in three days at Pan Pacific Games. Australia retains Bledisloe Cup. Runner Cathy Freeman wins gold in world championship 400 metres. Jesse Martin from Melbourne becomes the youngest person to sail around the world unassisted. Australian Women's Netball team wins the world championship for the eighth time. Australia wins Rugby Union World Cup for the second time.

Books

This is a selection of much-loved Australian books. Many have won national and international literary awards and so deserve to be included. Others are favourites which many Australians have on their bookshelves and regard as old friends.

Books for adults

Non-fiction

Adams, David (ed.)	*The Letters of Rachel Henning*
Adam-Smith, Patsy	*The Anzacs*
Arnell, Stan	*One Man's War*
Atkinson, Alan	*The Europeans in Australia*
Baker, Mark Raphael	*The Fiftieth Gate*
Barry, Paul	*The Rise and Rise of Kerry Packer*
Betts, Katharine	*The Great Divide*
Blainey, Geoffrey	*The Tyranny of Distance*
Cayley, N.W.	*What Bird Is That?*
Clark, Manning	*A Short History of Australia*
Conway, Jill Ker	*The Road from Coorain*
Cronin, Leonard	*Key Guide to Australian Wild Flowers, Trees, Mammals* (series of three)
Dunlop, E.E.	*The War Diaries of Weary Dunlop*
Durack, Mary	*Kings in Grass Castles*
Dutton, Geoffrey	*Snow on the Saltbush*
Facey, A.B.	*A Fortunate Life*
Flanagan, Richard	*A Terrible Beauty: A History of the Gordon River*
Gill, Alan	*Orphans of the Empire*
Greer, Germaine	*The Whole Woman*
Grey, Jeffrey	*A Military History of Australia*
Horne, Donald	*The Lucky Country*
Hughes, Robert	*Art of Australia*
James, Clive	*Unreliable Memoirs*
Kelly, Paul	*State of the Nation*

Leunig, Michael   *The Penguin Leunig*
Marr, David   *Patrick White: Letters*
Morgan, Sally   *My Place*
Park, Ruth   *The Companion Guide to Sydney*
Pierce, Peter   *The Country of Lost Children*
Read, Peter   *The Meaning of Lost Places*
Reynolds, Henry   *Why Weren't We Told?*
Robb, Peter   *Midnight in Sicily*
Rolls, Eric   *A Million Wild Acres*
                       Sojourners
Summers, Anne   *Damned Whores and God's Police*
Thorpe, Billy   *Most People I Know Think That I'm Crazy*

Fiction

Astley, Thea   *It's Raining in Mango*
Birtles, Dora   *The Overlanders*
Boldrewood, Rolf   *Robbery Under Arms*
Bradley, James   *The Deep Field*
Capp, Fiona   *The Last of the Sane Days*
Carey, Peter   *Oscar and Lucinda*
                       Jack Maggs
Cato, Nancy   *All the Rivers Run*
Clarke, Marcus   *For the Term of His Natural Life*
Cleary, Jon   *The Sundowners*
Cohen, Bernard   *Blindman's Hat*
Corris, Peter   *The Empty Beach*
d'Alpuget, Blanche   *Turtle Beach*
Dark, Eleanor   *The Timeless Land*
Davies, Julian   *The Beholder*
Davison, Liam   *The Betrayal*
Day, Marele   *Lambs of God*
Dessaix, Robert   *Night Letters*
Drewe, Robert   *The Drowner*
Earls, Nick   *Bachelor Kisses*
Falconer, Delia   *The Service of Clouds*
Flanagan, Richard   *The Sound of One Hand Clapping*
Foster, David   *In the New Country*
Franklin, Miles   *My Brilliant Career*
Garner, Helen   *Monkey Grip*
Gilling, Tom   *The Sooterkin*
Grenville, Kate   *Lilian's Story*
                       The Idea of Perfection
Hardy, Frank   *Power Without Glory*
                       But the Dead are Many
Hasluck, Nicholas   *Our Man K*
Hazzard, Shirley   *Transit of Venus*

Herbert, Xavier	*Poor Fellow My Country*
Hospital, Janette Turner	*Last Magician*
Hughes, Robert	*The Fatal Shore*
Ireland, David	*A Woman of the Future*
Johnston, George	*My Brother Jack*
Jolley, Elizabeth	*The Well*
	An Accommodating Spouse
Keneally, Thomas	*The Chant of Jimmie Blacksmith*
	Schindler's Ark
Kinsella, John	*Genre*
Koch, Christopher	*Highways to a War*
Lawson, Henry	*While the Billy Boils*
Lindsay, Joan	*Picnic at Hanging Rock*
Lucashenko, Melissa	*King Hit*
Lurie, Morris	*Two Brothers Running*
McCullough, Colleen	*The Thorn Birds*
McKie, Ronald	*The Mango Tree*
Malouf, David	*An Imaginary Life*
Niland, D'Arcy	*The Shiralee*
Park, Ruth	*The Harp in the South*
Pascoe, Bruce	*Shark*
Prichard, Katharine S.	*Coonardoo*
Richards, Tim	*The Prince*
Richardson, Henry H.	*The Fortunes of Richard Mahony*
Rothwell, Nicholas	*Heavan and Earth*
Rudd, Steele	*On Our Selection*
Sayer, Mandy	*Mood Indigo*
Scott, John	*Before I Wake*
Shute, Nevil	*A Town Like Alice*
Stead, Christina	*The Man Who Loved Children*
Tennant, Kylie	*The Battlers*
Tsiolkas, Christos	*Loaded*
Walker, Brenda	*Poe's Cat*
Weller, Archie	*Land of the Golden Clouds*
West, Morris	*The Devil's Advocate*
White, Patrick	*The Tree of Man*
	The Twyborn Affair
Winton, Tim	*Cloudstreet*
	The Riders
Yahp, Beth	*Crocodile Fury*

Books for older children and teenagers

ABC Books	*Sizzling Hot Jokes for Kool Kids*
Baillie, Allan	*The Last Shot*
Caswell, Brian	*A Cage of Butterflies*
Hartnett, Sonya	*Sleeping Dogs*
Hathorn, Libby	*Ghostop*
Jinks, Catherine	*Eye to Eye*
Kelleher, Victor	*Fire Dancer*
Lowry, Brigid	*Guitar Highway Rose*
Metzenthen, David	*Gilbert's Ghost Train*
Moloney, James	*A Bridge to Wiseman's Cove*
Orr, Wendy	*Peeling the Onion*
Park, Ruth	*Playing Beatie Bow*
Pausacker, Jenny	*Getting Somewhere*
Southall, Ivan	*Ash Road*
Stafford, M.	*Amy's Place*
Thiele, Colin	*Storm Boy*
Turner, Ethel	*Seven Little Australians*
Wheatley, N. & Ottley, M.	*Luke's Way of Looking*
Winton, Tim	*Lockie Leonard, Legend*
Zurbo, Matt	*Idiot Pride*

Books for younger children

ABC Books	*Bananas in Pyjamas series*
Baker, Jeannie	*Where the Forest Meets the Sea*
Bruce, Mary Grant	*A Little Bush Maid*
Carey, Peter	*The Big Bazoohley*
Carr, Roger Vaughan	*The Butterfly*
Clement, Rod	*Grandpa's Teeth*
Fienberg, Anna & Barbara	*Tashi and the Genie*
Freeman, Pamela	*Victor's Quest*
Gamble, Kim	*Come the Terrible Tiger*
Gibbs, May	*Adventures of Snugglepot and Cuddlepie*
Gleeson, Libby	*Hannah Plus One*
Graham, Bob	*Queenie the Bantam*
Gunn, Aeneas	*We of the Never Never*
Hann Syme, Marguerite	*Chickpea*
Hathorn, Libby	*Thunderwith*
Honey, Elizabeth	*What Do You Think?*
Jennings, Paul	*The Gizmo*
Jennings, Paul & Gleitzman, Morris	*Wicked (Parts 1 to 6)*

Kidd, Diana   *I Love You, Jason Delaney*
Klein, Robin   *The Listmaker*
Lindsay, Norman   *The Magic Pudding*
Marsden, John   *Burning for Revenge*
McLean, A. & J.   *Josh*
Moloney, James   *Swashbuckler*
Morgan, Sally   *Just a Little Brown Dog*
Morimoto, Junko   *The Two Bullies*
Morrow, Robin   *Beetle Soup*
Pedley, Ethel   *Dot and the Kangaroo*
Riddle, Tohby   *The Great Escape from City Zoo*
Rodda, Emily   *Rowan and the Keeper of the Crystal*
Rule, H. &
 Goodman, S.   *Gulpilil's Stories of the Dreamtime*
Steele, Mary   *A Bit of a Hitch*
Wall, Dorothy   *The Adventures of Blinky Bill*
Walker, Kate   *I Hate Books!*
Whatley, B. &
 Smith, R.   *Dectective Donut and the Wild Goose Chase*
Wheatley, Nadia &
 Rawlings, Donna   *My Place*
Winton, Tim   *Blueback*
Wrightson, Patricia   *Rattler's Place*

Poetry

Dawe, Bruce   *This Side of Silence*
Dennis, C.J.   *Song of the Sentimental Bloke*
Dobson, Rosemary   *The Three Fates*
Dutton, Geoffrey   *Night Flight and Sunrise*
Gilmore, Dame Mary   *Passionate Heart and Other Poems*
Harwood, Gwen   *The Lion's Bride*
Hewett, Dorothy   *What About the People!*
Hope, A.D.   *The Wandering Islands*
Lawson, Henry   *Poetical Works of Henry Lawson*
McAuley, James   *Music Late at Night*
Murray, Les   *Subhuman Redneck Poems*
O'Brien, John   *Around the Boree Log*
Oodgeroo Noonuccal   *My People*
Paterson, A.B. 'Banjo' *The Man from Snowy River and*
                       Other Verses
Porter, Dorothy   *The Monkey's Mask*
Riddell, Elizabeth   *From the Midnight Courtyard*
Slessor, Kenneth   *Five Bells*
                       Beach Burial
Stewart, Douglas   *Fire on the Snow*
Wright, Judith   *Woman to Man*

Drama

Balodis, Janis	*Too Young for Ghosts*
Beynon, Richard	*The Shifting Heart*
Buzo, Alex	*Norm and Ahmed*
Davis, Jack	*Kullark (Home)*
	The Dreamers
Elliot, Sumner Locke	*Rusty Bugles*
Kenna, Peter	*A Hard God*
Lawler, Ray	*Summer of the Seventeenth Doll*
Nowra, Louis	*Inside the Island*
	Precious Women
Porter, Hal	*Eden House*
Rayson, Hannie	*Room to Move*
Symour, Alan	*The One Day of the Year*
David Williamson	*Corporate Vibes*

Films

For the poor, working and privileged classes alike, the advent of the cinematograph brought brightness to an otherwise isolated and relentlessly dismal existence which many Australians led at the beginning of the 20th century. Most of the population of almost four million faced unemployment, sickness and poverty, and the moving picture show brought a chance to escape with snippets of nostalgia of a kinder European way of life. As a result people flocked in their thousands to especially built theatres where the 'magic shadow shows' were watched with awe. The colourful lights, music and lavish edifices of these picture houses, together with low admission fees, created a remarkably popular pastime.

Key: P = producer, D = director, W = writer, A = actor

Take 1: **Silent films**

The first film show took place in Melbourne's Opera House in 1896 and a month later the first cinema, 'The Salon Lumiere', was opened in Pitt Street, Sydney. In 1900, the Limelight Department of the Salvation Army, realising the impact of visual presentations, equipped a film unit which began to make religious epics. Newsreels were introduced in 1911 by T.J. West and by 1921 Australia had developed a flourishing, low-budget film industry which catered for over 800 picture theatres then operating.

There were 250 silent movies made in Australia before the 'talkies' were introduced in 1928.

Date	Film title/credits

1898 *Our Social Triumphs*
     Salvation Army Films – Joseph Perry (P)
1900 *Soldiers of the Cross*
     Salvation Army Films (P)
1906 *The Story of the Kelly Gang*
     J. & N. Tait (P), Charles Tait (D)
1907 *Robbery Under Arms*
     J. & N. Tait (P)
1911 *Captain Midnight*
     Cosens Spencer (D)
1914 *The Silence of Dean Maitland*
     Raymond Longford (P,D&W)
1916 *Mutiny on the Bounty*
     Raymond Longford (P,D&W), Lottie Lyell (A)
1919 *The Sentimental Bloke*
     Raymond Longford (P,D&W), Lottie Lyell (A)
1920 *On Our Selection*
     Raymond Longford (D)
1926 *The Moth of Moonbi*
     Charles Chauvel (D)
1927 *The Kid Stakes*
     Tal Ordell (D)
     For the Term of His Natural Life
     Norman Dawn (D), George Fisher (A)

Take 2: **The talkies**

Despite the enthusiasm of the early Australian producers, feature film production had reached crisis point by 1927 and the industry began to fade. Always working on slim budgets and lacking government support, producers found very few Australian films made a profit. As well, the distributors of British and American flims began to flood the Australian market and for the next 30 years our film industry was overshadowed as Australian producers found it impossible to compete. However, some films were extremely successful.

Date	Film title/credits

1933 *The Squatter's Daughter*
     Ken G. Hall (P&D), Jocelyn Howarth (A)
     In the Wake of the Bounty
     Charles Chauvel (P,D&W), Errol Flynn (A)
1940 *Forty Thousand Horsemen*
     Charles Chauvel (P&D), Elsa Chauvel (W), Chips Rafferty (A)

1946 *The Overlanders*
        Harry Watt (P,D&W), Chips Rafferty (A)
1947 *Bush Christmas*
        Ralph Smart (D)
1949 *The Rats of Tobruk*
        Charles Chauvel (P&D), Elsa Chauvel (W), Peter Finch (A)
      Sons of Matthew
        Charles Chauvel (P,D&W), John O'Malley (A)
      Eureka Stockade
        Harry Watt (D&W), Chips Rafferty (A)
1951 *Captain Thunderbolt*
        Cecil Holmes (D)
1955 *Jedda*
        Charles Chauvel (P,D&W), Ngaria Kunoth (A)
1958 *Smiley*
        Anthony Kimmins (P,D&W), Colin Petersen (A)
1960 *The Sundowners*
        Fred Zinneman (D)
1966 *They're a Weird Mob*
        Michael Powell (P&D), Richard Imrie & Emeric Pressburger (W),
        Walter Chiari (A)

Take 3: **The 1970s surge**

During the 1970s the Australian film industry at last began to expand
and make a mark once again on the world stage. The government
became directly involved and a national film and television school
was established, which trained some incredibly talented people who
produced many films that won international acclaim. Here is a
selection of the most successful box office hits.

Date   Film title/credits

1971 *Wake in Fright*
        George Willoughby (P), Ted Kotcheff (D), Evan Jones (W),
        Gary Bond (A)
      Walkabout
        Nicolas Roeg (D)
1972 *The Adventures of Barry McKenzie*
        Phillip Adams (P), Bruce Beresford (D),
        Barry Humphries (W), Barry Crocker (A)
1973 *Alvin Purple*
        Tim Burstall (P&D), Alan Hopgood (W),
        Graeme Blundell (A)
1974 *The Cars That Ate Paris*
        Hal & Jim McElroy (P), Peter Weir (D&W),
        Terry Camilleri (A)

1975 *Picnic at Hanging Rock*
      Pat Lovell (P), Peter Weir (D), Clifford Green (W),
      Rachel Roberts (A)
      The Removalists
      Margaret Fink (P), Tom Jeffrey (D), David Williamson (W),
      John Hargreaves (A)
      Sunday Too Far Away
      Gil Brealey & Matt Carroll (P), Ken Hannam (D),
      John Dingwall (W), Jack Thompson (A)
1976 *Caddie*
      Anthony Buckley (P), Donald Crombie (D), Joan Long (A),
      Helen Morse (A)
      The Devil's Playground
      Fred Schepisi (P,D&W), Arthur Dignam (A)
      Don's Party
      Phillip Adams (P), Bruce Beresford (D), David Williamson (W),
      John Hargreaves (A)
      Leisure
      Bruce Petty (animated)
      Storm Boy
      Matt Carroll (P), Henri Safran (D), Sonia Borg (W),
      Greg Rowe (A)
1977 *The Getting of Wisdom*
      Phil Adams (P), Bruce Beresford (D), Eleanor Witcombe (W),
      Susannah Fowle (A)
1978 *The Chant of Jimmie Blacksmith*
      Fred Schepisi (P,D&W), Tommy Lewis (A)
      Newsfront
      David Elfick (P), Phillip Noyce (D), Bob Ellis (W),
      Bill Hunter (A)
1979 *Breaker Morant*
      Matt Carroll (P), Bruce Beresford (D), John Hardy
      & David Stevens (P), Bryan Brown (A)
      My Brilliant Career
      Margaret Fink (P), Gillian Armstrong (D), Eleanor Witcombe (W),
      Judy Davis (A)
      Mad Max
      Byron Kennedy (P), George Miller (D&W), Mel Gibson (A)

Take 4: **Films of the 1980s**

Investors in films in the early 1980s were allowed generous tax
concessions. This resulted in a spate of people entering the
industry with very little knowledge of how it worked. At times
creativity was compromised in the great quest for monetary
gains. Although many films of quality were made, some were of
dubious value.

1980   *The Club*
       Bruce Beresford (D), David Williamson (W)
1981   *Gallipoli*
       Ben Gannon, Pat Lovell & Robert Stigwood (P),
       Peter Weir (D), David Williamson (W), Mel Gibson (A)
       Mad Max 2
       Byron Kennedy (P), George Miller (D&W),
       Mel Gibson (A)
       Puberty Blues
       Margaret Kelly (P&W), Bruce Beresford (D),
       Nell Schofield (A)
       The Winter of Our Dreams
       Richard Mason (P), John Duigan (D), Bryan Brown (A)
1982   *The Man from Snowy River*
       Geoff Burrowes & Simon Wincer (P), George Miller (D),
       Fred Cullen & John Dixon (W), Tom Burlinson (A)
       Monkey Grip
       Pat Lovell (P), Ken Cameron (D&W), Helen Garner (W),
       Noni Hazlehurst (A)
       The Year of Living Dangerously
       Peter Weir, James & Jim McElroy (P), Peter Weir (D),
       C.J. Koch & David Williamson (W), Mel Gibson (A)
1983   *Careful, He Might Hear You*
       Jill Robb (P), Carl Schultz (D), Michael Jenkins (W),
       Wendy Hughes (A)
       Phar Lap
       Richard Davis & John Sexton (P), Simon Wincer (D),
       David Williamson (W), Tom Burlinson (A)
1984   *Annie's Coming Out*
       Don Murray (P), Gil Brealey (D), Chris Borthwick
       & John Patterson (W), Tina Arhondis (A)
       My First Wife
       Paul Cox & Jane Ballantyne (P), Paul Cox (D), Bob Ellis (W),
       John Hargreaves (A)
1985   *Bliss*
       Anthony Buckley (P), Ray Lawrence (D&W), Peter Carey (W),
       Barry Otto (A)

DID YOU KNOW?

It is estimated that making a feature film in
Australia is approximately one-tenth the cost of
making it in Hollywood.

Burke & Wills
> Graeme Clifford & John Sexton (P), Graeme Clifford (D),
> Michael Thomas (W), Jack Thompson (A)

1986 *Backlash*
> Bill Bennett (P,D&W), David Argue (A)
> *Crocodile Dundee*
> John Cornell & Jane Scott (P), Peter Faiman (D), Paul Hogan (A)
> *The Fringe Dwellers*
> Sue Milliken (P), Bruce Beresford (D&W), Kristina Nehm (A)

1987 *Dead Calm*
> Phillip Noyce (D), Sam Neill (A), Terry Hayes (SC)
> *Evil Angels*
> Fred Schepisi (D), Robert Caswell & Fred Schepisi (W),
> Meryl Streep & Sam Neill (A)
> *High Tide*
> Sandra Levy (P), Gillian Armstrong (D), Laura Jones (W),
> Judy Davis (A)
> *The Lighthorsemen*
> Ian Jones (P), Simon Wincer (P,D&W), Peter Phelps (A)
> *The Year My Voice Broke*
> Terry Hayes, George Miller & Doug Mitchell (P),
> John Duigan (D), Noah Taylor (A)
> *Young Einstein*
> Yahoo Serious (D&A), Yahoo Serious & David Roach (W)

1989 *Sweetie*
> John Maynard (P), Jane Campion (D), Gerard Lee (W),
> Genevieve Lemon (A)

Take 5: Films of the 1990s

Australia has been an excellent venue for local and overseas film-makers. The combination of endless homegrown talent, both in acting and production, reasonably secure government support and the best film-making facilities outside Hollywood has seen an exciting transition in our film industry. This remarkable buoyancy, coupled with the willingness of Aussies to take a risk, has resulted in new and diverse productions which have taken the world by storm.

Date   Film title/credits

1990 *The Crossing*
> Sue Seeary (P), George Ogilvie (D), Russell Crowe (A)
> *Flirting*
> Terry Hayes, George Miller & Doug Mitchell (P),
> John Duigan (D), Noah Taylor (A)

Golden Braid
   Paul Cox (P,D&W), Chris Haywood (A)
Proof
   Lynda House (P), Jocelyn Moorhouse (D), Hugo Weaving (A)
1991 *Death in Brunswick*
   Bryce Menzies & Timothy White (P), John Ruane (D&W),
   Sam Neill (A)
1992 *Dingo*
   Rolf de Heer (P&D), Mark Rosenberg (W), Colin Friels (A)
Fern Gully: The Last Rainforest
   Bill Kroyer (P), Peter Faiman (D), Jim Cox (W),
   Robin Williams (A)
The Last Days of Chez Nous
   Jan Chapman (P), Gillian Armstrong (D), Helen Garner (W),
   Lisa Harrow (A)
Strictly Ballroom
   Tristram Myall (P), Baz Luhrmann (D&W), Paul Mercurio (A)
Romper Stomper
   Ian Pringle (P), Geoffrey Wright (D&W), Russell Crowe (A)
1993 *The Heartbreak Kid*
   Ben Gannon (P), Michael Jenkins (D&W), Claudia Karvan (A)
The Piano
   Jan Chapman (P), Jane Campion (D&W), Holly Hunter (A)
The Silver Brumby
   Colin South (P), John Tatoulis (D), Russell Crowe (A)
1994 *The Adventures of Priscilla, Queen of the Desert*
   Michael Hamlyn (P), Stephan Elliott (D&W),
   Hugo Weaving (A)
Bad Boy Bubby
   Rolf de Heer (P,D&W), Nicholas Hope (A)
Broken Highway
   Lauren McInnes (D&W), Aden Young (A)
Muriel's Wedding
   Lynda House (P), P.J. Hogan (D&W), Toni Collette (A)
Spider and Rose
   Lyn McCarthy (P), Bill Bennett (D&W), Ruth Cracknell (A)
The Sum of Us
   Kevin Dowling (P), Geoff Burton (D), David Stevens (W),
   Jack Thompson (A)
1995 *Angel Baby*
   Jonathon Shteinman (P), Michael Rymer (D&W),
   John Lynch (A)
Babe
   George Miller (P), Chris Noonan (D&W), Magda Szubanski (A)
1996 *Cosi*
   Richard Brennan (P), Mark Joffe (D), Louis Nowra (W),
   Ben Mendelsohn (A)

Doing Time for Patsy Cline *(1997).*

Love and Other Catastrophes
  S.A. Efthymiou (P), Emma-Kate Croghan (D), Yale Bregman
  & Helen Bandis (W), Frances O'Connor (A)
Lilian's Story
  Marian MacGowan (P), Jerzy Domaradzki (D),
  Steve Wright (W), Ruth Cracknell (A)
Not Fourteen Again
  Gillian Armstrong (P&D)
Shine
  Jane Scott (P), Scott Hicks (D), Jane Sardi (W),
  Geoffrey Rush (A)
Rats in the Ranks
  Robin Anderson (P&D), Bob Connelly (P)
1997 *Black Rock*
  David Elfick (P), Steven Vidler (D), Nick Enright (W),
  Laurence Breuls (A)
The Castle
  Debra Choate (P), Rob Sitch (D), Michael Caton (A)
Doing Time for Patsy Cline
  Chris Kennedy (P,D&W), Matt Day (A)
Idiot Box
  Glendys Rowe (P), David Caesar (D&W), Ben Mendelsohn (A)
Kiss or Kill
  Bill Bennett (P,D&W), Matt Day (A)
Oscar and Lucinda
  Timothy White (P), Gillian Armstrong (D), Laura Jones (W),
  Cate Blanchett (A)
The Quiet Room
  Rolf de Heer (P,D&W), Chloe Ferguson (A)
The Well
  Sandra Levy (P), Samantha Lang (D), Laura Jones (W),
  Miranda Otto (A)
1998 *The Boys*
  John Maynard (P), Rowan Woods (D), Stephen Sewell (W),
  David Wenham (A)

The Well *(1997)*.

Dance Me to My Song
> Rolf de Heer (P,D&W), Heather Rose (W&A)

Head On
> Jane Scott (P), Anna Kokkinos (D), Mira Robinson (W),
> Alex Dimitirades (A)

Radiance
> Ned Lander (P), Rachel Perkins (D), Louis Nowra (W),
> Rachel Maza (A)

The Interview
> Bill Hughes (P), Craig Monahan (D&W), Hugo Weaving (A)

The Sound of One Hand Clapping
> Rolf de Heer (P), Richard Flanagan (D&W), Kerry Fox (A)

1999 *The Craic*
> Marc Gracie & David Foster (P), Ted Emery (D), Jimeoin (P,W&A)

Erskineville Kings
> Alan White (P&D), Anik Chooney (W), Hugh Jackman (A)

Holy Smoke
> Jan Chapman (P), Jane Campion (D&W), Kate Winslet (A)

In a Savage Land
> Bill Bennett (D), Rufus Sewell (A)

Praise
> Martha Coleman (P), John S. Curran (D), Andrew McGahan (W),
> Sacha Horler (A)

Redball
> Daniel Scharf (P), John Hewitt
> (D&W), Belinda McClory (A)

Siam Sunset
> Al Clark (P), John Polson (D),
> Max Dann (W), Linus Roache (A)

Strange Fits of Passion
> Bryce Menzies (P), Elise McCredie
> (D&W), Michela Noonan (A)

Two Hands
> Marian MacGowan (P), Gregor
> Jordan (D&W), Bryan Brown (A)

Redball *(1999)*.

Advance Australia Fair

*The original words and music were supposedly written and composed by
Peter Dodds McCormick in about 1878. In 1983 a new version of the
song was adopted by the Australian government as the national anthem.*

Australians all let us rejoice,
For we are young and free,
We've golden soil and wealth for toil;
Our home is girt by sea;
Our land abounds in nature's gifts
Of beauty rich and rare;
In history's page, let every stage
Advance Australia fair.

Beneath our radiant Southern Cross
We'll toil with hearts and hands,
To make this Commonwealth of ours
Renowned of all the lands;
For those who've come across the seas
We've boundless plains to share;
With courage let us all combine
To Advance Australia fair.
In joyful strains then let us sing,
Advance Australia fair.

Kookaburra Sits on the Old Gum Tree

*This song is widely known overseas. It is one of many songs about
Australia which is taught in schools in other countries. For information
about kookaburras, see page 268.*

Kookaburra sits on the old gum tree,
Merry, merry king of the bush is he,
Laugh! kookaburra, laugh! kookaburra,
Gay your life must be.
Kookaburra sits on the old gum tree,
Eating all the gum nuts he can see,
Stop! kookaburra, stop! kookaburra,
Please leave some for me.

My Country

Dorothea Mackellar (1885–1968)

This poem, written in 1908, epitomises for most Australians the deep feelings of pride and love they have for their country. Although the young poet was born in England, she came to Australia as a child. It was then that she began to love this 'sunburnt country'.

The love of field and coppice,
Of green and shaded lanes,
Of ordered woods and gardens
Is running through your veins;
Strong love of grey-blue distance,
Brown streams and soft,
   dim skies –
I know but cannot share it,
My love is otherwise.

I love a sunburnt country,
A land of sweeping plains,
Of ragged mountain ranges,
Of droughts and flooding rains.
I love her far horizons,
I love her jewel-sea,
Her beauty and her terror –
The wide brown land for me!

The stark white ringbarked
   forests,
All tragic to the moon,
The sapphire-misted
   mountains,
The hot gold hush of noon.
Green tangle of the brushes,
Where lithe lianas coil
And orchids deck the tree-tops
And ferns the warm dark soil.

Core of my heart, my country!
Her pitiless blue sky,
When sick at heart, around us,
We see the cattle die –
But then the grey clouds
   gather,
And we can bless again
The drumming of an army,
The steady, soaking rain.

Core of my heart, my country!
Land of the Rainbow Gold,
For flood and fire and famine,
She pays us back threefold;
Over the thirsty paddocks,
Watch, after many days,
The filmy veil of greenness
That thickens as we gaze.

An opal-hearted country,
A wilful, lavish land –
All you who have not
   loved her,
You will not understand –
Though earth holds many
   splendours,
Wherever I may die,
I know to what brown country
My homing thoughts will fly.

DID YOU KNOW?

The saying 'Beyond the black stump' originated from the Black Stump Run, a tract of inhospitable, desolate land west of Coolah, New South Wales. Local Aborigines called it 'the place where the fire went out' referring to the lack of vegetation and the extremely harsh conditions.

Waltzing Matilda

A.B. 'Banjo' Paterson (1864–1941)

This song was written at the turn of the century at Dagworth Station, near Winton in Queensland, by one of Australia's favourite poets. The words given here are slightly modified from the original, and have become the most popular version. The song depicts a crafty wanderer of the outback, a swagman, whose only comfort against his harsh life is his 'Matilda', his blanket roll. He is caught for sheep-stealing but before the troopers can arrest him, he defiantly jumps into the billabong (waterhole) making it clear he would rather drown than be taken prisoner.

However, 'Waltzing Matilda' is far more than a song about a crafty swaggie. It seems to embody the rebellious spirit of early Australia, reminding us of the harsh beginnings of white settlement. It is a song which evokes great emotion and which lives in the hearts of many Australians.

Once a jolly swagman camped
  by a billabong,
Under the shade of a coolibah
  tree,
And he sang as he watched and
  waited till his billy boiled,
'Who'll come a-waltzing Matilda
  with me?'

Chorus
'Waltzing Matilda, waltzing
  Matilda,
'Who'll come a-waltzing Matilda
  with me?'
And he sang as he watched and
  waited till his billy boiled,
'Who'll come a-waltzing Matilda
  with me?'

Down came a jumbuck to drink
  at the billabong,
Up jumped the swagman and
  grabbed him with glee,

And he sang as he shoved that
  jumbuck in his tuckerbag,
'You'll come a-waltzing Matilda
  with me.'

Up rode the squatter mounted
  on his thoroughbred,
Down came the troopers, one,
  two, three,
'Whose that jolly jumbuck
  you've got in your
  tuckerbag?
You'll come a-waltzing Matilda
  with me.'

Up jumped the swagman and
  sprang into the billabong,
'You'll never take me alive',
  said he.
And his ghost may be heard as
  you pass by that billabong:
'Who'll come a-waltzing Matilda
  with me?'

Click Go the Shears

There is a great camaraderie in shearing sheds. It is back-breaking work and the champion shearer (the ringer) is continually challenged by his mates, especially the old men of the shed (the snaggers), who are well past their prime. To get an easy sheep to shear, with no belly wool, and beat the ringer would mean a feather in the snaggers' caps.

But shoddy workmanship is frowned upon and the snagger has to be quite crafty. At the end of the run the shearers gather to quench their thirst at the nearest pub. Their philosophy is 'Work hard, drink hard and die hard'.

Out on the board the old
　　shearer stands,
Grasping the shears in his thin,
　　bony hands,
Fixed is his gaze on a bare-
　　bellied 'joe',
Glory if he gets her, won't he
　　make the ringer go.

Chorus
Click go the shears boys, click,
　　click, click,
Wide is his blow and his hands
　　move quick,
The ringer looks around and is
　　beaten by a blow,
And curses the old snagger with
　　the bare-bellied 'joe'.

In the middle of the floor in his
　　cane-bottomed chair
Sits the boss of the board, with
　　eyes everywhere;
Notes well each fleece as it
　　comes to the screen,
Paying strict attention that it's
　　taken off clean.

The tar-boy is there, awaiting in
　　demand,
With his blackened tar pot in his
　　tarry hand;

Sees one old sheep with a cut
　　upon its back,
Hears what he's waiting for,
　　'Tar here, Jack!'

Shearing is all over and we've all
　　got our cheques,
Roll up your swag, boys, we're
　　off on the tracks;
The first pub we come to, it's
　　there we'll have a spree,
And everyone that comes along,
　　it's 'Have a drink with me!'

Down by the bar the old
　　shearer stands,
Grasping his glass in his thin
　　bony hands;
Fixed is his gaze on a green-
　　painted keg,
Glory, he'll get down on it, ere
　　he stirs a peg.

There we leave him standing,
　　shouting for all hands,
Whilst all around him every
　　'shouter' stands;
His eyes are on the keg which is
　　now lowering fast,
He works hard, he drinks hard,
　　and goes to hell at last!

The Man from Snowy River

A.B. 'Banjo' Paterson
One of the best-known story/poems in Australian literature.

There was movement at the station, for the word had passed around
That the colt from old Regret had got away,
And had joined the wild bush horses – he was worth a thousand
pound,
So all the cracks had gathered to the fray.
All the tried and noted riders from the stations near and far
Had mustered at the homestead overnight,
For the bushmen love hard riding where the wild bush horses are,
And the stock-horse snuffs the battle with delight.

There was Harrison, who made his pile when Pardon won the cup,
The old man with his hair as white as snow;
But few could ride beside him when his blood was fairly up –
He would go wherever horse and man could go.
And Clancy of the Overflow came down to lend a hand,
No better horseman ever held the reins;
For never horse could throw him while the saddle-girths would stand –
He learnt to ride while droving on the plains.

And one was there, a stripling on a small and weedy beast;
He was something like a racehorse undersized,
With a touch of Timor pony – three parts thoroughbred at least –
And such as are by mountain horsemen prized.
He was hard and tough and wiry – just the sort that won't say die –
There was courage in his quick impatient tread;
And he bore the badge of gameness in his bright and fiery eye,
And the proud and lofty carriage of his head.

But still so slight and weedy; one would doubt his power to stay,
And the old man said, 'That horse will never do
For a long and tiring gallop – lad, you'd better stop away,
Those hills are far too rough for such as you.'
So he waited, sad and wistful – only Clancy stood his friend –
'I think we ought to let him come,' he said;
'I warrant he'll be with us when he's wanted at the end,
For both his horse and he are mountain bred.

'He hails from Snowy River, up by Kosciuszko's side,
Where the hills are twice as steep and twice as rough;
Where a horse's hoofs strike firelight from the flint-stones every stride,
The man that holds his own is good enough.
And the Snowy River riders on the mountains make their home,
Where the river runs those giant hills between;

I have seen full many horsemen since I first commenced to roam,
But nowhere yet such horsemen have I seen.'

So he went; they found the horses by the big mimosa clump,
They raced away towards the mountain's brow,
And the old man gave his orders, 'Boys go at them from the jump,
No use to try for fancy riding now,
And, Clancy, you must wheel them, try and wheel them to the right.
Ride boldly lad, and never fear the spills,
For never yet was rider that could keep the mob in sight,
If once they gain the shelter of those hills.'

So Clancy rode to wheel them – he was racing on the wing
Where the best and boldest riders take their place,
And he raced his stock-horse past them, and he made the ranges ring
With the stockwhip, as he met them face to face.
Then they halted for a moment, while he swung the dreaded lash,
But they saw their well-loved mountain full in view,
And they charged beneath the stockwhip with a sharp and sudden dash,
And off into the mountain scrub they flew.

Then fast the horsemen followed, where the gorges deep and black
Resounded to the thunder of their tread,
And the stockwhips woke the echoes, and they fiercely answered back
From cliffs and crags that beetled overhead.
And upward, ever upward, the wild horses held their way,
Where mountain ash and kurrajong grew wide;
And the old man muttered fiercely, 'We may bid the mob good day,
No man can hold them down the other side.'

When they reached the mountain's summit, even Clancy took a pull –
It well might make the boldest hold their breath;
The wild hop scrub grew thickly, and the hidden ground was full
Of wombat holes, and any slip was death.
But the man from Snowy River let the pony have his head,
And he swung his stockwhip round and gave a cheer,
And he raced him down the mountain like a torrent down its bed,
While the others stood and watched in very fear.

He sent the flint-stones flying, but the pony kept his feet,
He cleared the fallen timber in his stride,
And the man from Snowy River never shifted in his seat –
It was grand to see that mountain horseman ride.
Through the stringybarks and saplings, on the rough and broken ground,
Down the hillside at a racing pace he went;
And he never drew the bridle till he landed safe and sound
At the bottom of that terrible descent.

He was right among the horses as they climbed the farther hill,
And the watchers on the mountain, standing mute,
Saw him ply the stockwhip fiercely; he was right among them still
As he raced across the clearing in pursuit.
Then they lost him for a moment, where two mountain gullies met
In the ranges – but a final glimpse reveals
On a dim and distant hillside the wild horses racing yet,
With the man from Snowy River at their heels.

And he ran them single-handed till their sides were white with foam;
He followed like a bloodhound on their track,
Till they halted, cowed and beaten; then he turned their heads for home,
And alone and unassisted brought them back.
But his hardy mountain pony he could scarcely raise a trot,
He was blood from hip to shoulder from the spur;
But his pluck was still undaunted, and his courage fiery hot,
For never yet was mountain horse a cur.

And down by Kosciuszko, where the pine-clad ridges raise
Their torn and rugged battlements on high,
Where the air is clear as crystal and the white stars fairly blaze
At midnight in the cold and frosty sky,
And where around the Overflow the reed-beds sweep and sway
To the breezes, and the rolling plains are wide,
The man from Snowy River is a household word today,
And the stockmen tell the story of his ride.

Ballad of the Drover

Henry Lawson (1867–1922)

Lawson is one of Australia's best-loved writers, with his vivid descriptions of the self-reliant bush folk of the turn of the century. His poems depict the 'hard times' endured by people employed in the pastoral industry and praise the courage with which they faced adversity. There is a gentle humour which reflects the feeling of 'mateship' which is familiar to most Australians. This is an abridged version of 'Ballad of the Drover'.

Across the stony ridges,
Across the rolling plain,
Young Harry Dale, the drover,
Comes riding home again.
And well his stock-horse bears him,
And light of heart he is,
And stoutly his old packhorse
Is trotting by his knee.

Up Queensland way with cattle
He's travelled regions vast,
And many months have
   vanished
Since home-folks saw him last.
He hums a song of someone
He hopes to marry soon;
And hobble-chains and camp-
   ware
Keep jingling to the tune.

An hour has filled the heavens
With storm-clouds inky black;
At times the lightning trickles
Around the drover's track;

But Harry pushes onward,
His horses' strength he tries,
In hope to reach the river
Before the flood shall rise.

When flashes next the lightning,
The flood's grey breast is blank;
A cattle-dog and packhorse
Are struggling up the bank.
But in the lonely homestead
The girl shall wait in vain –
He'll never pass the stations
In charge of stock again.

Across the flooded lowlands
And slopes of sodden loam
The packhorse struggles bravely
To take dumb tidings home;
And mud-stained, wet, and
   weary,
He goes by rock and tree,
With clanging chains and
   tinware
All sounding eerily.

Lake Macquarie, New South Wales.

The Man from Ironbark

A.B. 'Banjo' Paterson
As sophistication developed among city-dwellers at the end of the 19th century, there was a growing tendency to regard the bushman as a rural clown. This is a whimsical glimpse of the way one such 'clown' dealt with the situation.

tote – a record and distribution of a bet
yokel – a country bumpkin
peeler – policeman

It was the man from Ironbark
   who struck the Sydney town,
He wandered over street and
   park, he wandered up and
   down,
He loitered here, he loitered
   there, till he was like to drop,
Until at last in sheer despair he
   sought a barber's shop.
''Ere! shave my beard and
   whiskers off, I'll be a man of
   mark,
I'll go and do the Sydney toff
   up home in Ironbark.'

The barber man was small and
   flash, as barbers mostly are,
He wore a strike-your-fancy
   sash, he smoked a huge cigar:
He was a humorist of note and
   keen at repartee,
He laid the odds and kept a
   'tote', whatever that may be,
And when he saw our friend
   arrive, he whispered 'Here's a
   lark!
Just watch me catch him all
   alive, this man from Ironbark.'

There were some gilded youths
   that sat along the barber's wall.
Their eyes were dull, their heads
   were flat, they had no brains
   at all;
To them the barber passed the
   wink, his dexter eyelid shut,

'I'll make this bloomin' yokel
   think his bloomin' throat is
   cut.'
And as he soaped and rubbed it
   in he made a rude remark:
'I s'pose the flats is pretty green
   up there in Ironbark.'

A grunt was all reply he got; he
   shaved the bushman's chin,
Then made the water boiling
   hot and dipped the razor in.
He raised his hand, his brow
   grew black, he paused awhile
   to gloat,
Then slashed the red-hot razorback across his victim's throat;
Upon the newly shaven chin it
   made a livid mark –
No doubt it fairly took him in –
   the man from Ironbark.

He fetched a wild up-country
   yell might wake the dead
   to hear,
And though his throat, he knew
   full well, was cut from ear
   to ear,
He struggled gamely to his feet,
   and faced the murderous foe:
'You've done for me! you dog,
   I'm beat! one hit before I go.
I only wish I had a knife, you
   blessed murderous shark!
But you'll remember all your life
   the man from Ironbark.'

He lifted up his hairy paw, with
  one tremendous clout
And landed on the barber's jaw,
  and knocked the barber out.
He set to work with tooth and
  nail, he made the place a
  wreck;
He grabbed the nearest gilded
  youth, and tried to break his
  neck.
And all the while his throat he
  held to save his vital spark,
And 'Murder! Bloody murder!'
  yelled the man from Ironbark.

A peeler man who heard the
  din came in to see the show;
He tried to run the bushman in,
  but he refused to go.
And when at last the barber spoke,
  and said, ''Twas all in fun –
'Twas just a harmless little joke,
  a trifle overdone.'

'A joke!' he cried. 'By George,
  that's fine; a lively sort
  of lark;
I'd like to catch that murdering
  swine some night in
  Ironbark.'

And now while round the
  shearing floor the listening
  shearers gape,
He tells the story o'er and o'er,
  and brags of his escape.
'Them barber chaps what keeps
  a tote, by George, I've had
  enough,
One tried to cut my bloomin'
  throat, but thank the Lord
  it's tough.'
And whether he's believed or
  not, there's one thing to
  remark,
That flowing beards are all the
  go way up in Ironbark.

Bell-birds

Henry Kendall (1839–82)
*An excerpt from a poem which captures the rhythm of the cascading
waterfalls in the forest, the home of the bellbirds* (see page 267).

By channels of coolness the
  echoes are calling,
And down the dim gorges
  I hear the creek falling;
It lives in the mountain, where
  moss and the sedges
Touch with their beauty the
  banks and the ledges;
Through breaks of the cedar
  and sycamore bowers
Struggles the light that is love
  to the flowers.
And, softer than slumber, and
  sweeter than singing,
The notes of the bellbirds are
  running and ringing.

Margaret River, Western Australia.

PLATYPUSES, PLANTS, PARROTS

For millions of years the fauna of Australia evolved in isolation, and many different forms came from relatively few ancestral types. As a result, Australia has some of nature's strangest creatures, which draw enthusiastic zoologists and tourists to study them at first hand.

Mammals

Australia has about 230 species of mammals and almost half are marsupials, the pouched mammal. The balance consists of placental mammals (having a placenta which nourishes the embryo) and monotremes, the lowest order of egg-laying mammals (having one opening for digestive, urinary and genital organs).

Drysdale River

Purnululu

Millstream–Chichester

Rudall Riv

Karijini

Collier Range

Kalbarri

Goongarrie

Cape A

Frank

Stirling Range

Fitzgerald R

D'Entrecasteaux

DID YOU KNOW?

There are 2987 National Parks and Nature Conservation Areas in Australia, with a total area of 30 304 378 hectares, equivalent to 3.9% of the area of the continent. In addition, there is an area of 34 380 000 hectares of the Great Barrier Reef Marine Park offshore from the Queensland coast. With 1 700 000 hectares in the new Great Australian Bight Marine Park, Australia now has the two largest marine parks in the world.

Gurig

Jardine River

Kakadu

Mungkan Kandju

Nitmiluk

Lakefield

Daintree

Great Barrier Reef Marine Park

Gregory

Lawn Hill

West MacDonnell

Watarrka

Carnarvon

Uluru–Kata Tjuta

Great Sandy

Witjira

Simpson Desert

Lake Eyre

Lake Torrens

Sturt

Oxley Wild Rivers

Lake Gairdner

Gammon Ranges

Mootwingee

Goulburn River

Wollemi

Barrington Tops

larbor

Flinders Ranges

Blue Mountains

Yengo

Murray–Sunset

Kanangra–Boyd

Morton

Namadji

Deua

Flinders Chase

Wyperfeld

Kosciuszko

Wadbilliga

Little Desert

Alpine

South East Forest

eat Australian Bight arine Park

Grampians

Yarra Ranges

Snowy River

Croajingolong

Cradle Mountain–Lake St Clair

Franklin–Gordon

Southwest

Marsupials

Most of the world's marsupials are found in Australia.

Bandicoot

This small rat-like marsupial of the *Peramelidae* family is interesting because of its zoological likeness to the kangaroo and possum families, and yet it is insectivorous (insect-eating) and resembles the flesh-eating native cat. Bandicoots are found in most parts of Australia.

Koala

Phascolarctos cinereus
This enchanting little animal is unique to Australia. It is not a member of the bear family, but is a marsupial; it has a pouch which opens downwards. The koala is a tree-dweller, drowsing during the day and becoming more active in the evening, feeding on vast quantities of gum leaves which have a high oil content.

Kangaroos.

This enables it to go without water for long periods of time. The koala is Queensland's animal emblem.

Kangaroo

Perhaps Australia's best-known marsupial and the national animal emblem. There are 69 different species belonging to the superfamily, *macropodoidea*, which can be further broken down into two sub-families, the *macrodidea* (kangaroos, wallabies, wallaroos, paddymelons, tree kangaroos and forest wallabies) and the *potoroidae* (potoroos, rat kangaroos and bettongs).

The largest is the red kangaroo, *Macropus rufus*, which has a body length from 2.5–2.9 metres, a tail length from 71–100 centimetres and can weigh between 85–100 kilograms. It is the Northern Territory's animal emblem. The smallest group is the musk rat kangaroo, *Hypsiprymnodon moschatus*, which has a body length from 15–20 centimetres and can weigh between 450–500 grams. This tiny animal is thought to be the connecting link between the possum and kangaroo families.

Kangaroos of all kinds have one thing in common – they are bipedal (two-footed) with powerful back legs and long flat feet. They have a remarkable hopping action which uses less energy than four-footed animals; however, it prevents them from easily moving backwards.

Adapting well to varying conditions, particularly

drought, the kangaroo has a unique, continous flow of reproduction, with one joey outside the pouch, which will still suckle, one inside suckling and one embryo on hold. Thus the female can produce offspring long after the male has disappeared.

Marsupial mole

Notoryctes typhlops
This small animal lives in the desert regions of southern and western Australia. It is eyeless and has no claws, unlike a true mole. It tunnels with its fleshy feet through loose sand, and is rarely seen because it stays underground.

Numbat

Myrmecobius fasciatus
This unique striped marsupial is found only in the south-west corner of Western Australia. It is considered to be an endangered species as it is widely hunted by feral animals.

It has sharp front claws and a sticky tongue with which it attacks ant and termite nests. However, it can open only the weakest nests, and is unable to completely destroy them as it can't burrow in far enough. Although it is a marsupial, strangely it has no pouch. Instead, the young (usually four) cling with their mouths to the mother's underside until old enough to fend for themselves. The numbat is Western Australia's animal emblem.

Possums

Australian possums, or phalangers, are herbivorous marsupials which live in trees. They belong to four main families: ringtails and large gliders; brushtails and cuscus; feathertail and pygmy possums; and honey possums. They are shy, nocturnal creatures. Some are capable of gliding, but it is not considered true flight. They have a pouch, but also carry their young on their backs.

The greater glider possum, *Petauroides volans*, is an elusive creature which usually finds a home in the hollow of a gum tree. It is capable of gliding or volplaning from one tree to another by an extension of skin along the sides of the body and limbs, which when extended forms a sort of parachute.

DID YOU KNOW?

One of the world's tiniest mammals is Australia's only fishing bat, which is 2.5 centimetres long and weighs only 4.5 grams. It fishes in the dark, detecting prey by sonar signals sent back from water ripples. The bat's abnormally large claws enable it to swoop for fish just below the surface and be airborne in a split second.

Tasmanian devil.

Leadbeater's possum, *Gymnobelideus leadbeateri*, is a tiny possum which lives only in Victoria, over an area of 100 square kilometres extending from Marysville, north-east of Melbourne, to Tanjil Bren. After 1909 it was thought to be extinct, but it was rediscovered in 1961, again at Marysville. It is the animal emblem of Victoria.

Tasmanian devil

Sarcophilus harrisii

The Tasmanian devil is the largest surviving carnivorous (meat-eating) marsupial. It is nocturnal and very shy, belying its name. It is the size of a fox terrier but has strong enough teeth to consume a whole sheep, including the skull. Usually there are litters of four which remain in the pouch for several months.

Tasmanian tiger

Thylacinus cynocephalus

Also known as the thylacine, this is the largest carnivorous marsupial in the world. It is presumed extinct, although there have been many unconfirmed sightings. Thylacines at one time were very common, but a bounty placed upon them caused widespread destruction. The last one was caught in 1933 and died in Melbourne in 1936. They are wolf-like but are not related to the canine family. As a rule the litter numbers four, the young remaining in the pouch for perhaps three months before they are ready to leave the 'nursery'.

Wombats

The wombat is a powerful, thickset, burrowing marsupial found only in Australia. The common wombat, *Vombatus ursinus,* is a forest-dweller and the hairy-nosed wombat, *Lasiorhinus latifrons* is a plains-dweller. It is not a very sociable animal. The wombat has a bony plate in its rump which can be used to kill any predator which might follow it down its burrow, by crushing it against the roof of the burrow.

Because of their instinct to go through things rather than around, wombats are often considered stupid and destructive. However, they have a brain proportionally larger than any other marsupial, indicating high intelligence. The hairy-nosed wombat is South Australia's animal emblem.

Placental mammals

Australia's placental mammals comprise bats, the dingo, marine mammals and rodents. Placental mammals produce fully developed young.

Bats

Bats are the only true flying mammals. They are warm-blooded and are covered in fur, and nourish their young with milk. They can fly long distances, using echolocation to find their way. As a result they have highly developed senses of smell and hearing. Bats are represented in Australia by 58 species including the fruit bat, *Chiroptera pteropodidae*, and the rare ghost bat, *Macroderma gigas*, of central Australia, which is a cannibal bat living on smaller species of its own kind and other animals.

Dingo

Canis familiaris dingo
This dog is regarded as indigenous to Australia and is presumed to have evolved from dogs brought from Asia 3000 to 8000 years ago by the ancestors of the Australian Aborigines. They are stealthy nocturnal hunters and often set up a continual chorus of dismal howls, much like the Northern Hemisphere wolf.

Dingo.

Marine mammals

Sea lions, of the family *Otariidae*, and seals of the family *Phocidae* are ocean mammals found on Australia's southern coastline. Seals have limited mobility on land as they have to drag their hind limbs; sea lions, with more use of their hind limbs, are more mobile.

Dugongs, *Dugong dugon*, are completely herbivorous. They graze on sea grasses on the ocean bottom just as sheep graze in a paddock.

Rodents

There are numerous species of native Australian rodents. They are not as prolific in breeding habits as introduced species so they are not as widespread, nor are they considered a pest.

Monotremes

Echidna

Tachyglossus aculeatus
This bizarre creature and the platypus are the world's only egg-laying mammals. The echidna, or spiny anteater, has sharp claws and a long, sticky, ribbon-like tongue with which it gathers up ants and termites at lightning speed. It has no teeth, and relies on its stiff spines for protection.

It lays a single egg which is carried and hatched in a temporary but commodious pouch formed from folds of skin. The female has no teats; the milk is exuded into the pouch and is licked up.

Platypus

Ornithorhynchus anatinus
This animal, unique to Australia, is the world's strangest aquatic mammal. It has often been considered a living fossil and may be the missing link between reptiles and mammals. It has webbed, clawed feet and a duck-like bill, which is fleshy and sensitive for foraging for food. It has beaverlike fur and a tail, lays eggs and suckles its young, and just to make things more complicated, the male has a poisonous spur behind its back leg, the function of which is not known. It inhabits the eastern watercourses, making its burrow entrance above the waterline. The platypus is the animal emblem of New South Wales.

Reptiles and amphibians

Australia has about 140 species of snake, 360 species of lizard, two species of crocodile, 15 species of freshwater tortoise and six species of marine turtle.

Crocodiles

Both species of Australian crocodile are found in our northern waters. The freshwater crocodile, *Crocodylus johnstoni*, is not dangerous to people; however, the saltwater species, *C. porosus*, which can grow to seven metres long, is very dangerous. Both are protected, as it is felt that they are endangered. Not only are they hunted for their skins, but it is believed low-flying aircraft disturb the females so that they leave their eggs unprotected and vulnerable to predators.

Frogs

There are approximately 130 species of frog in Australia, but no salamanders. Australia's native frogs include a diverse array of tree frogs, marsh frogs and burrowing frogs. The golden swamp frog, from the genus *Limnodynastes*, is the most widely distributed frog in Australia.

The gastric brooding frog, *Rheobatrachus silus*, was first discovered in 1973. It is unique in the animal world because the female inhibits its gastric juices and turns its stomach into a uterus. It swallows the fertile eggs, which turn into fully developed young in the temporary 'nursery'. The young then emerge through the frog's mouth.

The water-holding frog of Australia, *Cyclorana platycephalus*, appears above ground only after rain. As it is a desert creature, it has long spells in its cocoon-like chamber below ground. During wet times, it fills the chamber with water and then sits in the water during drought.

The corroboree frog, *Pseudophryne corroboree*, grows to three centimetres long and is pale green with black markings.

The cane toad of South America, *Bufo marinus*, was introduced into Australia in 1935 to control cane-borer beetles. It failed to do this, and since then has spread in plague proportions along the east coast and across northern Australia.

Lizards

Australian lizards range in size from 5.5 centimetres to 2.4 metres long. The great perentie or goanna, *Varanus giganteus*,

DID YOU KNOW?

Through the ignorance of new settlers to the country and varying policies over the last 200 years, imported plants, animals, insects and sea creatures have slowly invaded and damaged our unique environment. These include the rabbit, hare, horse, donkey, deer, camel, fox, pig, goat, sheep, cow, rat, mouse, dog, cat and water buffalo. Other introduced species include cane toads, starlings and Indian Mynahs, bitou bush, water hyacinth, lantana, Patersons curse, prickly pear and blackberry bush, and sea creatures such as striped mussels, European carp and mosquito fish as well as insects, including the European and papernest wasp.

is the second-largest lizard in the world.

Perhaps the most popular lizard is the frill-necked lizard, *Chlamydosaurus kingi*. It has a vivid frill of skin which is normally folded back. Under attack, it unfolds the frill, sways to and fro, opens its mouth wide and hisses. However, it does not readily attack, and if in doubt runs at great speed on its back legs.

The blue-tongue lizard, of which *Tiliqua scincoides* is the most common, belongs to the skink family of lizards. They are the most prevalent in Australia.

The moloch or thorny devil, *Moloch horridus*, is well protected from predators by its ability to camouflage itself. It also has skin armour so sharp that no animal could eat it without injuring itself.

Snakes

Of the 140 species of snake found in Australia, approximately 100 are venomous. The non-venomous snakes include pythons, blind snakes, file snakes and some colubrid snakes. The largest is the amethystine or scrub python, *Liasis amethystina*, which grows to about seven metres and the smallest are the carpet python, *Morelia spilota variegata*, and diamond python, *M. spilota spilotes*, both of which reach a length of 2–4 metres.

Among the venomous snakes is the death adder, *Acanthophis.* It grows to a length of about 60 centimetres and its venom is more potent than that of the Indian cobra. It has a broad, flat, constricted head, and a short, thin tail.

The tiger snake of the species *Notechis* is distributed throughout the southern part of the continent. This aggressive and dangerous snake does not grow more than two metres in length but the venom is more powerful than that of any other land snake. It is coloured from tan to olive, with dark bands across the body.

The 3.4 metre taipan, *Oxyuranus scutellatus*, of Queensland, is one of the world's most venomous land snakes. One snake carries enough venom to kill 23 000 mice. It is brown and is Australia's largest venomous species.

There are over 30 species of sea snake found in our northern waters, the most common of which is the yellow-bellied sea snake, *Pelamis platurus.*

Earthworms

The world's largest earthworm, *Megascolides australis,* is found in Gippsland in Victoria. It grows to 3.56 metres in length and 1.9 centimetres in diameter.

Insects

Australia has over 50 000 species of insect. There are about 350 species of butterfly, 7600 species of moth, 18 000 species of beetle and 900 species of ant.

Cicadas

There are over 200 species of Australian cicada, having such fanciful names as double drummer, *Thopha saccata;*

cherry nose, *Macrotristria angularis*; red-eye, *Psaltoda moerens*, and black prince and green Monday (or greengrocer), *Cyclochila australasiae*. The nymphs (the young) live beneath the ground for several years before hatching, living on sap tapped from the roots of trees. They finally emerge, and within weeks they mate and die.

It is only the male cicada which sings so deafeningly. A collection of them can produce a noise in excess of 120 decibels, equal to the noise produced by a loud rock band.

Termites

Australia's magnetic termite, *Amitermes meridionalis*, builds a nest approximately four metres high, three metres long and one metre wide. The narrow end points north–south, and so the nest is called a meridional or compass nest. The nests have been used as direction finders by lost travellers.

Arachnids

The funnel-web spider, *Atrax robustus*, is the most poisonous spider in Australia. The male is five times more toxic than the female. It is found only in a small area of coastal New South Wales.

The male red-back spider, *Latrodectus hasseltii*, is one-third the size of the female and is reputed to be non-poisonous. The female, on the other hand, is highly venomous.

Marine organisms

The Great Barrier Reef

This largest and most intricate expanse of coral reef in the world extends along the Queensland coast for more than 2000 kilometres, covering a total area of almost 260 000 square kilometres.

The earth's largest structure created by living creatures, the reef began forming more than 10 000 years ago. It is a complex ecological maze of fortress-like structures composed of dead coral, over which living coral forms a mantle. The living coral, made up of millions of coral polyps, produces a limestone secretion for support and protection. These tiny marine animals, whose growth and reproduction build onto the remains of their ancestors, in turn create a still larger and more complex coral colony.

Between the outer Barrier Reef and the coast, ridges of small reefs have developed. Here, corals of brilliant colours

DID YOU KNOW?

Sharks have caused more deaths in Australia than anywhere else. Even so, since 1791 fewer than 100 people have been killed.

and fantastic designs live in the sheltered waters: mushroom coral, brain-like coral with intricate cerebral engravings, organ-pipe and gorgonian corals, and delicate traceries of lace in the shapes of fans and ferns. There are 'table-tops' and many-pointed antlers and sturdy stag-horn branches; brightly coloured fish dart about the coral, clams open to display their velvet-soft linings of many hues, and anemones, with decoy fish cradled in their tentacles, feed on anything that comes within reach.

Blue-ringed octopus

Hapalochlaena maculosus
This small octopus is found over vast areas, from intertidal waters to waters 40–50 metres deep. Often it takes the colour of its background, but when, irritated it lights up electric-blue rings around its body. Normally it is not aggressive, although if it is handled and stings, the sting can prove fatal. The first recorded death was in 1956.

The octopus's body is about the size of a 20-cent piece, and the tentacles are 7–8 centimetres long. It can live up to one year.

In the north-west corner of the continent a slightly larger version of the species occurs, *H. lunulosa*. It has not yet been proven whether the sting is poisonous.

Crown-of-thorns starfish

Acanthaster planci
This starfish, approximately 30 centimetres in diameter, is widespread in the Pacific region. It is not deadly, but because the spines are quite toxic, it is hard to handle. In recent years abnormal growth in numbers has occurred, not only in Australian coral reefs but as far afield as East Africa and Guam, giving rise to the belief that the increase is more a result of natural phenomena than the pollutants in our seas. The starfish attacks only living coral, and there is a widely held opinion that, because the Barrier Reef mainly comprises dead coral, the relatively small amounts of living coral destroyed are no great threat to the vastness of the reef. Layers of spines of the starfish have been found in calcified coral set down over hundreds of years, indicating perhaps that outbreaks may come in cycles.

Sea wasp

Chironex fleckeri
This creature is found in Australian tropical waters during the summer months. It is often referred to as the box jellyfish because of its cubic shape. Roughly the size of a wine cask, it has a simple branched tentacle flowing from each corner of the cube, which is extremely dangerous. In fact, the sea wasp is considered to be the most poisonous creature in our seas. A sting can cause death within minutes. Radio warnings are given when sea wasps are sighted, and intending swimmers are well advised to change their plans.

Australia is richer in birdlife than most other countries. There are over 700 different kinds, including bower-builders, lyrebirds, magpies, butcherbirds and song larks.

Bellbird

Manorina melanophrys
Bellbirds are found in open forests and sheltered dells on the east coast. They have a loud bell-like note, and can often be heard by travellers at sharp bends in a road where the bushland drops away into a gully. In contrast to their beautiful song, they are small and nondescript in appearance.

Black swan

Cygnus atratus
The black swan is unique to Australia and is the only species of swan on the continent. It is distributed throughout the country, building its nest, about one metre in diameter, among reeds in swamps and feeding on aquatic plants and animals. It has a trumpet-like call. It is Western Australia's bird emblem.

Bowerbird

The satin bowerbird, *Ptilonorhynchus violaceus,* is found only in Australia and New Guinea. The male builds a decorated bower with a series of archways, and fills the area with objects to attract the female to a mating dance. She in turn builds her nest in the trees, where she lays her eggs.

Brolga

Grus rubicunda
The brolga or native companion is the only Australian crane. It is a swamp dweller, found mostly on the inland plains. Flocks of brolgas perform a stately mating dance, using their long legs to perfect the formal routine of the dance.

Emu

Dromaius novae-hollandiae
The emu is the unofficial bird emblem of Australia. It is flightless, stands about 1.5 metres high and is Australia's largest bird. It is closely related to the cassowary and next in size to the ostrich. The dark-green eggs average nearly one kilogram in weight. These are hatched by the male, who sits on them for eight weeks before the chicks appear.

Despite its name, the mallee emuwren, *Stipiturus malachurus,* is Australia's smallest bird. It gets its name because its tiny tail is similar in shape to an emu feather.

Honeyeaters

The helmeted honeyeater, *Meliphaga cassidix*, is one of the

DID YOU KNOW?

No part of Australia is further than 1000 kilometres from the sea.

Kookaburra.

rarest birds in the world. It is found only in southern Victoria, east of Port Phillip Bay. This is the only bird species restricted to that state, although it belongs to the larger group of over 80 species of honeyeater. It has a yellow crest or helmet and a yellow tuft behind each ear, with a distinctive black face. The helmeted honeyeater is the bird emblem of Victoria.

Kookaburras

Unique to Australia, these birds are the largest of the kingfishers. There are two types: the laughing jackass of the eastern states, *Dacelo gigas*, and the blue-winged kookaburra, *D. leachi*, of the north and north-west. They breed in families, so older offspring help raise the fledglings. They 'laugh' raucously in chorus, marking out their territory. They live on reptiles, small mammals, mice and sometimes fish. The kookaburra is the bird emblem of New South Wales. A well-known song about it is on page 246.

Lyrebirds

The male lyrebirds, *Menura novae-hollandiae* and *M. alberti*, have a fancy gauze-like tail which gives this unique bird its name. The female is nondescript in appearance. Lyrebirds are ground feeders, and build incubation mounds for nests which keep the interior at 30°C. They have a wide vocal range and are splendid mimics.

DID YOU KNOW?

The flightless wood hens of Mt Gower, Lord Howe Island, are amongst the rarest birds on earth.

Parrots

There are more than 50 species of Australian parrot. Among them are galahs, *Cacatua roseicapilla;* sulphur-crested cockatoos, *Cacatua galerita;* rosellas, of the genus *Platycercus;* lorikeets, of the genera *Trichoglossus* and *Glossopsitta;* and budgerigars, *Melopsittacus undulatus*. Parrots are usually found in semi-arid areas, gathered together in large flocks.

Penguin

The only species residing in Australian waters is the fairy or little penguin, *Eudyptula minor*. Phillip Island, near Melbourne, is the home of the best-known colony. Tourists flock to Phillip Island to watch the evening penguin parade, as the birds waddle back to their nests after a day's fishing.

Swift and swallow

The migratory spine-tailed swift, *Hirundapus caudacutus*, is known as the storm-bird. It is often seen soaring high in the sky before and after a storm, feeding on the insects trapped in the turbulence. It rarely lands, and spends much of its life in the sky.

The welcome swallow, *Hirundo neoxena*, also spends long hours soaring. These birds can feed their young without landing on the nest. They hover over the fledglings and drop the food.

Wedge-tailed eagle

Aquila audax
With an average wingspan of 2.5 metres, this bird is Australia's largest raptor. It is clearly recognisable by its huge broad wings and the long, wedge-shaped tail. The general colour is dark brown, with a chestnut neck. The legs are feathered right down to the feet. Its hooked beak and strong talons clearly mark the wedge-tailed eagle as a bird of prey. It is found throughout Australia, but is more common in the arid centre than on the coastal plains. It is the Northern Territory's bird emblem.

Plants

Although Australia is predominantly arid, with vast desert areas, there are many other vegetation regions, such as rainforests, savanna grasslands, scrub, mallee, heath and alpine areas.

Australian plants in general are characterised by their drought-resistant qualities. They have tough spiny leaves and thick bark to resist evaporation. They are also very fire-resistant, and many plants need a fierce blaze to germinate seeds and rejuvenate.

The Australian land flora comprises over 12 000 species of flowering plants and is dominated by *Eucalyptus* (over 550 recognised species), *Melaleuca* (paperbark), *Leptospermum* (tea-tree), *Callistemon* (bottlebrush), *Banksia* (honeysuckle), *Acacia* (wattle), *Casuarina* (she-oak) and *Xanthorrhoea* (blackboy).

The eucalypt is the most dominant tree in Australia, and has tough, durable wood. It is able to resist the ravages of fire by sending out shoots from the trunk, which keep the tree alive until the branches recover. The bark, leaves and branches are constantly shed, which creates fuel for bushfires. As well, eucalyptus oil is highly flammable. During a bushfire, the oil creates a gas which can form fireballs. This is nature's way of keeping the fire alive so as to burn and then rejuvenate the Australian bush.

Forests

On the northern and eastern coastlines of the continent are vast areas of forest, which experience rainfall ranging from 1000 to 2500 millimetres per year. In the broad-leaved rainforests of the north, buttressing fig trees, interlacing lianas, cabbage fan palms, entanglements of lawyer vines, eucalypts, nettle trees and fungi create a dank and brooding atmosphere.

The open forests around the top end of the Northern Territory and on the east coast are less formidable and dense. Here, eucalypts such as mountain ash, *Eucalyptus regnans*, spotted gum, *E. maculata,* and hoop pine,

Araucaria cunninghamii, dominate the landscape, with the perennial plants like prickly Moses, *Acacia ulicifolia*, and purple coral-pea, *Hardenbergia violacea*, flowering in spring. In the New South Wales and Tasmanian forests, the waratah, *Telopea speciosissima,* blooms with its crimson composite flower, 10 centimetres wide, on a single straight stem. The waratah is the floral emblem of New South Wales.

The Cooktown orchid, *Dendrobium bigibbum,* is native to tropical Queensland and has been chosen as the floral emblem of that state. It has purple flowers about four centimetres across. The orchid grows in rocks and trees in well-watered areas of Cape York Peninsula.

Grasses and woodlands

These areas are to be found mainly 200–300 kilometres inland from the north and east coasts. There is a greater distance between the trees than in the forests, and the tree crowns are quite large. Here the eucalypt abounds, and varieties such as yellow box, *Eucalyptus melliodora,* white cypress pine, *Callitris columellaris,* Darwin stringy-bark, *E. tetrodonta,* and

DID YOU KNOW?

After much agitation by conservationists to protect the natural bushland around cities, the world's first green ban was placed on Kelly's Bush, Hunters Hill, Sydney, in 1972 by Jack Mundey of the Builders' Workers Union.

river red gum, *E. camaldulensis*, flower in spring and summer.

The gradual blending of woodland into grassland produces a more sporadic grouping of trees intermingled with varieties of grasses, such as kangaroo grass, *Themeda australis*, and blue devil, *Eryngium rostratum*.

An unusual plant of the grasslands is the subterranean orchid, *Rhizanthella gardneri*. It is found in the wheat belt of south-east Western Australia. It exists wholly beneath the soil and does not disturb the surface. Farmers found this elusive plant while ploughing. It is thought that it could become extinct because of loss of natural habitat.

Scrub and mallee

This is a diverse community of shrubby plants where the most dominant, the Mallee eucalyptus, is no more than eight metres high. It is restricted to the south-eastern and south-western regions of the country where many Australian wildflowers grow. The saw banksia, *Banksia serrata,* grows in this area. It was named after Sir Joseph Banks, the botanist who came with Captain Cook on the *Endeavour.*

Banksia species are considered to be the honeysuckle trees of Australia. Like most Australian plants, they need an extremely hot fire to germinate their seeds. May Gibbs, the Australian author of children's books, immortalised this tree by creating the Bad Banksia

The desert boab tree.

Men characters in *Snugglepot and Cuddlepie.*

Golden wattle, *Acacia pycnantha*, is Australia's floral emblem. It is one of 850 species of Australian acacia found in scrublands. The bark is a source of gum arabic, used in tanning. Wattle has fragrant golden-yellow flowers.

The common pink heath, *Epacris impressa*, is Victoria's floral emblem. It occurs mainly in southern parts of Victoria, chiefly in the wetter foothill country, the coastal heathlands, the Grampians and the Little Desert scrub. It grows to about 1200 metres above sea level.

Deserts

The true desert prevails over vast regions of the inland. Here, the land receives unpredictable and extremely low rainfall, temperatures are extreme, and evaporation exceeds precipitation. These adverse conditions not only create a variety of dry salt lakes and dry riverbeds but produce a complex mosaic of plant communities. Plants adapt by growing spindly leaves and tough bark to stop evaporation in the extreme heat. Again, the eucalypts, coolibah, *E. microtheca*, and ghost gum, *E. papuana*, dominate the desert trees. The unusual boab tree has branches which look like the roots of the tree. Aborigines believe that the tree lives upside down. It has adapted well to desert conditions by storing water in its trunk.

Porcupine grass, such as *Triodia irritans*, and saltbush, *Atriplex vesicaria*, are the dominant plants in Australian desert areas. They are tough grasses with rounded tussocks and sharp, pointed leaves. Being drought-resistant, the seeds are dispersed by the dried plant tumbling in the wind.

Sturt's desert rose, *Gossypium sturtianum,* is a small bushy plant growing to a height of 1.5 metres, with dark-green leaves. The petals of the flowers are mauve, with deep-red markings at their base. Sturt's desert rose is an arid-zone plant of the Northern Territory,

Wollemi pines (Wollemia nobilis).

and it was adopted for the territory's emblem in 1974. It was named for Charles Sturt, an inland explorer (see page 14).

Sturt's desert pea, *Clianthus formosus,* is South Australia's floral emblem. It is a creeper with brilliant scarlet and black flowers and grows only in dry, sandy country.

DID YOU KNOW?

Two small stands of prehistoric conifers were discovered by a bushwalker in 1994 in an isolated rainforest gorge 150 kilometres from Sydney. It was one of the world's rarest plants, the Wollemi pine (*Wollemia nobilis*), thought to be long extinct. At the time of the discovery, it was estimated that there were only 38 adult pines and 200 juveniles. Considered living fossils, their lineage stretches back 90 million years and their discovery was hailed as the botanical find of the century.

In the early days of the colony the precarious food supplies resulted in a staple diet of meat and cheese, tempered with some vegetables and wheat products. The food was mainly based on English fare, and by 1900, regardless of our long hot summers, the preference for hot meals with plenty of meat persisted. In fact, Australians were recognised as the greatest meat-eaters in the world. Even the middle class rarely ate fresh fruit or salads and Australia's wonderful variety of seafood was largely unrecognised.

There was little change in dietary habits until the postwar immigration years, when the introduction of cuisines from many lands widened Australia's culinary horizons.

While there is now a more cosmopolitan attitude to the selection of food, many traditional recipes from the early days remain popular.

Lamingtons

These small cakes were popularised by Queenslanders in the early 1900s.

3/4 cup butter
3/4 cup caster sugar
3 eggs
1/2 teaspoon vanilla
1 cup self-raising flour
1/2 cup plain flour
1/2 cup milk
chocolate icing
desiccated coconut

Beat butter and sugar until creamy. Add two eggs, one at a time, and beat well.

Add vanilla and half the sifted flour. Mix well. Add milk, the remaining flour and the third egg, and mix until smooth.

Place in a well-greased lamington tin (or baking dish) and bake for 30 minutes in a preheated moderate to slow oven. Cool and cut into small squares.

Spear each square on a carving fork, dip in chocolate icing, drain, and toss in desiccated coconut.

Famous cornflour sponge cake

3 eggs, separated
pinch salt
1/2 cup caster sugar
1/4 teaspoon vanilla
2/3 cup cornflour
1 slightly rounded tablespoon
    plain flour
1 level teaspoon
    baking powder

Preheat oven to 190°C (375°F).
    Beat egg whites with salt until soft peaks form. Gradually beat in sugar, a little at a time, then continue beating until the whites are stiff.
    Add egg yolks and vanilla. Beat until combined. Sift together, three times, cornflour, plain flour and baking powder. Add to egg mixture. Carefully and lightly fold into mixture with wooden spoon. Do not stir.
    Divide batter evenly between two greased and lightly floured 20-centimetre round sandwich pans. Bake for 18–20 minutes.

Pumpkin scones

These moist, delicious scones are old favourites.

1 level tablespoon butter
3 level tablespoons sugar
1 egg
3/4 cup cooked
    mashed pumpkin
2 cups self-raising flour
pinch salt
1/4 cup milk

Cream butter and sugar, add egg and mix. Fold in pumpkin.
    Sift flour and salt and fold in with milk.
    Knead well. Roll out the dough and cut it into circles with a scone-cutter. Bake in a hot oven for 15 minutes.

Queensland blue pumpkin soup

The Queensland blue is a variety of pumpkin which is noted for its flavour and keeping qualities. The quantities given will serve six people.

3/4 cup butter
41/2 cups peeled chopped
    pumpkin
1/2 cup chopped onion
2 cups water
3 tablespoons plain flour
1 cup milk
1 egg yolk

Melt 1/2 cup butter in a heavy pan, add pumpkin and onion and steam for seven minutes with the lid on, stirring occasionally. Add water and simmer until the pumpkin is very tender. Press through a sieve or puree in a blender with a little milk.
    Melt the rest of the butter and stir in flour. Gradually add the puree of pumpkin and the remaining milk, stirring constantly. Simmer for 4–5 minutes.
    Just before serving, combine egg yolk with a little of the pumpkin mixture, then stir into the soup.

Billy tea

To be found where old mates yarn.

Place a billycan of fresh stream water onto the hot coals of a fire. When the water is boiling, sprinkle in a handful of tea leaves and allow to boil for one minute. Drop in a green gum leaf or two for flavour. Allow the brew to stand by the fire for two minutes. Tap billycan sides with stick to settle the tea leaves, and pour tea into mugs. Some old-timers 'swing the billy' of boiling tea around their heads. This is a sure way of making a good brew.

Peach Melba

This dessert was named for the famous opera singer, Dame Nellie Melba.

3 large peaches
vanilla ice-cream
whipped cream
raspberry syrup

Cook the peaches carefully so that they do not break. Drain, cut in half, and chill. Place cut side up in individual dishes. Fill each with a scoop of ice-cream and top with whipped cream. Pour raspberry syrup around peaches.

Pavlova

The pavlova was created in 1935 by chef Bert Sachse while he was working at Perth's Esplanade Hotel. He made it in honour of the hotel's most distinguished guest of previous years, the great prima ballerina Anna Pavlova. It is now considered to be a national dish. This popular party dessert consists of a shell of meringue filled with whipped cream and fresh fruit.

4 egg whites
pinch salt
1 1/4 cups caster sugar
1 teaspoon vinegar
2 teaspoons cornflour
whipped cream
fruit to decorate

DID YOU KNOW?

The average Australian can expect to eat during his or her lifetime: 17 beef cattle, 92 sheep, 4005 loaves of bread, 165 000 eggs, half a tonne of cheese, eight tonnes of fruit and 10 tonnes of vegetables.

Heat oven to moderate. Mark a 20 centimetre circle on greaseproof paper. Brush paper with oil and place on a greased oven tray.

Beat egg whites and salt at high speed until they are stiff but not dry. Gradually add sugar, a tablespoon at a time, beating well after each addition. The meringue should be smooth and glossy, and hold firm peaks.

Remove beaters and sprinkle vinegar and cornflour over the top of the mixture. Fold in lightly.

Spoon mixture onto the greased paper circle and spread evenly. Make a depression in the middle with the back of a spoon.

Place in bottom half of oven and immediately reduce heat to low. Bake for $1^1/2$ hours. Turn off heat and allow pavlova shell to cool in the oven.

When cool, fill shell with whipped cream and decorate with strawberries, sliced kiwi fruit or passionfruit.

Vegemite pinwheels

These are made from the famous Kraft product Vegemite, a favourite of many Australians. The quantities given will make about 36 pinwheels.

2 cups self-raising flour
1 good pinch cayenne pepper
1 teaspoon dry mustard
2 tablespoons butter
$1^1/2$ cups grated cheese
$^1/3$ cup water
Vegemite

Sift dry ingredients together. Rub in butter and add cheese. Mix to a firm dough with water.

Turn out onto a floured board and knead well. Roll pastry into a rectangle. Spread with Vegemite and roll into a long coil. Cut into pinwheel slices and place them flat on a greased tray.

Bake in a hot oven for 10–15 minutes.

DID YOU KNOW?

In an election for the Waverley Municipal Council in Sydney in 1859, Elizabeth Cadman, the wife of ex-convict John Cadman, the superintendent of government boats, was the first woman in Australia to demand to be allowed to vote. The Cadmans lived in the building now known as Cadman's Cottage from 1816 to 1845. It is now part of the Sydney Cove Maritime Museum and is the oldest house in Sydney.

Bush brownie
A stockman's stand-by.

1¹/2 cups self-raising flour
1 teaspoon each of ginger,
   all-spice and nutmeg
³/4 cup butter
¹/2 cup brown sugar
2 cups mixed fruit
1 egg
1 cup milk

Sift dry ingredients. Rub in butter and add fruit. Mix in egg and milk, beaten well together.

Pour into a greased tin and bake for 30–40 minutes in a moderate oven. Serve sliced and buttered.

Anzac biscuits
A crisp, tasty treat with good keeping qualities. Often sent to Australian soldiers by loving families. The quantities given will make about 36 biscuits.

¹/2 cup butter
1 tablespoon golden syrup
¹/2 teaspoon bicarbonate of soda
2 tablespoons boiling water
1 cup uncooked rolled oats
1 cup desiccated coconut
1 cup plain flour
1 cup brown sugar
2 teaspoons ground ginger

Melt butter and golden syrup in a large pan over low heat. Add bicarbonate of soda mixed with boiling water.

Combine dry ingredients in a mixing bowl, then pour melted mixture into the centre and mix to a moist but firm consistency.

Drop slightly rounded teaspoonfuls of mixture onto a cold greased tray. Cook for 10–15 minutes in a moderate oven. Cool on a wire rack.

Drover's damper
Traditionally made by bushmen, who sometimes cooked the dough in the hot ashes of a fire. The outside was burnt but the damper was broken open and only the centre eaten. Here is a sophisticated version of the basic recipe. It is excellent with pumpkin soup.

2 cups self-raising flour
¹/2 teaspoon salt
2 teaspoons sugar
1 tablespoon butter
1 cup milk

Sift flour and salt. Add sugar and rub in butter. Mix in milk to make a medium-soft dough. Knead lightly on a board until smooth. Pat into a round shape, place in a tin and glaze with milk. Bake in a hot oven, reducing heat until cooked (20 minutes). Turn onto a tea towel, wrap and cool. Serve with butter and golden syrup ('cocky's joy') or jam.

Variations: To make fruit or grated cheese damper use one cup of either ingredient, added to basic recipe. Beer damper can be made by substituting beer for milk.

English is spoken in many countries, but the Australian brand is unmistakable. To the British our 'G'day, mate' will be curious, to the Americans it will be delightful, and to a homesick Aussie it will be music to the ears.

Here is a guide to some common Aussie expressions and their meanings.

ace – excellent

'ang on – wait a moment

arvo – afternoon

'avago – have a go (usually 'ya mug' – you fool – is added); try harder

barbie – barbecue

bewdy or *bewdy bottler* – good; the best

beyond the Black Stump – far from the city; the outback

bingle – minor car accident

bludger – layabout, one who wants something for nothing, person who does no work or very little

bluey – a swag or blanket roll

bombed out – unsuccessful; *also* drunk

by crikey – an expression of surprise

cactus – useless, broken

cark it – to die

cashed up – having plenty of ready money

cheesed (off) – bored; fed up

chewy – chewing gum

chook – a domestic fowl

chook raffle – a lottery in which the prize is a chicken; usually held in a 'pub' (hotel)

chuck a wobbly – go berserk

cobber – friend

cocky – know-all; *also* a small farmer

come a cropper – to fall heavily

cot case – a drunk or exhausted person, fit only for bed

deadhead – a stupid person

dead marine – an empty beer bottle

dead set – certain; assured; used as an exclamation meaning 'really!'

dead set against it – uncooperative

dinky-di – genuine

do your lolly (melon; nana; loaf) – to get very angry

dob in – to betray or report someone to the authorities; *also* to nominate someone for an unpleasant task *don't get off your bike* – calm down

drongo – stupid person

dry as a drover's dog – extremely thirsty

dunny – an outside toilet

esky – a portable icebox (brand name)

fair crack of the whip – ease up

fair dinkum – honest; genuine

fair enough – all right; acceptable

fair go – a chance; *also* an appeal for fairness

flake (out) – to collapse; to fall asleep

flat out like a lizard drinking – lying prone; *also* rushed; extremely busy

flush – having plenty of money

fossick – to search for something

freak out – to have an extreme reaction (good or bad) to something

full as a goog (tick; boot) – drunk

game as Ned Kelly – very brave (Ned Kelly was a daring bushranger [robber] in 1878)

garbage – an exclamation meaning 'What rubbish, I don't believe you!'

g'donya – good for you, well done

get nicked – to be caught

go off like a bucket of prawns in the sun – to create commotion

good one – an exclamation of approval

goodo – yes, all right

gutful – more than enough

have tickets on yourself – to be conceited

hit the deck – to duck; to put your head down

hit the tin – to put money in the kitty; to contribute to a collection of cash

hoon – a stupid or uncultivated person; also a fast or reckless driver

---

DID YOU KNOW?

The name 'gum tree' was first used by Sir Joseph Banks at Botany Bay in 1770, when he recorded a tree having gum exudations (later known as eucalyptus gum).

hooroo – goodbye

kick in – to help out with money

knock – to criticise, find fault

knocker – a person who makes derogatory remarks

larrikin – mischievous, wild or carefree person

like a hornet in a bottle – furious

like a possum up a gum tree – moving fast

like a rat up a drainpipe – moving even faster

lingo – language

loaded – extremely wealthy; *also* very drunk

mate – good or best friend; *also* used to greet someone as in 'G'day mate'

matilda – a blanket roll carried by a swagman

m'oath – my oath; on my oath

mug – fool

mulga – rough country

no-hoper – incompetent person; social misfit

nosh-up – a good meal

nick – to steal

nick off – to go away; expression meaning 'lose yourself!'

nifty – stylish; clever; shrewd to the point of dishonesty

ocker – the archetypal uncultivated Australian man

outback – the inland country far away from cities

prang – minor car accident

rack off – to go away; expression meaning 'lose yourself!'

ring-in – a substitute

rort – to con

sangers – sandwiches

she'll be apples, she's sweet – it'll be fine

shonky – poor quality

DID YOU KNOW?

The first point in Australia which is touched by the morning sun is Mount Warning, near Murwillumbah in New South Wales, and the last touching point in the evening is Dirk Hartog Island, near Exmouth in Western Australia.

shout – to buy drinks for everyone

sickie – a day taken off work, but not necessarily because of illness

skip – Australian-born (from Skippy the kangaroo)

skite – a bragger

smoko – break from work (originally for a cigarette)

snags – sausages

stinker – an objectionable person

stone the crows – exclamation of astonishment

swag – a blanket roll of light bedding

swagman – a man who travels around the country on foot and takes odd jobs

ratbag – a rogue; an eccentric person

rubbish – to criticise; to mock

ta-ta – bye-bye

tinnie – a can of beer

too right – an exclamation meaning 'I quite agree'

top drop – a good beer

true blue – genuine

twit – a fool

ute – open-backed van

veg out – relax

wag – to play truant

wheelie – a noisy skidding turn while driving

whinge – to complain

whopper – something surprisingly big

wowser – a killjoy; a prudish teetotaller

write-off – a total loss

wuss – spoilsport

yakka – hard or heavy work

yobbo – a stupid or uncultivated person

zonked (out) – tired out; exhausted